Praise for *Customer Loyalty*

"Sales people will find Griffin's book interesting, practical, and profitable."
　　　—American Marketing Association

"Jill Griffin offers a clear path to competitive leadership in any industry. *Customer Loyalty* provides examples over and over again that a company keeps its customers by providing value every day."
　　　—LOUISE R. COOPER, vice president, OEM Sales,
　　　　Prodigy

"*Customer Loyalty* offers hundreds of examples to show how to turn customers into advocates for your business. More importantly, Jill Griffin offers detailed advice on how to create a loyalty-driven culture as a fundamental part of your business strategy."
　　　—MICHAEL L. POWELL, executive vice president,
　　　　Revlon Professional Products, North America

"Learn the finer points of cultivating—and keeping—loyal customers from Harley-Davidson and other companies with devoted clients."
　　　—Money Book Club

"Today's competitive markets require that we not only sell and service more customers than ever before but that we stay closer to each one. *Customer Loyalty* offers real-world solutions and examples for achieving this level of customer contact and building solid customers relationship."
　　　—MARGARET C. CRANK, former director of marketing,
　　　　MCI Telecommunications Corporation

"Improving customer loyalty is a vital investment for every organization. Using *Customer Loyalty's* blueprint for creating loyalty systems, a company can enhance its customer equity."
　　　—LAURA PATTERSON, director of customer marketing and
　　　　brand strategy, Motorola Semiconductor Products

D0182251

Customer Loyalty

How to Earn It, How to Keep It

Jill Griffin

Jossey-Bass Publishers • San Francisco

FIRST PAPERBACK EDITION PUBLISHED IN 1997.
THIS BOOK WAS ORIGINALLY PUBLISHED BY LEXINGTON BOOKS.

Substantial discounts on bulk quantities of Jossey-Bass books are available to corporations, professional associations, and other organizations. For details and discount information, contact the special sales department at Jossey-Bass Inc., Publishers (415) 433-1740; Fax (800) 605-2665.

For sales outside the United States, please contact your local Simon & Shuster International Office.

Jossey-Bass Web address: http://www.josseybass.com

Manufactured in the United States of America

Library of Congress Cataloging-in-Publication Data

Griffin, Jill.
  Customer loyalty : how to earn it, how to keep it / by Jill Griffin.
    p. cm.
  ISBN 0-02-912977-X
  ISBN 0-7879-0860-6 (paperback)
    1. Consumer satisfaction.   2. Customer service.   3. Customer relations.   I. Title.
HF5415.5G75   1995
658.8'12—dc20   94-36213
                                                                        CIP

HB Printing 10 9 8 7 6 5 4 3
PB Printing 10 9 8 7 6 5 4 3 2 1

The Jossey-Bass
Business & Management Series

To my grandmother, Ada Faircloth Marsh, who first introduced me to writing and its possibilities.

To my husband, J. Mack Nunn, whose endless love and belief in me have brought a whole new dimension to the term "loyalty."

Contents

Preface

I grew up in Marshville, North Carolina, a small town of about 1,500 people located close to the South Carolina border. Like many small towns in the 1960s, Marshville boasted a busy town square made up of mom-and-pop businesses. Guion's Drug Store, Audrey's Dress Shop, Collins Brothers Market, and Perkins Dry Cleaners were all owned and operated by local people.

Audrey, Mr. Collins, and the others were behind the counters of their shops everyday serving customers, most of whom they knew on a first-name basis. We came to these stores as much for the latest gossip and news as we did for prescriptions, hamburgers, and dry cleaning.

By big city standards, our buying choices were limited, but we didn't know it. Local businesses satisfied our needs and, in return, won our loyalty.

For most businesses—whether large or small—these good old days are gone forever. In today's competitive business climate, aiming for customer satisfaction is no longer enough. Many customers who are satisfied with a product or service will defect to buy a competitor's product without hesitation, forcing many businesses to spend more and more money to attract new customers.

To maintain a dependable clientele and curtail the expense of wooing new customers, businesses must go beyond their usual concerns about customer satisfaction and take steps to ensure greater loyalty. You can't go back to the old days and old ways of doing business, but you *can* build a new and similar sense of community with your customers.

The results will be:

- loyal clients, who will, in turn, become your best advertisers
- smaller new-customer development costs, and
- a bottom line you can celebrate.

That's what this book is all about.

A special thanks to Thorn Bacon and Judy Barrett, who offered critical input to the manuscript throughout the development process, and to Dr. Robert Peterson, who provided me with up-to-the-minute research on customer loyalty. Acknowledgments are also owed, along with gratitude, to my editor Beth Anderson and literary agent Jeff Herman. And finally, a big thank you to my ace team of MBA interns from the University of Texas for their many hours of research.

Customer Loyalty

1

Customer Loyalty

The Way to Many Happy Returns

While customer satisfaction is necessary to any successful business, we are learning that satisfaction alone is not enough to build a loyal customer base. In the 1980s, *customer satisfaction* was the watchword for businesses. Everyone was rushing around to find ways to make customers happy by meeting and even exceeding their expectations. The theory was that if customers are satisfied, they will buy more and will do so more often. Books, articles, and seminars touted such buzzwords as *customer service, service quality*, and *service excellence*. Behind all these buzzwords was the belief that customer satisfaction produces positive financial results, especially in repeat purchase. Yet the latest research findings suggest otherwise: High levels of customer satisfaction do not necessarily translate into repeat purchases and increased sales. Consider these findings:

- Forum Corporation reports that up to 40 percent of the customers in its study who claimed to be satisfied switched suppliers without hesitation.[1]
- *Harvard Business Review* reports that between 65 and 85 percent of customers who chose a new supplier say they were satisfied or very satisfied with their former supplier.[2]
- Dr. Peter ZanDan, whose company Intelliquest conducts market research studies for computer manufacturers worldwide, reports that in more than 30,000 interviews, his company has never

found high levels of customer satisfaction to be a reliable predictor of repeat purchase.

- Research conducted by the Juran Institute reveals that in excess of 90 percent of top managers from more than 200 of America's largest companies agree with the statement "Maximizing customer satisfaction will maximize profitability and market share." Yet, less than 2 percent of the 200-plus respondents were able to measure a bottom-line improvement from documented increases in levels of customer satisfaction.[3]

Most managers assume that a positive correlation exists between customer satisfaction scores and customer buying behavior. The general belief is that increasingly higher satisfaction scores from a customer are followed by increases in the customer's share of spending, rate of referral, and willingness to pay premium prices. Yet, as the findings above illustrate, this correlation is unreliable. Satisfaction levels do not necessarily translate into higher sales and profits.

What accounts for this disparity? Why would customers indicate one thing, yet do another? A number of factors contribute to the problem. Often customers, at the time they are queried about their satisfaction, are unaware of their future decisions to act. For example, a software company analyzed the satisfaction ratings of a group of customers taken a short time before they defected to a competitor and found the ratings virtually identical to those of an equally large group of customers who remained with the company. Yet these reportedly satisfied customers went to a competitor once they became aware of the greater value.

Another reason satisfaction scores are unreliable is that people often use these surveys as a way to communicate desires beyond the norm of sufficiency. This is often the case with price. The Juran Institute reported that for more than 70 percent of businesses studied, price scored first or second as the feature with which customers were least satisfied. Yet when nearly all of the customers who had shifted spending to competing suppliers were interviewed, in no case were more than 10 percent of the lost customers motivated to switch because of price. In addition, representative samples of customers who had exhibited the most loyalty in terms of buying behavior were as likely to report the same level of dissatisfaction with price as the lost customers.[4]

Perhaps the biggest reason for the disparity between satisfaction ratings and repeat purchase is the measurement of satisfaction itself. Recent studies confirm that current satisfaction measurement systems are not a reliable predictor of repeat purchase. Some of the most convincing evidence is found in the research of Dr. Robert Peterson of the University of Texas. Peterson found that in most surveys of customer satisfaction, a whopping 85 percent of an organization's customers claim to be "satisfied" but still show a willingness to wander away to other providers.[5]

This lack of correlation between customer satisfaction and repeat purchase may be partly due to the difficulty of accurately and reliably measuring customer satisfaction. Satisfaction measures are largely "self-reported," which means that a customer answers a series of questions, usually in the form of a written survey. A number of factors can inflate self-reported satisfaction ratings, including the following:[6]

- *Question formation.* Questions posed in positive terms ("How satisfied are you?" vs. "How dissatisfied are you?") get more favorable responses. The majority of satisfaction survey questions are posed in positive terms.
- *Measurement timing.* Measurements taken immediately after purchase are likely to yield more favorable responses than measurements taken later.
- *Mood of respondent.* A respondent's overall mood at the time of the survey can affect response.

An additional factor contributing to overstated customer satisfaction ratings is customers' reluctance to admit they made a bad purchase. They feel a low satisfaction rating reflects badly on their purchase behavior or judgment. Therefore, they will compensate by distorting their satisfaction with a higher-than-deserved rating.

Given the many problems with satisfaction measurement, it is little wonder that many companies are failing to find a strong relationship between their customers' satisfaction measures and economic performance. For example, the CEO of a manufacturing company that produces industrial equipment was feeling intense frustration with the lack of results from his firm's satisfaction program when he remarked, "It gives me a warm feeling to know that the customer satisfaction score is up again for the fourth straight year. Now can someone tell me why profitability and market share are down again?"[7]

From the customer's inclination to overstate satisfaction to the questionable extrapolation of data into sales and profit projections, one thing is certain: Current satisfaction measurement systems cannot be used as reliable predictors of repeat purchase.

The New Measurement: Customer Loyalty

If customer satisfaction is unreliable, then what measurement is tied to repeat puchase? The measurement is *customer loyalty*. In the past, efforts to gain customer satisfaction have attempted to influence the attitude of the customer. The concept of customer loyalty is geared more to *behavior* than to attitude. When a customer is loyal, he or she exhibits purchase behavior defined as nonrandom purchase expressed over time by some decision-making unit. The term *nonrandom* is key. A loyal customer has a specific bias about what and from whom to buy. His or her purchase is not a random event. In addition, the term *loyalty* connotes a condition of some duration and requires that the act of purchase occur no less than two times. Finally, the term *decision-making unit* indicates that the decision to purchase may be made by more than one person. In such a case, a purchase decision can represent a compromise by individuals in the unit and can explain why individuals are sometimes not loyal to their most preferred product or service.

Two important conditions associated with loyalty are customer retention and total share of customer. Customer retention describes the length of relationship with a customer. A customer retention rate is the percentage of customers who have met a specified number of repurchases over a finite period of time. Many companies operate under the false pretense that a "retained" customer is automatically a loyal customer. For example, the CEO of a burgeoning computer hardware company boasted, "We haven't got a loyalty problem; we've retained virtually every customer we've ever sold to." But on closer inspection, the executive discovered that at least 50 percent of retained customers (those who made at least one purchase annually after the initial sale) were buying add-on systems and services from competitive vendors.[8] Retention was not the problem, but share of customer was.

A firm's share of customer denotes the percentage of a customer's budget spent with the firm. For example, a firm captures 100 percent, or total, share of a customer when the customer spends his or her entire budget for the firm's products or services on that firm. Whenever a firm's competitor captures a percentage of the customer's budget, then the firm has lost that portion, or "share," of the customer.

In the ideal, both customer retention and total share of customer are essential to loyalty. There are, however, some situations, such as government accounts, where customers are restricted from purchasing from just one vendor. In such a case, earning a 50 percent share of the customer, for instance, may be the most the firm can accomplish. Likewise, in many packaged goods categories buyers can be and frequently are multibrand loyal. For example, a customer may be equally loyal to two beers, Michelob and Amstel, buying one this week and the other the next. In such circumstances, market conditions and product usage can dictate the limits of loyalty.

If customer retention and total share of customer are essential for loyalty, how are these buying behaviors achieved? An important first step is to notice how a number of well-established business strategies actually work against the development of customer loyalty. The most frequently used of these strategies is market share.

Why a Market Share Strategy Can Limit Loyalty

Since the 1970s, American companies have waged a fierce battle to win market share. In short, building market share by attracting new customers was considered *the* way to maximize profits. The belief was so popular that over the last two decades, most leading U.S. firms pursued a market share strategy with the expectation that it was the surest way to the greatest profits. The pursuit of market share has made many companies more concerned with finding new customers than with holding on to old ones. Statistics show that on average, American businesses spend seven times more money attracting new customers than trying to keep existing ones. Says Bain & Co. consultant Frederick F. Reichheld, "Ask a bank manager how many new accounts he signed up last month and he will probably know off the top of his head. Ask the same person how many accounts he has lost in the past month and you will most likely draw a blank stare."

Table 1–1 compares the strategy of building market share with that of building loyalty. Note that both strategies are used under the same market conditions (low-growth, saturated markets), but that is where the similarities end. Success and failure in a market share strategy are evaluated in regard to competitors, while success and failure in a loyalty strategy are evaluated in terms of retention and share of customer.

Attracting Price Shoppers, Not Loyalty Seekers

Because more effort is required to create customer switching than to maintain the status quo, costs are generally higher for the market share strategy than for the loyalty strategy. For example, in the market share strategy, companies often use a host of short-term marketing tools (coupons, sales promotions, discounted prices, etc.) to woo customers from competitors. While often creating a short-term boost in sales, these actions alone rarely create lasting value for customers, many of whom eventually leave for a competitor.

Consider the outcome of the "coffee wars." In the 1980s, three major brands—Folgers, Maxwell House, and Hills Brothers—dom-

TABLE 1–1

Increasing Market Share v. Building Loyalty

	Market Share Strategy	Loyalty Strategy
Goal	Buyer switching	Buyer loyalty
Market condition	Low-growth or saturated markets	Low-growth or saturated markets
Focal point	Competition	Customers
Measure of success	Share of market relative to competition	Share of customer Customer retention rate

inated the ground coffee market. Each had roughly a third of the market and equally loyal consumer franchises. At one of the companies, a decision was made to implement an aggressive promotional plan to stimulate trial purchase among drinkers of competitive brands. The plan included heavy couponing to stimulate switching. The strategy worked so well that the other brands initiated similar programs. As a result, a massive war over market share began and heavy promotional activity became the industry standard. The results were disastrous for coffee manufacturers. Now, a decade later, brand loyalty has been eroded and many buyers view coffee as a commodity rather than a preferred brand.

In the never-ending quest to build market share, these coffee manufacturers traded their brand-loyal customers for those who are price sensitive and eroded their profits in the process. In addition, by turning the industry into a commodity market, barriers to entry were lowered, thus inviting new competitors to the market. Now, in addition to battling each other, the original big three face an expanded list of competitors and a significantly more competitive marketplace.

As the coffee industry illustrates, misused sales promotions can turn loyal customers into price-sensitive buyers. Research shows that such short-term marketing tools can increase the price sensitivity of all consumers. As a result, companies find themselves in a dilemma where they have little choice but to offer coupons and discounted prices because of continuous competitive promotions and strong customer conditioning. In these markets, customers feel cheated when they don't have a coupon rather than feeling rewarded when they do. In addition to the coffee industry, home delivery pizza is another industry that has created a situation in which customers are always searching for the lowest price. Customers who respond only to price cutting may churn orders, but they seldom become loyal customers. They buy from whatever vendor offers the lowest price.

When Heterogeneous Customers Meet Homogeneous Products

The problems with a market share strategy go even further. The pursuit of market share can actually work against the development of loyalty. Why? Because substantial gains in market share can increase the diversity of the company's customer base. As a result, the company is forced to serve an increasingly heterogeneous base of customers with a homogeneous set of products and services. This disparity can create a dangerous dynamic within the company: The service and attention once available to high-potential customers are undercut and diluted to provide for an increasing assortment of less promising customers. To make matters worse, these same high-potential customers are most likely receiving exceptional care and service from other companies in other industries. This positive experience with other companies makes them increasingly sensitive to and often intolerant of a company delivering anything less. It also makes them "ripe" for competitors that can offer a more specialized product or service tailored specifically for these customers' particular needs.

Serving heterogeneous customers with homogeneous products has been the downfall of a wide range of retailers, from department stores and variety stores to supermarkets, drugstores, and hardware stores. Caught in the middle and challenged on either side by specialty stores and volume discounters, many of these "all things to all people" stores have been forced to close their doors.

Those retailers that have successfully remained in the middle have changed their operations drastically. They have centralized management and downsized departments where they are unable to offer customers a clear advantage. Many have remodeled their stores to resemble a series of speciality stores under one roof. In fact, such stores as Nordstrom and Lord and Taylor are no longer considered department stores but, rather, departmentalized speciality stores. Relationship building with customers is a priority. For example, in many of these stores a computer program linked to cash registers records addresses of customers and their purchases. The stores use the data to alert shoppers of sales and new merchandise shipments that match their buying profiles.

Today's companies must manage a strange paradox: In the race to win market share and its promise of profit, a company risks (and often loses) its highest-margin customers and in doing so worsens rather than improves its profitability. A company interested in building a solid, loyal customer base uses a different approach from a company interested in simply building market share. Loyalty building requires the company to emphasize the value of its products or services and to show that it is interested in building a relationship with the customer. The company recognizes that its business is to build a stable customer base rather than make a single sale. This shift in emphasis is sometimes subtle, but it is necessary to create loyalty among customers and an understanding of the importance of loyal customers to the company.

When Leslie Otten opened Sunday River Skiway in Bethel, Maine, in 1980, he had a plan.[9] He intended to use all the well-established marketing techniques he'd learned about to grab a share of the market. By offering lower prices, longer hours, and more services, Otten expected to win his new customers by wooing them away from neighboring ski resorts. He knew that his resort was comfortable, attractive, and well managed, so there would be no reason for these new customers to be dissatisfied.

To Otten's dismay, he discovered that after five years of hard work, price cutting, creating customer incentives, sales, discounts, coupons, bonuses—doing whatever it took to get skiers to patronize his Skiway—results were less than satisfying. Sure, people came to his resort, just as they did others in the area, but profits were not growing and his marketing tactics were not paying off.

That was when Otten sat down and took a long hard look at what he'd been doing. What he found when he examined his five-year company history surprised him. With the major emphasis on tracking sales and profits from new customers, old customers were being ignored and they were dropping by the wayside. Otten also found that his staff was taking satisfied customers for granted. The staff assumed that Skiway didn't need to worry about losing those customers to the competition.

It was clear to Otten that he had to make a new plan to develop economic security for his business. The strategy he adopted flew in the face of standard procedures. Rather than striving for market share, engaging in competitive discounting wars, or luring new customers through short-term incentives, he decided to launch a campaign of "growing" customers. And the new plan is paying off big.

Instead of focusing only on increased services, price breaks, or longer hours, he is doing everything in his power to turn first-time skiers—those who have never been on the "boards" before—into loyal customers. Otten's plan includes making first-time visitors so enjoy skiing at his resort that they'll want to repeat the experience again and again.

Before Otten started courting first-time customers back in the winter of 1984–85, only 40 percent of the people who visited Sunday River ever returned. Now more than 75 percent return for more ski adventures. Those repeat enthusiasts are a major reason why gross revenues have increased from $6 million to $18.3 million. Pretax income has climbed almost fourfold, to $4 million a year.

Otten explained his strategy: "If I can turn a first-time customer into someone who skis five times a year, that's $165 in revenue. Given that, I want to make the experience—especially the first experience—of dealing with us as pleasant as possible."[10]

For people just learning to ski, the process can be particularly frightening. Otten wants to minimize their anxiety. As visitors approach his resort, signs instruct them to turn their radios to Sunday River's low-power transmitter. A friendly, soothing voice welcomes them and explains where various slopes and services can be found. To make the transition to a snowy world even more pleasant, Otten has stationed helpers at every step along the way. His most experienced instructors are assigned to new skiers. Staff members help new skiers select clothing, boots, skis, and accessories.

Unlike many business people who try to make their profit the first time the customer comes through the door, Otten barely breaks even on skiers new to his resort. Instead, he offers incentives for customers to come back—again and again and again. On their first visit, novices pay for their first lesson, but equipment (skis, poles, and boots) and lift ticket are all free. The student is also given the chance to sign up for two additional lessons that include the freebies. If students complete all three lessons, they are given a coupon for a fourth day of free skiing. Furthermore, Otten sells student poles, skis, boots, and bindings at cost.

The result of all this "nonprofit" activity is surprising. By the time skiers have finished the three lessons and free day at Sunday River Skiway, they are more than likely to have become loyal customers. They are familiar with the resort, the ski areas, the equipment, and the service. Not only are customers satisfied; they are virtually sold on the resort as the place to ski. Return skiers guarantee increasing profits and a stable growth rate.

The average American company loses 15 to 20 percent of its customers each year. Recognizing this pattern and its severe impact on corporate competitiveness and profitability, companies must move away from the long-accepted market share strategy to a radically different, more long-term approach to business—that of building customer loyalty. This reorientation will produce significant results. By increasing their rate of customer retention by as little as a few percentage points, banks, retailers, insurance brokers, distributors, health care providers, and software manufacturers can increase their profits by 25 to 100 percent.

The Longer the Loyalty, the Bigger the Rewards

The rewards of loyalty are long-term and cumulative. The longer a customer remains loyal, the more profit a business can reap from that single customer. Research shows that across a wide cross section of industries (credit cards, industrial laundry, auto servicing, industrial distribution), the longer a company retains a loyal customer, the more profit that customer will generate. For example, the expected profits from a fourth-year customer of an auto service company is more than triple the profits generated by that same customer in the first year. Companies can boost profits 25 to 85 percent by increasing retention by as little as 5 percent[11] (see Figure 1–1).

If you find these profitability improvements too good to be true, consider the following factors. Increased loyalty can bring cost savings to a company in at least six areas: (1) reduced marketing costs (customer acquisition costs require more dollars); (2) lower transaction costs, such as contract negotiation and order processing; (3) reduced customer turnover expenses (fewer lost customers to replace); (4) increased cross-selling success, leading to larger share of customer; (5) more positive word of mouth; and, assuming loyal customers are also satisfied, (6) reduced failure costs (reduction in rework, warranty claims, etc.)[12]

But the benefits of loyalty and its effect on profitability go well beyond cost savings. As usage increases, so do profit margins. For example, credit card companies spend an average of $51 to recruit a new customer. The new customer uses the card slowly at first, and the profit ratio is minimal. But second-year customers are a different matter. Provided they feel no major dissatisfaction with the

FIGURE 1–1

Reducing Defections 5 percent Boosts Profits 25 to 85 percent

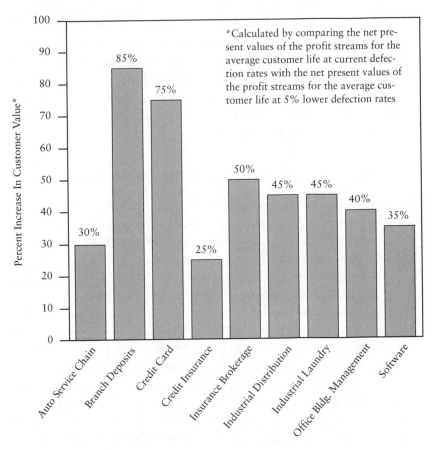

Source: Frederich F. Reicheld and W. Earl Sasser, Jr., "Zero Defections: Quality Comes to Services," *Harvard Business Review*, September–October 1990, 110.

company, they begin to use the card regularly and more often. The balance, and therefore the profit, grows. In the following years, they purchase even more, and profits rise again. In comparison to acquisition spending, there is less expense involved in keeping these customers, and so that original $51 investment really begins to pay off.

This trend is true across industries. For one industrial distributor, profits grew steadily the longer a customer remained with the company. At some point, profits level off, but even after eighteen years with one customer the distributor found that profits from that customer were still going up.

Otten, of Sunday River Skiway, says the motivating factor for his pursuit of lifetime customers is "greed." He offers five reasons for wooing a first-time customer into a lifetime buyer:

- Sales go up because the customer is buying more from you.
- You strengthen your position in the marketplace when customers are buying from you instead of your competition.
- Marketing costs go down when you don't have to spend money to attract that repeat customer, since you already have him or her. In addition, satisfied customers will tell their friends, thereby decreasing your need to advertise.
- You're better insulated from price competition because a loyal customer is less likely to be lured away by a discount of a few dollars.
- Finally, a satisfied customer is likely to sample your other product lines, thus helping you achieve a larger share of customer. (Otten sells and rents lodging at his resort. Since he started building a loyal customer base, real estate income is up 52 percent, to $5.8 million, with pretax earning up 440 percent, to $1.3 million.)[13]

In addition to these five factors, one other element also supports retention. When a company is spending less on acquiring new customers, it can also spend money to continually improve its product and/or service. That in turn can also help make customers more loyal.

The "Loyal Customer–Loyal Employee" Connection

When a company is spending less to acquire new customers, it can afford to pay employees better. Better pay prompts a chain reaction, with a host of benefits. Describing this chain reaction, Frederick Reicheld says, "Increased pay helps boost employee morale and commitment; as employees stay longer, their productivity rises and training costs fall; employees' overall job satisfaction, combined with knowledge and experience, leads to better service to customers; customers are then more inclined to stay loyal to the company; and as the best customers and employees become part of the loyalty-based

:em, competitors are inevitably left to survive with less desirable customers and less talented employees."[14]

As a rule, customers are more apt to become loyal if they develop a personal relationship with salespeople. A customer who regularly buys from the same person comes to rely on that person's help in making purchasing decisions. Salespeople also find it easier to deal with the same customer again and again rather than having to establish new relationships. This symbiotic relationship is beneficial both to the business and to the customer. In general, a repeat customer is likely to be satisfied, and if an employee is dealing with satisfied customers, he or she is likely to enjoy the job more, do a better job, and remain with the company. A national automotive service chain implemented a customer retention program. In a year, the company increased its retention rate by seven percentage points and reduced mechanic turnover to a fraction of former levels.

All businesspeople recognize that training a new employee costs both time and money, and that during the training period and for a time following, the employee is not functioning at maximum efficiency. If a company is able to retain good employees, satisfaction both inside and outside the company improves.

The Cost of Losing a Customer

Just as customer retention has a positive impact on profitability, customer defection can have a negative impact on profitability. The very reasons why a loyal customer is so profitable are the same reasons why a lost customer is so detrimental. Simply stated, it costs less to sell and service a loyal customer. New customers are more costly. Therefore, defections by long-term customers can cause dramatic losses and affect the bottom line much more quickly than those by new customers can. It is difficult for companies to realize how expensive it is to lose a customer. (I analyze those losses in detail in Chapter 9.) Today's accounting systems are designed to show short-term gains and losses and do not help a business track the benefits of maintaining a relationship with a customer over a long period of time. Expected cash flows over a loyal customer's lifetime cannot be evaluated given the current systems. Yet it is clear that a satisfied, loyal customer can contribute a great deal to the financial bottom line of any company.

Consider the experience of Charles Cawley, president of MBNA America, a Delaware-based credit card company. Cawley recognized that customer defections could indicate areas where a company needed improvement. In 1982, Cawley called a meeting of all 300 MBNA employees and reported that he had had many letters from unhappy customers. He declared that from that point on, the company was going to work hard to keep these people happy and keep them as customers. To accomplish that goal, the company began asking questions of customers who were defecting. Why were they leaving? What were their problems? What did they want in a credit card company? Once the information was gathered, the company put together a plan of action and went to work. Products and processes were regularly adjusted to reflect the changing needs of the customer base.

As a result, fewer customers left the company. Eight years later, MBNA enjoyed one of the lowest customer defection rates in the industry. Some 5 percent of its customers left every year—half the rate for the remainder of the industry. Although the difference between 5 and 10 percent may seem insignificant, it reflected a huge difference in profitability. Without any acquisitions, MBNA's industry ranking moved from thirty-eight to four. Profits soared sixteenfold.[15]

The best alternative to expensive, short-term marketing tactics is a strategy that encourages customer loyalty. To begin that strategy formulation, let's take a closer look at the dynamics of loyalty found in Chapter 2.

Summary

- High levels of customer satisfaction do not necessarily translate into repeat purchases and increased sales.
- Question formation, measurement timing, and mood of respondent inflate customer satisfaction ratings and make them a poor predictor of purchase behavior.
- Unlike customer satisfaction, which is geared more toward attitude, customer loyalty is behavior based and is defined as nonrandom purchase expressed over time by some decision-making unit.
- Two important conditions associated with loyalty are customer

retention and total share of customer. In the ideal, a loyal customer's purchase behavior reflects both of these conditions.

- The quest for market share can erode a firm's profitability and draw focus away from its most profitable customers.
- Loyalty is the result of paying attention to what it takes to keep a customer and then constantly providing it.
- Increased customer loyalty leads to higher profitability, higher employee retention, and a more stable financial base.

2

A Closer Look at Loyalty

Customers are smarter than they used to be. In the 1980s, people were eager to spend and acquire, to base their buying decisions on a whim or an impulse, but the 1990s have changed all that. Just look at the businesses that are booming today: Wal-Mart, discount malls, and no-frills grocery stores. Consider these two buyers:

Leah Gorman, a forty-one-year-old San Francisco housewife, did her part to advance conspicuous consumption in the 1980s. Admits Gorman, "Five years ago [in 1986], if I saw an outfit for one of my boys that would look darling, I bought it. I'd never give it a second thought. If I was a little tired, we'd just go out to dinner. It wasn't an issue."[1] Now Gorman is a new breed of consumer. She buys groceries at shoppers' warehouses and is concentrating her efforts to see that her budget goes farther and lasts longer. "I pay a quarter of what I used to," reports Gorman.[2]

Marcie Everett, whose young family moved to Philadelphia from New York, is changing her buying patterns as well: "I figured out that we really didn't need the very latest electronic gadgets or the most up-to-the-minute wardrobes. I shop much more carefully now. All of a sudden, we realized that we have to look toward the future, and spending everything we have right now is foolish."

These new kinds of buyers are not only limiting their spending; they are also spending more wisely. They want real value for their money, and they are representative of hundreds of thousands of individuals and businesspeople in the market today.

How do we win the loyalty of these discerning consumers? Rewards are enormous for the company that can successfully develop, maintain, and enhance the loyalty of these savvy buyers. Managing customer loyalty begins with understanding how and why it develops. We begin this process by dissecting the customer purchase cycle.

Loyalty and the Purchase Cycle

Each time a customer buys, he or she progresses through a buying cycle. A first-time buyer goes through five steps: First, a customer becomes aware of a product and, second, makes an initial purchase. Next, the buyer moves through two attitude formation phases—one called "postpurchase evaluation" and the other termed "decision to repurchase." If the decision to repurchase is "yes," the fifth step, repurchase, ultimately follows. The sequence of repurchase, postpurchase evaluation, and decision to repurchase forms a repurchase loop that is repeated a few times or hundreds of times during a customer's relationship with a company and its products and services (see Figure 2–1).

For example, a residential real estate agent may sell homes to a family once, twice, or maybe three times in the life cycle of the re-

FIGURE 2–1
The Purchase Cycle

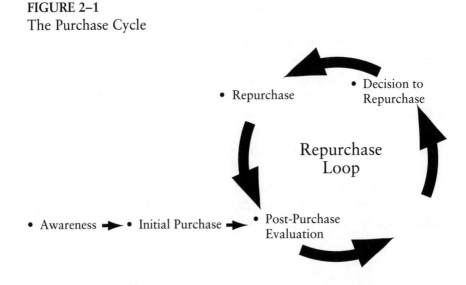

lationship. Following initial purchase, the repeat purchase cycle would be repeated two or three times. At the other extreme, dry cleaners may repeat the cycle more than forty-five times each year for a family. With each revolution of the repurchase loop, the potential exists to either strengthen or weaken the bond with the customer. The stronger the bond, the greater the loyalty and the more benefit to you as a marketer. Let's take a closer look at each step.

Step 1: AWARENESS. The first step toward loyalty begins with the customer's becoming aware of your product. It is at this stage that you begin to establish the all-important "share of mind" required to move your product or service ahead of your competitor's in the minds of prospective customers. Awareness can come about in a variety of ways: advertising, direct mail, trade press, word-of-mouth communication, and marketing activities such as in-store displays. At the awareness stage, a potential customer knows that you exist, but there is little bond between you. At this point, another company's advertising or marketing ploy can steal the customer away before you even get started.

Step 2: INITIAL PURCHASE. The first-time purchase is a crucial step in the ability to nurture loyalty. The first purchase is a trial purchase, and the company can impress the customer positively or negatively with the product, the employees, the service, and even the physical surroundings. Once this first purchase is made, you then have the opportunity to truly begin nurturing a loyal customer.

Step 3: POST PURCHASE EVALUATION. After the purchase is made, the customer consciously or subconsciously evaluates the transaction. If he or she is satisfied or at least is not dissatisfied enough to consider switching to a competitor, Step 4—decision to repurchase—is a possibility. As discussed earlier, most customers rate themselves as at least "satisfied" with the product they are using. But satisfaction alone does not give a company a strategic advantage. Auto analyst J. D. Powers agrees: "A satisfied buyer is a repeat buyer—maybe." For example, data show that the Acura automobile has an outstanding customer service rating (147, while the industry average is 118). Nevertheless, only half the car owners said they intended to purchase an Acura again.

Step 4: DECISION TO REPURCHASE. The commitment to repurchase is the most crucial attitude for loyalty—even more essential than satisfaction. Simply stated, without repeat patronage, loyalty does not exist. The motivation to repurchase comes from a favorable attitude toward the product or service that is high in comparison to attitudes toward potential alternatives. Decision to repurchase is often a natural next step when a customer feels a strong emotional bond with the product. Airstream recreational vehicles, certain cigarette brands, and Macintosh computers have successfully created emotional bonds with some customers.

As we will explore in later chapters, not every company offers a product that creates an emotional bond. Another powerful way to gain a customer's decision to repurchase is to establish the idea in the customer's mind that switching to a competitor will cost the customer—in terms of time, money, or performance. For example, Volvo emphasizes safety, certain photo processors offer the convenience of sixty-minute film developing, and Timex watches offer durability—qualities the customer might have to give up were he or she to choose a competitor's product.

Step 5: REPURCHASE. The final step in the cycle is the actual repurchase. In order to be considered a genuinely loyal customer, the customer must buy again and again from the same business, repeating Steps 3 through 5 (the repurchase loop) many times. Barriers to switching can support customer repurchase. The truly loyal customer will reject the competition and repurchase from the same company whenever an item is needed. This is the kind of customer that businesses need to court, serve, and nurture.

Remember Sunday River Skiway's Leslie Otten, discussed in Chapter 1? Once Otten has created a frequent buyer, he fights to keep him or her. Otten understands that continually cycling the skier through the repurchase loop is essential to building loyalty. He employs both emotional-bonding and cost-saving appeals to strengthen repurchase. New skiers are sent a certificate celebrating their completion of the learn-to-ski program. He has created a frequent-skier program—modeled after airline frequent-flyer programs—that rewards customers with a free day of skiing after as few as five visits, and customers receive mailings describing special promotions. "We want to stay top of mind," says Otten. "We've worked too hard to have people forget us."[3]

Attachment: A Prerequisite to Loyalty

As demonstrated by the five-step purchase cycle, two factors are critical for loyalty to flourish: (1) an attachment to the product or service that is high compared with that to potential alternatives and (2) repeat purchase. Let's look at each of these factors more closely, beginning with an examination of how a buyer forms a favorable attachment.[4]

The attachment a customer feels toward a product or service is shaped by two dimensions: the degree of preference (the extent of the customer's conviction about the product or service) and the degree of preceived product differentiation (how significantly the customer distinguishes the product or service from alternatives.) When these two factors are cross-classified, four attachment possibilities emerge, as shown in Figure 2–2.

Attachment is highest when the customer has a strong preference for a product or service and clearly differentiates it from competitive products. For example, it is this highest attachment toward a Manhattan hair salon and its staff that prompts a friend of mine, who lives in New Jersey, to drive two hours round-trip into the city every six weeks for hair color services. Each trip costs her in excess of $90 for hair services and $22 for city parking. While less expen-

FIGURE 2–2
Four Relative Attachments

Product Differentiation

		No	Yes
Buyer Preference	Strong	Low Attachment	Highest Attachment
	Weak	Lowest Attachment	High Attachment

sive, more convenient hair care services are readily available closer to her home, she feels strongly about getting the "right" hair color service and perceives the Manhattan salon as clearly superior to other service providers.

An attitude that is weak toward a company's product or service but differentiates it from competitors' offerings translates to high attachment and may in turn contribute to loyalty. For example, an individual's attitude toward his or her auto mechanic may be mildly positive but much more so compared with that toward other mechanics. Therefore, these circumstances contribute to loyalty.

In contrast, a strong preference combined with little perceived differentiation may lead to multiproduct loyalty. This is particularly true in fast-moving consumer food goods. Sometimes a consumer chooses Ragú spaghetti sauce; other times, Prego. Sometimes the choice is Coke; other times, Pepsi. The customer has a set of two or three favorites, and situational factors like shelf positioning and in-store promotions will drive that particular purchase.

Finally, a positive but weak preference associated with no perceived differentiation would lead to lowest attachment, with repeat purchase less frequent and varying from one occasion to the next. For example, a homeowner who has his or her carpets cleaned sporadically may consult the yellow pages of the telephone directory and call a different carpet cleaning service each time.

Four Types of Loyalty

After attachment, the second factor that determines a customer's loyalty toward a product or service is repeat patronage. Four distinct types of loyalty emerge when low and high attachments are cross-classified with high and low repeat purchase patterns (see Figure 2–3).

No Loyalty

For varying reasons, some customers do not develop loyalty to certain products or services. For example, I know a manager of a travel agency who goes anywhere in town to get a haircut—just as long as it costs him $10 or less and he doesn't have to wait. He rarely goes to the same place two consecutive times. To him, a haircut is a

FIGURE 2–3
The Four Types of Loyalty

Repeat Purchase

		High	Low
Relative Attachment	High	Premium Loyalty	Latent Loyalty
	Low	Inertia Loyalty	No Loyalty

haircut regardless of where he receives it. (The fact that he is almost bald may have something to do with it!) His low attachment toward hair services combined with low repeat patronage signifies an absence of loyalty. Generally speaking, businesses should avoid targeting "no loyalty" buyers because they will never be loyal customers; they will add little to the financial strength of the business. The challenge is to avoid targeting as many of these people as possible in favor of customers whose loyalty can be developed.

Inertia Loyalty

A low level of attachment coupled with high repeat purchase produces inertia loyalty. This customer buys out of habit. It's the "because we've always used it" or "because it's convenient" type of purchase. In other words, nonattitudinal, situational factors are the primary reason for buying. These buyers feel some degree of satisfaction with the company, or at least no real dissatisfaction. This loyalty is most typical for frequently bought products. It's exemplified by the customer who buys gas at the station down the street, dry cleaning from the store down the block, and shoe repair from the nearby cobbler. These buyers are ripe for a competitor's product that can demonstrate a visible benefit to switching. It is possible to turn inertia loyalty into a higher form of loyalty by actively courting the customer and increasing the positive differentiation he or she perceives about your product or service vs. others available. For example, a dry cleaner that offers home delivery or extended hours could make its customers aware of this fact as a way to provide differentiation of its service quality vs. that of competitors.

Latent Loyalty

A high relative attitude combined with low repeat purchase signifies latent loyalty. When a customer has latent loyalty, situational effects rather than attitudinal influences determine repeat purchase. For example, I am a big fan of Chinese food and have a favorite Chinese restaurant in my neighborhood. My husband, however, is less fond of Oriental food, and so despite my loyalty, I patronize the Chinese restaurant only on occasion and we go instead to restaurants that we both enjoy. By understanding situational factors that contribute to latent loyalty, a business can devise strategies to help combat them. For example, the Chinese restaurant might consider adding a few all-American dishes to its menu to pacify reluctant patrons like my husband.

Premium Loyalty

Premium loyalty, the most leverageable of the four types, prevails when a high level of attachment and repeat patronage coexist. This is the preferred type of loyalty for all customers of any business. At the highest level of preference, people are proud of discovering and using the product and take pleasure in sharing their knowledge with peers and family. Loyal Swiss army knife users are constantly telling friends and neighbors how valuable the knife is, how many handy uses it has, and how often they have used it in a day, a week, or a month. These customers become vocal advocates for the product or service and constantly refer it to others. When I was starting my business, a friend was newly inspired by the *Quicken* software program that automates one's checkbook. He insisted on bringing his program over and demonstrating it to me on my computer. He was displaying premium loyalty.

Loyalty Management: How It Can Work

Premium loyalty, or the lack of it, was a major reason for stagnant sales for Leegin Creative Products, Inc., a belt manufacturing company in Industry, California.[5] Company owner Jerry Kohl had watched with frustration as sales remained in the $9 million range for almost a decade. The $10 million barrier seemed impossible to break. Then, in the summer of 1986, Kohl went off to Harvard Business School for the first of three annual sessions in the Owner/President Management program. In the course of the seminar, Kohl realized the crux of his company's problem: Leegin was a belt manufacturer just like every other belt manufacturer. In the minds of Leegin customers, there were no real penalties or substantial trade-offs for buying from a competitor. In other words, Leegin had created no attachment through customer preference or product differentiation. As a result, many Leegin retailers had either no loyalty or, at best, inertia loyalty for the company's leather products.

Kohl set out to serve his customers in a way that none of his competitors did. He looked for ways to distinguish Leegin by helping his customers sell more belts and make more money.

Kohl hit upon the idea of the computer as a sales aid. What if all Leegin salespeople carried laptop computers on all sales calls? What if their computer system allowed them to tell customers which belts had been selling in other regions and which ones had not? What if, with the punching of a few buttons, customers could see an analysis of this year's sales compared with last year's or the number of belts sold—by individual style, by category, or by color? Such a system, Kohl reasoned, could help both the buyer and the seller to make informed decisions and be a big justification for being a loyal retailer of Leegin products.

Such a system was implemented at Leegin, and as a result, profits have risen steadily. In 1987, the company hit $10.8 million; in 1988, $15 million; and in 1989, $20 million. At the end of 1992, Leegin recorded revenues of $47 million—five times its mid-1980s level. In 1993, the company's revenues jumped to $64 million. Leegin's pretax income in the past three years has hovered around 10 percent of sales. Its debt-to-equity ratio dropped from 3:1 in 1989 to 1.1:1 in 1993.

Using computers has made life easier for both employees and customers. Salespeople do not have to put on a big sales pitch and try to twist arms to make sales; the information makes the sale. It also allows customers to select their inventory and maximize their own profits by buying belts that are selling well in their particular store. One men's store owner that deals with Leegin says, "Thanks to them, we make a lot of money in the small space we use for belts. It's probably one of the most profitable centers in the store."[6] Customers are able to trust the veracity of the information Leegin salespeople present, and loyalty grows as the system works. The intent to repurchase is there because it would be foolish for the customer to give up the service he or she receives.

Loyalty Management: Reactive or Proactive?

"Doctoring" the inertia, latent, or no-loyalty conditions of your current customers and finding ways to upgrade them to premium loyalty are one aspect of loyalty management. An even more proactive approach is to start from the earliest stages of customer development and devise ways to nurture and enhance loyalty throughout the customer's history with your company. This way, you can better manage the development of loyalty and minimize—or in some cases even avoid—such conditions as inertia or latent loyalty.

A friend of mine has grown children who were born fourteen months apart. She recently saw her son graduate from Harvard and her daughter graduate from Baylor Medical School. I was commenting on her children's accomplishments and asked her what her secret to successful parenting was. She thought a minute and then said she felt that, during their childhood, she had intuitively recognized "windows of opportunity" when the youngsters would be most receptive to learning new things. Art, music, writing, travel to Europe—she had somehow known when to introduce these things into their lives so that they were most apt to have the greatest impact.

In our relationships with our customers, there are also windows of opportunity in which to "seed" loyalty. Some of the opportunities come early in the relationship. Others come later. The ultimate quality (and profitability) of the relationship with the customer is a direct result of how much loyalty a customer feels for your product or service. The greater the loyalty, the more benefit to you as a marketer.

Beginning in Chapter 3 and continuing throughout the book, we will trace the evolution of loyalty over the life cycle of the customer, identify the windows of opportunity, and present strategies for anchoring high levels of loyalty at each stage of customer development.

Summary

- Every time a customer buys, he or she advances through a buying cycle. Each step of the buying cycle is an opportunity to seed loyalty.
- Depending on the nature of the product or service, a customer may repurchase a few times or hundreds of times in the course of the relationship. With each repurchase exists an opportunity to strengthen or weaken the bond with the customer.
- A customer's level of attachment coupled with the level of repeat purchase defines the condition of loyalty.
- There are four types of loyalty: no loyalty, latent loyalty, inertia loyalty, and premium loyalty. The goal is to upgrade as many of your customers as possible into premium loyalty by converting them from the other types.
- "Doctoring" the inertia, latent, or no-loyalty conditions of your current customers and finding ways to upgrade them to premium loyalty are one aspect of loyalty management.
- A more proactive approach to loyalty management is to start from the earliest stages of customer development and devise ways to nurture and enhance loyalty throughout the customer's history with your company.

3

Growing a Loyal Customer

The Seven Key Stages

For most shoppers, produce is a generic product—tomatoes are tomatoes, mushrooms are mushrooms, lettuce is lettuce. Most of us don't have a favorite brand of lettuce, but Frieda Caplan, chairman and founder of Frieda's Finest, has created a well-known and thriving company based on selling produce with a difference. Buyers look for Frieda's name because she realized years ago that she was really in the business of serving her customers rather than selling produce. Frieda first tested this philosophy in 1957, when for two weeks she was left on her own to watch over Giumarra Brothers, a Los Angeles produce supplier. Only a clerk at the time, Frieda promised a buyer for a major grocery store chain that she could provide enough mushrooms for the store's major advertising campaign at Thanksgiving time. Frieda was unaware that demand for fresh mushrooms peaks at Thanksgiving—the same time supplies are also the most limited.

In the produce industry, there is little time for written contracts and paper verifications. Verbal commitments are the way business is done, and once Frieda had committed to providing the mushrooms, she had to provide them. How did she honor her commitment? She hustled. She coaxed. When necessary, she pleaded. In some cases, she even packed her new baby into her station wagon and drove out to the mushroom farms and helped pack the mushrooms herself. Then she delivered them to her client.

Frieda realized that satisfying customers and keeping them buying were the task facing anyone interested in building a successful business. Today Frieda and her two daughters run a business that concentrates on building loyalty within their customer base. To do that, they add value to the produce by providing extras that make their produce stand out from everyone else's. Seminars, advertising assistance, and product selection assistance are a few of the tools the company uses to help retailers maximize sales of Frieda's produce. She provides what the retailers need and also helps them sell to their customers. For consumers, Frieda offers explanatory labels that describe how the product can be used and publishes a free newsletter for any customer who wants to receive it.

Typically, the produce supplier puts the tomatoes, lettuce, or kiwi fruit on the shelf and it's up to the retailer to sell it. Frieda realized that she would be building her own business and that of her customers, the retailers, if she helped market the produce. Instead of providing unusual fruits such as kiwi and hoping someone would want them, Frieda provided information on the fruits, and she encouraged chefs and restaurants to use them and develop recipes—in short, she developed the market that then created customer demand for the product. She proved that being proactive in winning loyalty brings big rewards.[1]

Customer Defined

The definition of the word *customer* provides important insights into why businesses need to develop and nurture customers rather than simply attract buyers. *Customer* is derived from the root word *custom*. The word *custom* is defined by the *Oxford English Dictionary* as meaning "to render a thing customary or usual" and "to practice habitually."

A *customer* is a person who becomes *accustomed* to buying from you. This *custom* is established through purchase and interaction on frequent occasions over a period of time. Without a strong track record of contact and repeat purchases, this person is not your customer; he or she is your "buyer." A true customer is "grown" over time.

The Loyal Customer: A Working Definition

As we discussed in Chapter 1, many companies in the 1980s counted on customer satisfaction as a guarantee of future success but were disappointed to find that satisfied customers might shop elsewhere without a moment's hesitation. Customer loyalty, on the other hand, seems to be a much more reliable measure for predicting sales and financial growth. Unlike satisfaction, which is an attitude, loyalty can be defined in terms of buying behavior. A loyal customer is one who

- makes regular repeat purchases;
- purchases across product and service lines;
- refers others; and
- demonstrates an immunity to the pull of the competition.[2]

There is a common denominator that runs through all these behaviors and helps explain why loyalty and profitability are so inextricably linked: Each behavior, either directly or indirectly, contributes to sales.

Let's look at each of these behaviors in the context of Harley-Davidson, Inc., a company with perhaps the most loyal customer base in the United States.

Harley-Davidson: An American Classic of Loyalty

Harley-Davidson celebrated its ninetieth birthday on June 12, 1993, boasting a 63 percent market share. Some 100,000 people celebrated the anniversary, including 18,000 members of the Harley-Davidson Owners Group (HOG). Hotel rooms were sold out for a sixty-mile radius. It was a justifiably proud day for the American manufacturer.

Things weren't always this rosy. At the start of the 1980s, few people gave Harley-Davidson much chance of surviving, and certainly no one predicted that the company would come back with such remarkable vigor. Harley was the last surviving U.S. motorcycle maker, and the company was being run out of business by Japanese manufacturers. The company realized that without some major changes, it was on the verge of extinction and thus went to work to correct a host of quality problems on its product line. By 1987, thanks to greatly improved products, Harley regained its market momentum. Since that time, the Harley motorcycle has continued to grow in popularity and loyalty among older Americans who can afford the average $10,000 bike.

Was the turnaround simply a matter of better manufacturing? Hardly. Although the Harleys are now better-made bikes, the major boon to business came from developing a loyal customer base. The company identified the "typical" Harley-Davidson owner and began to meet that person's needs. Although the media often present Harley owners as bearded, tattooed, and scary, most customers are ordinary middle-class or upper-middle-class citizens who work for a living—the man or woman next door. These people enjoy their motorcycles as a hobby or sport. The bikes are fun; they are exciting; they are grown-ups' toys that enhance everyday life. And Harley-Davidson customers are loyal. Once they become HOGs, they remain HOGs. Look at Harley owners in the context of our four-pronged definition of loyal customers:

MAKES REGULAR REPEAT PURCHASES

Richard Inzerillo, a lawyer, and his wife, Deborah, have gone from zero to five Harleys in just fifteen months, and with each purchase they're trading up. The West Islip couple started with an Electra Glide in August 1991, bought a Sportster that September, traded in the Sportster with thirty-three miles on it a month later, bought two Softails, then replaced the Electra Glide with an Ultra Classic Electra Glide and purchased a custom Softail and, most recently, a Nostalgia.

One segment of the Harley customer base is referred to as RUBs (Rich Urban Bikers). These people enjoy having new bikes, having a bunch of different bikes, and fixing up their bikes. They buy new models as they are offered; then they spend additional money customizing them. New seats, new exhaust pipes, and new headlights are just a few of the options that keep the customers coming back again and again. The HOG-wild Inzerillos, for example, spent $4,000 a piece on accessories for their Softails. But it's not just the RUBs who pamper their Harleys. Working-class men and women are spending big dollars to retool the bikes too.

PURCHASES ACROSS PRODUCT AND SERVICE LINES

Not only do customers buy one Harley after another, but they are constantly buying accessories for their bikes. Some customers take a $10,000 bike and add additional items that raise their investment in the machine dramatically. One customer has $28,000 invested in his bike. Whenever something new comes out, the loyal customers are waiting in line to buy it.

Over the past five years, the company's line of branded merchandise—available only at Harley dealers and promoted through a glossy catalog—has taken off. These products, which are only peripherally related to the bikes themselves, are an important growth area for the company. The goods range from $500 Harley black leather jackets down to $65 fringed bras and even $12 shot glasses.

Marty Altholtz sold bikes for twenty-five years, but finds that now a big part of his business involves selling accessories for bikers and others who just enjoy the Harley image. "We've turned into a miniature Macy's," says Altholtz.[3] Harley-Davidson offers key chains, mugs, pins, belt buckles, pen and pencil sets, shot glasses, knives, sunglasses, cuff links, piggy banks, playing cards, wallets, caps, T-shirts, sneakers, snow globes, paperweights, and ashtrays. There are Harley-Davidson sweatshirts, coats, and, of course, leather jackets.

REFERS OTHERS

Michelle Russo, a twenty-five-year-old secretary with the Long Island Railroad, had a boyfriend. He had a Harley. Before long, she had a Harley too. Although Michelle began with little interest in owning a motorcycle, her boyfriend constantly reminded her what a great machine his Harley was and what fun they would have if she rode too. Michelle's boyfriend convinced her not to buy a motorcycle, but to buy a Harley. She began with a Sportster, considered a starter bike by Harley owners. Now she is moving up to a Low Rider, another Harley model. Harley people say there is no known cure for Harley fever, and it seems to be spreading. Membership in HOG numbers 100,000.

DEMONSTRATES AN IMMUNITY TO THE PULL OF THE COMPETITION

Harley owners refuse to admit that other kinds of bikes even exist. They are sure that if someone owns another kind of motorcycle, he or she must secretly be miserable. It isn't because Harleys are the fastest or leanest bikes on the road. They aren't; many Japanese models are faster, sleeker, and perhaps more economical. But Harleys are classics. Their owners consider them beautiful machines that provide a sort of transcendental riding experience. Getting there faster is not the point—getting there on a Harley is.

The Harley is a bike over which grown men have been known to weep, a bike commanding such love and loyalty that as many as 10 percent of its owners are said to have its name tattooed somewhere on their person.

Growing a Loyal Customer

How can other companies engender the same loyalty that Harley-Davidson has developed? To understand the process, consider nature and the lessons it provides. In my seminars, I show a slide of an acorn and ask my participants what an acorn becomes over time. An oak tree, of course. It doesn't happen in a day, a week, a month, or even a year—it's a long, step-by-step progression.

People grow into loyal customers by stages as well. The process is accomplished over time, with nurturing, and with attention to each stage of growth. Each stage has a specific need. By recognizing each of these stages and meeting those specific needs, a company has a greater chance of converting buyers into loyal customers and clients. Let's look at each of these stages one by one:

Stage 1: SUSPECT. Suspects include everyone who might possibly buy your product or service. We call them suspects because we believe, or "suspect," they might buy, but we don't know enough yet to be sure.

Stage 2: PROSPECT. A prospect is someone who has a need for your product or service and has the ability to buy. Although a prospect has not yet purchased from you, he or she may have heard about you, read about you, or had someone recommend you to him or her. Prospects may know who you are, where you are, and what you sell, but they still haven't bought from you.

Stage 3: DISQUALIFIED PROSPECT. Disqualified prospects are those prospects about whom you have learned enough to know that they do not need or do not have the ability to buy your products.

Stage 4: FIRST TIME CUSTOMER. First-time customers are those who have purchased from you one time. They can be customers of yours and still be customers of your competitor as well.

Stage 5: REPEAT CUSTOMER. Repeat customers are people who have purchased from you two or more times. They may have bought the same product twice or bought two different products or services on two or more occasions.

Stage 6: CLIENT. A client buys everything you have to sell that he or she can possibly use. This person purchases regularly. You have a strong, ongoing relationship that makes him or her immune to the pull of the competition.

Stage 7: ADVOCATE. Like a client, an advocate buys everything you have to sell that he or she can possibly use and purchases regularly. In addition, however, an advocate encourages others to buy from you. An advocate talks about you, does your marketing for you, and brings customers to you.

INACTIVE CUSTOMER OR CLIENT. An inactive customer or client is someone who was once a customer or client but has not bought from you in a period of time longer than the normal purchase cycle.

The Profit Generator* System and the Customer Stages

How the Profit Generator System Works

In my marketing seminars, I use the image of the Profit Generator system to illustrate the marketing challenges every company must address to be profitable (see Figure 3–1).

---

*Profit Generator is a registered trademark.

The Profit Generator° System

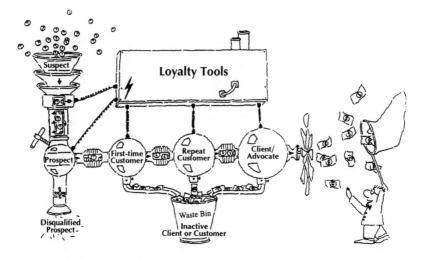

The Profit Generator system works like this: An organization funnels *suspects* into its marketing system, and these people are either qualified as high-potential *prospects* or disqualified. Disqualified prospects are filtered out of the system, while qualified prospects remain inside. The sooner a disqualified prospect is filtered out, the better for you. Wasting time and money on suspects who will not buy or are unable to buy cuts dramatically into your profits, so you want to identify disqualified suspects as quickly as possible. Qualified prospects are then focused upon with the goal of turning them into *first-time customers*, then *repeat customers*, and eventually *clients* and *advocates*. While moving them through the Profit Generator system into higher levels of loyalty, you also want to encourage customers to buy regularly from you and stop buying from your competition. Without proper care, first-time customers, repeat customers, clients, and advocates can become *inactive*, causing a company substantial losses in sales and profits. You'll notice that the globes representing each customer stage become progressively larger. This is because, despite the fact that the number of customers in each stage is smaller than that in the preceding stage, the further along in the system the customer gets, the more bottom-line profit the organization can enjoy.

Every business has customers and clients that fall into some if not all of these categories. A residential real estate company has homeowners as clients. These homeowners could transition through five stages: suspect, prospect, lister, seller, and advocate. A hotel chain catering to corporate travelers has the travel departments of major corporations as clients. Their customer stages could be suspect, prospect, first-time booker, repeat booker, client, and advocate. While the actual names of the customer stages may be modified, most organizations have customers that evolve through a similar transition.

Other applications to the Profit Generator system vary as well. For example, in many industries buyer monogamy (i.e., whether that person is buying only from you or is also buying from a competitor) is the client-stage litmus test. In some sectors like state government that cannot buy exclusively from one seller, this may not be a reasonable requirement. In those situations, the best a company can hope for is that it is one of two or three sellers used exclusively by that buyer. Depending on the nature of your business, these stages can be modified to address the specifics of your own buying situation.

The rule of thumb in working within the Profit Generator system is that the goal for you within each stage of development is to "grow" the relationship into the next stage of development. The goal of interacting with a prospect is to turn a prospect into a first-time customer, a repeat customer into a client, a client into an advocate. Once you reach the advocate stage, your job is to keep that person buying and referring. As we saw earlier with the definition of loyalty, a company can enjoy real profits when the customer has evolved into the latter stages of the Profit Generator process. Failure to "grow" customers to those advanced stages robs the company of profits and valuable referrals.

While we will devote a chapter to each of these stages in the remainder of the book, the following provides an overview of the evolutionary process.

Suspects and Prospects: Attracting Those with Long-Term Potential

The first job of any marketer is to identify suspects and prospects, qualify them, and move them to the first-time customer stage in the Profit Generator system. That is the most challenging and most expensive part of marketing. While the word *suspect* may sound harsh and contrary to this age of customer satisfaction, it serves as a reminder that at this stage in the relationship, we "suspect" that a person (or a company, in the case of business-to-business marketing) may have a need for our products and services, but without more information we cannot be sure.

The closer your suspects are in habits and needs to your established clients, the better the chance they will qualify as prospects and eventually become customers. Careful qualification of a suspect into a prospect is essential to preventing wasteful use of time and money.

To qualify as a prospect, someone must meet at least two key criteria: have the need for your product and/or service and have the ability to buy. In the thrill of the "hunt," many companies have pursued suspects with considerable marketing time and money, only to realize too late that the suspects never met the necessary criteria. With marketing resources in short supply, the sooner a suspect is identified as unqualified, the quicker the company can move on to those with longer-term potential.

Turning qualified prospects into buyers is where the "selling" begins. Research has found that this is becoming an increasingly prolonged process. A 1991 study of industrial sales calls found that the number of calls needed to close a sale is up almost 50 percent, from 4.3 calls in 1979 to 6.3 calls in 1991. This finding makes the qualifying process of a prospect more critical than ever.

First-Time Customers: The Art of the Transaction

The sale is not the objective of the marketing process—it's the beginning of a lifetime customer relationship. It is a rare case when a customer can be sold something only once. Even items that may be bought only once, such as a swimming pool or a set of encyclopedias, can generate peripheral sales, such as pool equipment or annual volumes.

The first-time customer stage is a crucial stage and coincides with the trial purchase portion of the purchase cycle outlined in Chapter 2. As we discussed in the earlier chapter, the first-time customer is essentially trying out your product or service. If a continuing relationship is going to be developed, it has to begin with the first purchase. If the first purchase is not satisfying to the customer, there will probably not be a second purchase. Such customers come to the purchase with a set of expectations gathered from a variety of sources. From the buying experience, they will form a set of perceptions. If their perceptions meet or, even better, exceed their expectations, there is a good likelihood they will be open to repurchase. If their perceptions fall below their expectations, the chances of repurchase are much less. A poor first-time buyer experience is a major handicap to a further deepening of the relationship.

At the first-time customer stage, the buyer and seller are in a "transaction" phase, wherein the customer is likely to pay close attention to timeliness, accuracy, and other facets of the products and services provided. Being a dependable seller is critical to launching a long-term relationship.

The three early stages of the Profit Generator system (suspect, prospect, first-time customer) are the most expensive areas for a marketer. As you progress through the stages, your marketing efforts can become more efficient.

Repeat Customers: Providing Value with Each Interaction

It is critical to keep your customers in the Profit Generator system and expand the business relationship. That's the fastest and easiest way to higher profits.

Once you have reached the customer or client stage, you have the opportunity to recognize each of your customers as individuals and offer products, services, and information tailored to their unique needs. Every interaction should be seen as an opportunity to add value. It is important that your interaction with repeat customers work to deepen the relationship. These customers will in turn respond with more information about themselves, will become gly loyal, and will continue to drive sales and profits up-

To achieve this level of bonding, you must move away from mass advertising to a private dialogue, conducted directly with each customer. Depending on your business, this can be through phone calls, newsletter, letters or salespeople. Customers want to feel that the company knows them. Follow-up marketing that is personalized to these customers can deepen your relationship with them, not just make a sale. The highest levels of human needs—those concerned with involvement and individualization—can be addressed as part of the seller-buyer relationship. These actions enable the repeat customers to view your business not just as a building at a particular address or not just as a phone number in their Rolodex, but as a company of human beings with whom they have formed a relationship.

Client Stage: Shifting from "Salesperson" to "Consultant"

At the client stage of the relationship, the buyer feels a real commitment to buy from you and proves it by buying every product or service of yours the person thinks he or she can reasonably use.

One of the benefits of the client stage is that the relationship has progressed in trust so that you can now be more proactive with the client. From the history that developed through the earlier customer stages, you have proved yourself dependable and accountable. You have now earned these people's confidence, and they increasingly seek your input for ideas and services. With this level of contribution, you add more value.

As such customers go out of their way to be served by you, even if doing so means paying more for your services, they cease to see you as a salesperson and, rather, see you as an ally and partner. When the relationship moves to this level, there is little a competitor can do to lure your customer away. You are perceived as being worth more than simply the product or service you sell.

Almost a year ago, I changed my long-distance carrier. I chose the new carrier because of its low rates. Over the next twelve months, I increasingly relied on my sales representative to provide me with input on a number of phone issues, including my office phone system, an outbound telemarketing setup, and a toll-free

line. Her input helped me save valuable time and money. Now when I have phone system questions, whether it involves long-distance or not, I usually consult her. While other long-distance carriers have approached me, some with even lower rates, I stay with my current carrier. Why? Because I find the advisory aspect of the relationship so valuable.

Advocacy: Your Best Advertising

When customers become advocates for your product or service, you have achieved a relationship of great closeness and trust. This is the most valued and sought-after level of bonding, where word-of-mouth advertising flourishes. The bond at this level is strong. But an element of risk has been added, because the original buyer's relationship with your company is now visible to others. Therefore, you must be prepared to follow through promptly and professionally and make the new customers feel as valued and important as the advocates who recommended them.

Inactive Customers and Clients: "Your Unharvested Acre of Diamonds"

From the moment a customer first buys from you, that person is vulnerable to being wooed away by a competitor or not buying altogether. Generally, the further the customer has progressed in the system, the more you stand to lose if he or she becomes inactive. When inactivity strikes, it is imperative to find out why customers fall out of the Profit Generator system and to win them back.

Reactivating customer relationships is frequently the most overlooked source for incremental profits. Research studies tell us that one's probability of selling an inactive customer is one in four.

If you call people who have discontinued a buying relationship, three great things will happen. First, you'll have an excellent opportunity to renew the business relationship. Studies have shown that if unhappy customers have an opportunity to talk to you about their problems—even if you don't do anything to fix the problems—they're twice as likely to buy from you again than if you had never talked to them. The second benefit is that you'll have begun to stop the negative publicity. Customers will know that you care about them and will tell others. Finally, as your last benefit, you'll identify what's wrong within your system so you can take immediate steps to correct the problem and prevent it from occurring with other customers.

Key questions that a company needs to address are "How many customers do we lose each year?" "What would it cost to keep these customers?" and "How does this cost compare with the cost of finding new customers?"

The Importance of the Big Picture

The Profit Generator system can put the importance of customer conversion and loyalty into perspective for every employee in an organization. As we began to see in Chapter 2, the profitability of a loyal customer is significant. A loyal client for Domino's Pizza, for example, is worth approximately $5,000 in sales over the life of a ten-year franchise contract. Phil Bressler, co-owner of five Domino's Pizza stores, discovered that it paid big dividends to explain to every order taker, delivery person, and store manager that a loyal customer was worth $5,000. For Phil, simply telling employees that customers were valuable was not nearly as effective as communicating the precise dollar amount: "It's so much more than they think that it really hits home."[4]

A similar philosophy is practiced by Ford Motor Company, which has found through research that the lifetime value of a single customer represents an asset worth about $142,000. Like Domino's Pizza, Ford finds that the benefits of communicating that fact to employees can help put day-to-day operations into perspective. An employee who is in charge of collecting overdue bills, for example, is less likely to view his customers as. . . . "delinquent deadbeats," but, rather, as valuable assets that must be nurtured.

Company employees are not the only ones with shortsighted vision. Until recent years, the completion of a sale was the end of the process for too many marketing strategists. Little or not time or money was allocated for creating a special relationship with the company's best customers. Most companies—whether selling goods or services—failed to grasp, must less calculate and record, the lifetime value of a customer. Most companies focused on making a sale rather than concentrating more marketing dollars on having that sale lead to a long-term profitable relationship.

One of the early pioneers of the "growing a customer" concept is car salesman Joe Girrard. Joe Girrard has been in the *Guinness Book of World Records* twelve times for being the world's greatest salesman—each year for eleven years running, he sold more new cars and trucks than any other human being. Joe's success was based on his realization that the sale is only a brief encounter—and that without a commitment on his part to establishing an ongoing relationship with the buyer, that encounter can lead nowhere. Joe says the whole process begins with an attitude: "I look at a customer as a long-term investment. I'm not just going to sell him one car and then tell him to shove it when he is not satisfied with that car. I expect to sell him every car he is ever going to buy. And I want to sell his friends and his relatives. And when the time comes, I want to sell his children their cars too. So when somebody buys from me, he is going to love that experience and he is going to remember it and remember me and talk about it to everybody he runs into who needs a car. I look at every customer as if he is going to be like an annuity to me for the rest of my life."

Scott Hanson Galleries operates with a keen focus on repeat sales. Hanson's galleries are situated in tourist spots like Sausalito, New Orleans, and Rodeo Drive in Beverly Hills. Visitors often browse and come away without buying any art, but it is much less likely that someone will buy from Hanson Galleries only once. The average Hanson customer makes seven purchases within the first three years, and the average Hanson invoice is a very respectable $4,200. Who is the Hanson Galleries customer? Middle-class art buyers looking for pieces to hang over their couches and mantels. The galleries retail limited-edition graphics by popular artists such as Marc Chagall, Thomas McKnight, and Peter Max.

How does this company achieve such a remarkable repeat purchase record among such an unlikely target market? By encouraging its staff to focus on two key things: attitude and follow-up. After fifteen years in the business, founder Scott Hanson has learned that the salespeople—called art consultants—have to view the walk-in visitors as a revenue stream, not as a one-shot sales possibility. With the right attitude on the part of the art consultant, the next goal is the prospect's attitude. To persuade a prospect to become a buyer, the art consultant must lead prospects through the three attitude steps: first, that buying art is OK and not frivolous; second, that they are capable of making intelligent art purchases; and third, that Hanson Galleries is a good place to buy art.

"Education is critical to our sales," says Hanson. "You buy a work and then everything that happens with that artist, you're notified. You now become knowledgeable about that artist and his work. You can talk about him with people at cocktail parties."[5]

"Our salespeople are not just selling a product," relates the director of the La Jolla, California, gallery, Joy Ortner. "They're finding out who you are, what you do, where you live, how big your home is, what color your walls are. That's the key to multiple acquisition." This customer information goes on cards kept on file and is key to the art consultant's follow-up by telephone. All consultants are required to spend roughly 50 percent of their time on the phone and the other half on the floor.

Mailings go out announcing new works, and clients get called before and after the announcements are sent. Sales Director Jennifer Walker confirms that this constant contact makes a difference. "Lots of our clients are doctors, businessmen," she says. "We get right through to them. The secretary will say, 'It's your art consultant.'"[6]

Each Hanson Galleries art consultant generally sells between $500,000 and $1 million in sales each year. These consultants succeed by changing attitudes and purchasing habits and by turning first-time buyers into loyal clients.

How a Database Can Increase Customer Loyalty

R. H. Macy started his first dry goods store on New York City's Sixth Avenue in 1858. His business grew because he knew each of his regular customers so well that he could anticipate their needs and even make a personal call when one of them was sick. Times have changed since Mr. Macy started his business. Companies have hundreds or thousands of employees. It is impossible for the huge department store that bears Macy's name today to turn back to the 1858 form of micromarketing, but it can use modern technology to approximate it. One key way an organization can approximate this quality of relationship is with a customer database.

Thanks to the computer, the names and addresses of customers or potential customers, coupled with information about their purchasing habits and preferences, can now be stored electronically and searched for items corresponding to certain criteria. For example, a salesperson could manually go through dozens of files to determine which clients have not placed an order in the past six months. A computer, however, fed the right search criteria, can identify those customers in moments, saving valuable time that can be spent with customers.

An up-to-date list of your current customers is the most valuable list you can own, because by definition it identifies people who have already made it into at least the second stage of the Profit Generator cycle. You can use the list to help motivate your current customers to buy more frequently and to spend more when they buy. In other words, your customer database moves you from a reactive to a proactive realm in business building. You no longer have to wait for them to contact you.

A database provides a company with the ability to segment names into the different stages in the Profit Generator system and to personally address each member of the subgroups with attention to his or her particular situation. Letters, offers, inquires, phone calls—all can be made with pinpoint accuracy to help your company build loyal customers. For example, a hair salon can isolate all repeat customers of the salon who are not users of perms or color services and send a special offer to them. A clothing store can identify repeat customers and clients that buy a particular line of clothing and, when the store sponsors a trunk show for that line, notify those particular customers. This addressability enables you to develop an ongoing relationship between your company and an individual customer, and by utilizing the tools of data processing you can track the relationship's progress and long-term profitability.

A Database in Action

Robert Sidell started California Cosmetics in 1985 with a distinct product advantage. Sidell had been successful for twenty-seven years as a Hollywood makeup artist. He had done the makeup for movies and TV series such as "The Waltons," *Body Heat,* and *E.T.* In the process, Sidell had developed specialized skin cleansers and toners for the stars he worked with. When he launched his retail cosmetics company in 1985, he found a ready market. In their first full year, Sidell and his partner, Paula Levey, generated $1.6 million in revenues. The second-year revenues reached $4 million, and the third year, $12 million, with net margins growing to 12 percent. Sidell discovered, however, that maintaining the aggressive growth and profits meant he had to constantly discover new customers. To support his increasing sales, his overhead continued to rise as a result of a growing advertising budget, additions to his product line, a larger payroll, and other expenses. Sidell called the vicious circle of increased sales leading to increased overhead his "treadmill".

So how did Sidell get off the treadmill? By using his customer database to sell more to *existing* customers. Sidell discovered that selling more to customers who had already bought from him was much less costly than finding new customer's. Before starting his new program, Sidell's average customer spent $30 a year. That meant he had to have 400,000 customers to produce $12 million in revenues. To hit $16 million with reliance on new customers, he would need 133,000 new customers. Simply by getting his existing customer base to spend an additional $10, however, he could reach his $16 million goal without the additional acquisition costs associated with new customers.

Sidell came upon his new strategy by accident. With sales typically down in the summer months, he instructed his service reps to call ten customers who had not placed orders in a while and find out why: "Eight placed an order right there. They had meant to give us a call but had been too busy or they had misplaced our catalog. But as soon as someone asked them to buy, they did. You don't have to kick me in the head for too long for me to realize something. We were missing a golden opportunity."

Recognizing the gold mine he had in his existing client base, Sidell went further. His sales reps routinely asked the birthdates of new customers. With this information, Sidell began to send his customers birthday presents—a set of three makeup brushes (each of which cost him 45¢). Along with the gift, he enclosed a $5 gift certificate and a birthday card. A remarkable 40 percent of the people who received the present placed another order.

The lesson? Take steps to nurture and build your relationships with your customers. By motivating the customer to buy from you once, you have already taken a big step in creating "share of mind" with that customer. Your company is not a stranger. The customer knows who you are. Your next step is to begin to treat the customer in a personal, individual way. He or she will respond. A marketing database is the key tool for making that happen.

Share of mind is a term marketers use to describe the dominance a customer perceives about a product vs. alternatives. Commenting on the opportunity for combining database technology with the customer's share of mind, direct mail veterans Stan Rapp and Tom Collins say, "When you join these two forces together, the share of mind and the customer database, it is as if you have ignited a second-stage rocket to boost your company into higher orbit. Now you can go to customers who are already favorably disposed to your product and company and offer them other products, services or benefits especially selected to fit their individual tastes. This deepens the share of mind and their resulting loyalty. Then these responses feed additional personal information into the customer database. This makes possible more and better benefits and services, which in turn deepens the share of mind—in an endless feedback loop."[8]

As business gets tougher, the leaders in nearly every industry are going to be the ones learning to use information technology to get back to the basics—the customer. Every business that wants to generate greater customer loyalty ought to be exploring new ways to use its customer database.

The Thrill of the Chase and Other Misconceptions

The Profit Generator system is about focusing marketing and selling efforts on a company's most promising future customers: those it already has. A new idea? Not at all. But most organizations give it lip service at best. Why? Maybe it's because it doesn't require buying fancy new technology or spending lots of media bucks or repositioning the company.

There are essentially three ways to do more business:

1. Have more customers.
2. Have more purchases.
3. Have more expensive purchases.

The Profit Generator system focuses on leveraging items 2 and 3. Currently, there seems to be a sense in marketing that landing new customers (acquisition programs) is more rewarding and exciting than holding on to current customers (retention programs) or increasing business volume among current customers. For some reason, the thrill of chasing new customers and of closing that first deal seems more challenging than keeping the customers you already have. Finding new customers often involves flashy advertising, new sales techniques, and different marketing approaches. This sometimes makes marketing people feel creative and aggressive, but in fact it is possible to be both creative and innovative in devising methods for keeping existing customers happy—and the financial rewards are much greater.

Market researchers Kevin J. Clancy and Robert S. Shulman call the constant search for new customers the "death wish paradox." Companies expend more energy and money into programs that result in less value. Even if the programs are successful in finding new customers, the cost is excessively high.

Research studies tell us that the probability of selling something to a prospect is about one in sixteen, while the probability or selling something to an existing customer is closer to one in two. Given these odds, it is amazing that more companies are not focusing on service and developing their existing customer base. Yet they don't. For example, the international marketing research firm Yankelovich Clancy Shulman reported that an upscale women's apparel maker was dissatisfied with its sales record. The results of Yankelovich's study showed that among the maker's best customers, the company was receiving only 22 percent of the dollars those customers spent on clothing. Furthermore, the study showed that among those who had once been good customers, 12 percent had not purchased from the company in more than a year. When inquiring into the company's marketing strategy, Yankelovich found that huge sums were being spent on finding new customers, but almost nothing was being spent on cultivating existing customers. As a result, the company continued to see high turnover among customers, high marketing expenses, and low customer loyalty.[9]

The Marketing Relationship as an Open System

The Science of Transformation

In 1977, a Belgian physical chemist, Ilya Prigogine, won the Nobel Prize in chemistry for the theory of dissipative structures. It explains an "irreversible process" in nature—toward higher and higher orders of life. This same theory can be applied to a company's system of marketing to its customers.

The chemist's theory is highly complex, but in the simplest terms it describes how certain structures are constantly changing and adapting to existing circumstances. These structures are both extremely stable and constantly changing—an apparent paradox. But it is both their flexibility and their ability to change that accounts for their stability. Structures that are rigid and fixed are much more easily toppled or broken. The same is true in business. The business that is constantly adjusting, changing, refiguring, and adapting to changing customer needs and marketplaces will be the strongest and most successful.

Reorganizing to a Higher Order

Prigogine's theory of dissipative structures can be seen in the evolution of a company as it goes about the business of retaining its customers. Often keeping customers means adding new products and services to meet customers' evolving needs. Companies that fail to use their knowledge of customers to develop the product or service those people will need next are leaving the door open for another company to lure them away. Although it is tempting to use new products to win whole new markets, it almost always makes better sense to stick with existing customer segments. Over time, the company can develop intimate knowledge of these people and can then make good intuitive market judgments. Also, it is easier to build sales volume with customers who already know the company than it is with newcomers.

One business that learned this lesson was Entenmann's of New

York, a loyalty leader in specialty bakery products sold through grocery stores. The company, constantly monitoring its sales, noticed a leveling-off process. To determine the reason why sales had stopped growing, Entenmann's monitored customer purchase patterns in each local market. As a result of asking the right questions, Entenmann's found that its core customers were growing older, and as a consequence of increasing health concerns, they were looking for more fat-free and cholesterol-free products. When the company contacted the customers directly and asked if they would buy fat- and cholesterol-free products from Entenmann's were these available, the customers said they would.

At that point, Entenmann's had a choice to make. It could create a new line of products for its existing customers or it could go all out to find new customers for its existing products. Entenmann's decided to rethink its position and set about developing a new line of fat- and cholesterol-free baked goods. These products would satisfy the needs of existing customers as well as appeal to other health-conscious suspects. The decision has proved to be a good one. The new product line has been highly successful. It has addressed the changing needs of the company's core clientele and even attracted new customers.

In another industry, USAA has established a remarkable 98 percent retention rate in the field of auto insurance. USAA has concentrated its efforts among military officers—a group perceived as difficult because they are moved to new locations often and without notice. USAA studied this narrow market and found a way to meet the needs of these clients. In addition, the company has developed new products to sell to this loyal customer base, increasing its profits at the same time that it individualizes its services. USAA now offers mutual funds, life insurance, health insurance, and credit cards—all tailored to the needs of military personnel.

The relationship that thrives between a company and its client is one that is open and responds to evolving needs. As the customer changes, the company changes; as the company changes, the customer's buying habits change as well. This dynamic, constantly changing and evolving relationship makes for better business for the company and better products and services for the customers.

Building a Loyal Clientele One Step at a Time

Marketing consultant Murray Raphel conducts seminars that deal with marketing questions. On one occasion, he held a seminar for owners of hockey teams. One of the owners asked, "How do I sell 10,000 tickets to our next game?"

Murray responded, "Sell them one at a time." It is important to keep in mind that each individual transaction with each individual customer is significant. It is impossible to consider your market as one homogeneous package. If you consider small pieces, you can get a much better handle on what works and what doesn't. Concentrating on individual sales, individual customers, and groups of customers will lead to overall improvement in sales and increased income much more quickly than trying to come up with grand schemes that will appeal to the whole universe.

That same philosophy of "pieces" can be applied to building client loyalty. Frieda Caplan, Harley-Davidson, Scott Hanson Galleries, and Robert Sidell all understand that loyalty doesn't happen overnight. Customer loyalty comes about gradually, over stages of development. Each of these companies has a plan to develop loyalty, not just a plan to make sales.

Summary

- An effective marketing strategy must include targeting new prospects and retaining current ones.
- A loyal customer displays four distinct purchase behaviors: makes repeat purchases, purchases across product and service lines, provides customer referrals, and demonstrates immunity to the pull of the competition.
- A customer's loyalty grows through seven stages: suspect, prospect, disqualified prospect, first-time customer, repeat customer, client, and advocate.
- Attitude and follow-up are essential to growing loyal customers. If a customer becomes inactive, measures should be taken to woo the person back.
- Computer databases are an important tool for building individual customer relationships.

- The ability to be flexible and adapt to the needs of customers is essential in a loyalty-based marketing system.
- Customers must be thought of as individuals and treated as such if they are to remain loyal and help your business grow and prosper.

4

Turning Suspects into Qualified Prospects

I n the 1950s, McGraw-Hill Business Publications developed a magazine advertisement that has become a classic. It shows a veteran buyer sitting solemnly in his chair facing the would-be salesperson and declaring:

I don't know who you are.
I don't know your company.
I don't know your company's product.
I don't know what your company stands for.
I don't know your company's customers.
I don't know your company's record.
I don't know your company's reputation.
Now—what was it you wanted to sell me?

The ad concludes:

Moral: Sales start before your salesman calls—with business
  publication advertising.[1]

This award-winning advertisement, developed more than forty years ago, still vividly illustrates the tasks and challenges companies face today in turning suspects and prospects into loyal customers. Today the stakes are even higher, since consumers are constantly being surrounded with marketing and sales messages at every turn. On an average day in America, $63,301,699 is spent on TV advertising and $80,547,945 on newspaper advertising.[2] It is estimated that the average American is exposed to well over 3,000 marketing messages a day.[3]

The average cost of a business-to-business sales call has been increasing at an annual rate of just over 11 percent, according to a recent survey by *Sales & Marketing Management* magazine. The companies surveyed reported that they have been able to raise prices only by an average of 5 percent over the past three years. As a result, costs of sales are growing continually, cutting into profits significantly. This same survey found that in most cases, it took seven sales calls to close a first sale, and that the cost of this first sale averaged $239. The results of this survey dramatically point out that selling to new customers is a costly business—in part because you are trying to lure away someone else's loyal customers.

We all recognize that some investment must be made to find new customers and convert suspects and prospects into customers. In order to do that as efficiently as possible, it is important that companies focus on three key marketing questions at an early stage:

- *Who to target*—how to identify those groups of people most likely to buy your products and services
- *How to position your products and services*—how to best position your product or service in the minds of your prospects to earn their dollars and their loyalty
- *How to qualify prospects*—how to focus on high-potential prospects rather than more mediocre suspects

Each of these considerations supports the key function of marketing at this stage in the Profit Generator system: to create the right conditions and lay the right foundation in the minds of well-chosen prospects so that sales can be made easily.

Who to Target

Developing loyal customers and clients begins by searching out the types of customers to whom a company can provide superior value and determining how best to reach those prospects. Many companies, particularly start-ups, suffer early defeat when they fail to discover how big their market is and how to approach it. With limited financial capability, they often shy away from the hefty price tags of research designed to help answer these crucial questions. Instead, they try a scatter-shot approach that in the long run wastes more money and still doesn't produce a good customer base.

Biosite Diagnostics took a different approach. This five-year-old biotechnology firm headquartered in San Diego was started by four former employees of Hybritech, a biotech unit of Eli Lilly and Company. Although resources were tight, the four men spent $150,000 for two market surveys to ascertain whether their new product had a market. In reality, the surveys did much more than simply tell them whether their product had a market. The research played a significant role in helping the fledgling company attract investors, redefine its target market, and redirect its business strategy.

Triage, Biosite's first product, is a small, disposable diagnostic device that tests urine for the presence of drugs in just ten minutes. Before market research was done, emergency rooms appeared to be the company's best initial market for the product. This market, however, was relatively small; moreover, there were already two large companies competing in the field. These facts tended to discourage potential investors.

The research firm surveyed potential users, including 400 physicians and laboratory technicians. In addition, focus groups were conducted among approximately 100 possible users of the device. As a result of the research, the company learned that while there were competitors in the market, the Biosite product had definite advantages over them. It was confirmed that emergency room physicians needed drug analysis in order to select treatment, but it was also discovered that they needed the information quickly. Biosite could produce the results several hours faster than its competitors. Biosite's device cut the testing time dramatically.

The surveys also indicated that while the doctors ordered the tests, the laboratory technicians chose the test to be administered. This information led to a two-pronged marketing thrust, directed at both doctors and laboratory staff.

In addition, the research showed that the company's proposed target market was larger than the young company could easily handle. Instead of stretching its resources to the breaking point, the company decided to find distributors to help fulfill the orders for the product. "We could have sold it ourselves, but it would have taken much more money and much more time," one of the partners explained.[4]

As a result of early testing, Biosite successfully introduced its first diagnostic product, with a second soon to follow. The company saw profits leap from $3 million to $8 million in a year's time. The information gained from the market research helped the company make cost-cutting, effective decisions while planning its marketing program. Instead of guessing, management made choices based on reliable information that provided them with specific targets for their sales force. They learned who needed the product, why it was needed, and the most cost-efficient way of getting the product to the customers.

While not all research studies have such a profound effect on companies, one thing is certain: A careful study of potential markets can save a company unnecessary costs and product delays.

Hitting the Bull's-Eye with Your Target Marketing

With marketing expenses continually on the rise, it is clear that the successful business is going to have to spend its money wisely. The problem is how to do that. The potential market for many products and services is huge—there are all sorts of people and organizations that might want to buy what you have to sell, but you can't possibly try to sell to every one of that amorphous mass.

That is why target marketing is so important. When you think about that possible market, you realize that some of your prospects are too far away, others can't afford your product, some want to shop locally, and others already have a supplier to whom they are loyal. There are many reasons why a suspect doesn't qualify as a good prospect. Target marketing lets you identify, within that broad market of all logically possible buyers, those prospects who are *most* likely to purchase your products and who offer the greatest return for your investment.

Why "target" marketing? Picture a target. Its bull's-eye is small but valuable, the first ring is somewhat larger but not quite as valuable as the bull's-eye, the second ring is larger and less valuable, the third ring is still larger and less valuable and so on, until the target area is complete. Off the target, there is no value. Using this same analogy, think in terms of your business. Your bull's-eye contains the greatest concentration of qualified prospects of any circle on the target. But every ring thereafter contains less and less of the individuals and organizations most likely to buy from you.

Suppose you need $100 in sales to break even and you have $15 to spend on marketing. Think of each dollar as an arrow. Every bull's-eye will bring in $10. The first ring is worth $6, the next ring $3, and the outer ring $1. Clearly, the more bull's-eyes you hit, the better off you will be. You'll *have* to have some bull's-eyes just to break even.

Obviously, you wouldn't just start flinging arrows every which way (though many companies' sales and marketing efforts do resemble such scatter-shot approaches). As with archery, you do better taking careful aim than aimlessly and randomly firing flights of arrows. Furthermore, your marksmanship will improve with practice.

As a marksman, you will also want to take factors besides the arrows and target into account. Archers consider the wind, the light, and the distance of the target. You should consider the market trends, the political climate, the competition, and other factors as you prepare your marketing strategy. The more you know, the better your aim will be.

You may be shooting at more than one target at a time. If your company has more than one good market, you can target each of them at the same time. If you do that, however, you must be aware that your strategy will have to be altered. There are still only so many marketing dollar-arrows that you have to shoot. You will need to think of each market as a separate target and design your strategy specifically for that bull's-eye.

Uncovering Your Natural Target Market

Like the partners at Biosite, Steve Tran understood the importance of identifying his target market. In June 1988, he wasn't selling enough cars at Mac Haik Chevrolet/Subaru in Houston, Texas, and he knew why. "The market is far too competitive to simply wait for customers to show up and buy from you. You have to bring them in," said Steve.[5]

As a first-generation immigrant from Vietnam, Steve, a former teacher, knew what it is was like to struggle with the language and cultural differences in the United States. He reasoned that other

Vietnamese in the Houston area felt the same pressure and might appreciate buying a car from someone who spoke their language and had a similar background.

Steve got the Houston phone book and compiled a list, by hand, of residents with Vietnamese surnames. He sent these folks a letter—in Vietnamese—with his picture on it. Included in his letter was the statement "I am Vietnamese and a former teacher. Like you, I always believe that no one can understand the needs and the taste of Vietnamese people better than a Vietnamese."[6]

Within four months after beginning his targeting strategy, Steve Tran was leading the dealership in sales, with almost half of his sales attributed to the business generated from his Vietnamese target market.

Targeting Loyalty-Based Customers

Establishing a successful Profit Generator system depends on attracting the type of customer who can buy again and again over a long period of time. Sam Walton, founder of Wal-Mart, the largest retailer in the world, reported in his autobiography, *Made in America*, "[Customer loyalty] is where the real profits in this business lie, not in trying to drag strangers into your stores for a one-time purchase based on splashy sales or expensive advertising. Satisfied, loyal repeat customers are at the heart of Wal-Mart's spectacular profit margins."

As you begin targeting your market, you begin to narrow down the universe in which you will try to sell your product or service. You want to discover the "right" customers, those who are likely to do business with you again and again. These are not necessarily the easiest customers to reach or even the most profitable in the short run.

Writing in the "Manager's Journal" column of the *Wall Street Journal*, business innovation specialist Michael Schrage says, "Contrary to popular belief, customer service doesn't begin with the customer's expectations of the business—it begins with the business's vision of the customer. Smart businesses pick customers—and learn from them. While some customers consistently add value along several dimensions, other customers are value-subtracters: What they cost in time, money and morale outstrips the prices they pay."[7]

As we saw from Chapter 1 and the conditions of loyalty, there are some customers who are just not loyal—no matter what you do to please them, they are ready to bolt at the drop of a hat. Your challenge as a marketer is to avoid targeting as many of these people as possible and instead concentrate your energy on those who can be developed into loyal customers.

Business consultant Frederick F. Reichheld has identified some qualities of customers who tend to be loyal: Customers who have been referred by others are apt to be more loyal than those who buy because of an advertisement. Those who buy at full price rather than on promotion, homeowners, middle-aged people, and those who live in rural populations tend to be more loyal. More mobile populations tend to lack loyalty because their constant moves interrupt their business relationships.[8]

Reichheld cautions, however, that generalizing about the "right" customers can overshadow the fact that a customer who is disloyal and costly for one company can be loyal and profitable for another. As we discussed in Chapter 3, USAA enjoys a remarkable 98 percent retention rate in the auto insurance industry with its targeting of military officers. Known for its frequent moves, this group of insurance customers was a problem segment for other insurance companies. Using a centralized database and a telephone sales force that customers can access from anywhere in the world, USAA has developed insurance products that cater to the military's particular needs and has made a substantial profit in doing so.

Ten Steps to Effective Targeting

Consider these steps in identifying and selecting your most profitable markets:

1.   *Survey the total market.* Continually identify all types and categories of people, industries, and others that might use your expertise or product.

2.   *Segment your markets.* Break down your list of potential markets into groups that have common characteristics. You might list people by their professions or industries by their products, for example.

3.   *Analyze your markets.* Discover as much as you can about

the market groupings you have segmented. Find out what they need, what they want, what they fear, and who they buy similar services from. Find out everything you can that will help you evaluate how much potential they offer to you and how you can go about selling to them.

4. *Study the competition.* Find out how your successful competitors go about selling. While you will not want to copy their approaches, you need to know what works in your market. Knowing what your competitors do also helps you decide how you will be able to cut into and capture some of their market.

5. *Stratify the market.* Rank various market segments by priorities. Your primary market should be the market segment you can reach the easiest with the lowest investment and with the greatest expectation of return. In the long run, return should be measured not simply on the basis of volume or sales but by profit. A number of factors can contribute to profitability, including the target group's proven responsiveness to marketing, its growth potential, its readiness and ability to make buying decisions, and the ease by which it can be reached through the media.

6. *Do an in-depth market analysis of your top markets.* Uncover as much information as you can about your most likely suspects, including what they read, what trends they are concerned about, and how they think. Find out who in your field they consider to be best and why.

7. *Analyze what marketing vehicles are most effective.* The fewer resources a company wastes marketing to people who will never be prospects, the more it can invest reaching and selling to its genuine prospects. Asking new buyers, "How did you hear about us?" can help you zero in on ways to reach new customers.

Frequency is the key to effective penetration. Studies have shown that when people hear about your company and products four or more times, they perceive you as credible. Choose marketing vehicles that enable you to afford and achieve such penetration. Carefully consider your marketing budget. If your funds allow you only a "flash in the pan" approach, you will probably be wasting your money and need to rethink your choice.

As a rule, the more focused and smaller the target market and the more clearly a company can identify individual prospects, the more cost efficient marketing becomes. Such direct marketing techniques as mailings, telephone calling, and personal selling can be very effective. On the other hand, if the target group is large and homogeneous, then mass-marketing techniques like television, newspapers, and radio work more efficiently.

8. *Test your markets.* To get a better idea of what will really work, you need to contact a few prospects in each of your high-potential markets. This will tell you which ones are easiest to sell to, which approach works best, and how receptive the prospects are. You may find that what you thought was your best market is really not as good as your second-best market. If you evaluate your sample in terms of cost, efficiency, and successful approach, you will learn a great deal that can save you time and money later.

9. *Analyze what is doable.* A recent sales force productivity study of 192 companies and nearly 10,000 sales representatives reported an average of seven calls to close a first sale. For most businesses, a "threshold" number of calls is required for each sale. Anything less than this threshold requirement makes all previous activity a waste. In establishing sales projections and quotas, consider such factors as how many contacts are required to reach threshold, the average number of calls per day a salesperson can make, and the number of sales days available per period. Considering these factors can help you realistically plan for sales results and help avoid the disappointments that accompany overstated projections and unrealistic expectations.

10. *Choose your markets.* Keep in mind that it's not how many target markets you can identify and open—it's how many you can profitably penetrate, market to, and serve. Treat your target market selection as an open-ended question, continually identifying and investigating new markets of opportunity.

The importance of targeting can be summarized like this: Before you do anything else, you need to find out *who* and *where* your best prospects are and *what* are the most efficient ways to reach them.

How to Position Your Products and Services

Once the target market has been identified, the next step is to create and communicate your message to the prospects throughout your market. Marketing is most effective when it provides information to the target market about the availability of a product or service that satisfies a want in that target market.

Many people erroneously believe that the "right" advertising and marketing can be used to change people's minds about what they want. This belief is questionable regardless of budget, but for smaller firms with limited resources, the cost of such a task is out of the question. Most firms simply cannot advertise enough to change customers' attitudes. It is much more practical and profitable to find out what those attitudes are and then organize your business in accordance with them.

In no industry is this more necessary than in retailing, which has an overriding mandate: Buy what the customer likes and your products will sell; buy what they dislike and your merchandise will sit on the shelf. Leslie Wexler, founder of the The Limited clothing stores, developed a simple and effective technique for addressing his customers. Says Wexler, "When we started the The Limited in 1963 with preppie clothes, I had in mind some fictional collegiate who went to Connecticut College for Women." Several years later Hollywood presented the same image Wexler had envisioned earlier: "She was Ali MacGraw in *Love Story*. And the question I always asked in buying merchandise was, Would she buy it? I was always banging my head against the question, Would the [Ali MacGrawesque character] buy this sweater or blouse?"[9]

When Wexler launched Victoria's Secret, the successful lingerie store chain, Cybill Shepherd was the character he had in mind. "She is naughty, but nice. Free-spirited. Has a good figure but she's not a Playboy bunny. She's more than 30 years old. She is very much her own person, but she is still pretty and sexy," Wexler explained.[10] "Would Cybill Shepherd buy this? is the question I always tell the buyers to keep in mind. In two years, five years, seven years, maybe it isn't Cybill Shepherd, it's whomever. But today it is."[11]

After three decades, Wexler has grown his company into five key businesses: Limited Stores, Express, Lane Bryant, Lerner, and Victoria's Secret, each with sales of more than $1 billion. Much of the success of these businesses is the result of the company's having a clear idea of who the target market is and what that market wants.

The credit card issuer Advanta has been turning in double-digit growth in revenues and profits while such large issuers as Citicorp and Chase Manhattan have seen an erosion in market share. Why? The company is particularly selective about it customers—keeping its MasterCards and Visas out of the hands of deadbeats—and it tailors card terms such as specific interest rates, payment schedules, and credit lines to each individual. The company does not accept applications but instead goes after the customers who fit its desired profile.

"We get enough information about the customer to know what doesn't satisfy them about the credit cards they have," said Richard Greenawalt, Advanta's president. "We try to play off that dissatisfaction."[12]

The company's micromarketing strategy of segmenting potential customers into detailed profiles and then tailoring product terms is in vast contrast to the industry's traditional way of issuing credit cards. Historically, credit card companies have mailed out generic credit card offers to anyone with a decent credit rating.

Advanta's microstrategy is paying big dividends. The company reports that its customers use its credit cards more frequently than others', and as an additional key to profits, a larger percentage of its customers maintain outstanding balances and pay finance charges. In the last four years, Advanta's credit card receivables have grown at a rate of 35 to 40 percent a year, compared with the industry growth rate of 6 percent. Moreover, the company reports lower credit card losses because its carefully selected customers predictably pay their bills more promptly than other cardholders.

Matching potential customers with their preferences of products and services has been the key to the success of The Limited and Advanta. Roger Thompson has had less success trying to change market preferences. When he opened a hair salon in North Dallas, Thompson, former artistic director for Vidal Sassoon, refused to do "big hair" so popular in Texas, preferring the more natural look—straight, short, and styled without gels, sprays, or teasing combs.

Roger Thompson's "natural" bent runs contrary to the regional trend for hair color. Hair color manufacturers like L'Oréal report that Dallas is one of the biggest markets for bleach. Even Texas Governor Ann Richards boosts big hair. Commenting on the governor's widely recognized white hairdo, gubernatorial hairdresser

Gail Huit proclaimed, "I rat the tar out of it. I spray the hell out of it. We get it up. We defy gravity."[13]

Not giving clients what they want has created a less-than-booming business for Thompson. Five months after the salon opened, three of the six stylists were let go. Prospects for repeat business are looking dim as well. Just ask Sue Eudaly, who, after being persuaded by a Thompson stylist to change from blond, found herself with brown hair she did not like and a $225 bill. "It was very depressing," said Eudaly, who showed her dissatisfaction by not leaving a tip. A few weeks later, Eudaly got another salon to bring back the blond. "The Roger Thompson Salon is very definitely New York," she said. "But they need to understand that this is Dallas, Texas."[14] Moral: Find out what your customers want and then give it to them.

Is It Image or Is It Character?

As stated earlier, marketing creates an environment that convinces prospects of the value of doing business with the company. The goal is to create a condition that makes a prospective customer want to do business with you. Although it may appear that you have sold a product, you have actually sold the perception of your company. You have planted an idea in your customer's mind about what doing business with you will be like. To keep generating new customers, as every thriving business needs to do, you should project a clear, simple, powerful image to those with the desire and ability to buy what you are selling.

One of the earliest lessons on positioning and projecting the right image or character can be found in the late 1930s and early 1940s, when Packard was America's prime luxury car. The Packard was the standard by which all other cars were compared. In terms of today's market, it was like Cadillac and Mercedes-Benz combined into one car. Everyone aspired to own a Packard. Then the company began a new advertising and marketing campaign. It decided to introduce a much cheaper car with the slogan "Now everyone can drive a Packard." Within one year, the company was in deep trouble. The luxury car buyers turned to Cadillac. The company did not realize that it was the exclusivity of its product that made it successful. As soon as "everyone" could drive a Packard, no one wanted to drive one.

Image-Driven Marketing: Friend or Foe?

For decades, large corporations have used image marketing to sell their wares, and as a result, image-driven campaigns such as "Fly the friendly skies" and "The heartbeat of America" have become familiar fixtures. When a company delivers customer value consistent with its image, customers respond in a positive way, as evidenced by the success of Carnival Cruise Lines.

Carnival's success stems from delivering a consistent message and travel product. Supporting its "fun ship" image, everything in the cruise ship's marketing message connotes fun. While traditional cruise advertising has promoted ports of call, Carnival's TV spots hype the ships—where vacationers spend 80 percent of their time during a cruise—and the activities on them, such as dining, nighttime entertainment, exercise facilities, dancing, and more fun. Even the ships themselves support the image of gaiety, with such names as *Mardi Gras* and *Fantasy*.

"We're 'Happy Valley,' not 'Death Valley,'" says Bob Dickinson, senior vice-president of sales and marketing for Carnival Cruise Lines, referring to the cruise industry's history of being a vacation haven for retirees. "If you tell people you're the 'fun ships,' you're going to attract people disposed to having fun."

To maximize the company's consumer base, Dickinson says, Carnival sees itself in the vacation industry, where virtually everyone is a prospect, rather than in the cruise industry. While almost two-thirds of Carnival customers are new to cruising, repeat business has doubled in the past five years. "If you like fun," says Dickinson, "you don't graduate away from fun."

Carnival Cruise Lines delivers a travel service consistent with its image, but many companies using image marketing do not. As a result, consumers' positive reception to image marketing is being replaced by increasing cynicism as buyers continually encounter situations where companies do not deliver on the promises implied by their image.

Character-Driven Marketing: The New Generation

A number of companies have seized this opportunity to build credible relationships by expressing their character rather than simply an image. Commenting on the difference between the two approaches, Peter Laundy, principal of Laundy Rogers Design, a New York City communications firm, said, "Image positioners compete; their actions invite analogies involving sports or war. They focus on winning and therefore on the competitor. Character expressers, on the other hand, are aware of competitors but are not as focused on battle. They chart their own course, independent of their competitors and in tune with their customers and their values. . . . A company that expresses character looks for situations that simultaneously build pride in the organization and loyalty in customers."[15]

Apple Computer, Ben & Jerry's, The Body Shop, Smith & Hawken, and Starbucks Coffee are all character expressers. These companies have carved out identities that attract those prospects destined to become loyal. Says Laundy, "Instead of blowing up minor differences between themselves and their competitors, these companies have built real differences deep into their products and organizations."[16] Anita Roddick founded The Body Shop, a cosmetic company, to help provide customers with products that supported their "well-being." In sharp contrast with long-standing cosmetic companies that stress sex appeal and instant rejuvenation, the company projects a deep sense of environmental responsibility and supports that character with herbal ingredients, a policy of no animal testing, and use of inexpensive, recyclable containers.

In regard to marketing communication, image expressers and character expressers are worlds apart. Explains Laundy, "Image positioners see communications—in their catalogs, brochures, direct mail pieces, annual reports, advertisements, and so on—as a message they want to get across. Character expressers see communications as an opportunity to demonstrate that their companies do what they say they do." For example, Ben & Jerry's has a highly visible program of social responsibility. Consider this passage from the "Independent Review of Social Performance Report" section of Ben & Jerry's 1990 annual report:

> Ben & Jerry's has yet to print nutritional information on packaging of its original super-premium ice cream; it has no paid parental leave; and it has only one minority in a senior management position. In the case of energy, due to inadequate recordkeeping the company is unable to report on energy conservation actions. Relations with franchises have im-

proved; even so, the company's communication with franchisees about the social mission have been uneven."[17]

Yes, the content is negative but the far bigger message about the company's behavior is very positive and reinforcing. While most annual reports are expensive chronicles that shareholders read with some "consider the source" suspicion, Ben & Jerry's annual report breaks new ground.

Another believer in character expression is Swatch founder Nicolas G. Hayek. Hayek's company single-handedly saved the Swiss watch industry by bucking traditional wisdom and keeping manufacturing of his inexpensive watch in high-wage Switzerland. This decision forced Hayek to find other ways to compete and was the genesis of his low-cost, unrepairable, flashy, and fun Swatch watch. In the ten years the company has been in business, 100 million watches have been sold and annual profits have soared to $286 million.

Hayek attributes his success in part to character expression. Explaining why character and not image has worked for him, Hayek says, "An image is passive and can be interpreted in different ways. A message about a product is immediately clear and understandable to everyone. It also must be honest."

"I sent the first message about Swatch when I created a 400-foot working Swatch and arranged to hand it over to one of the most prestigious banks in Frankfurt. The display was accompanied only by the words: Swiss. DM 60 [approximately $40]. The promotion sent the following message: High quality, because it was Swiss. Low price, because DM 60 was practically unheard of at the time. Provocative, because a 400-foot plastic watch was hanging on a stuffy bank building. And joy of life."[18]

Reflecting on the synergy built by character expression, Laundy adds, "Character instills pride in the organization and teaches employees how to behave when no one is looking over their shoulders. It delights customers, who refer new business, and journalists, who write good things about the company. Together, employees, suppliers, customers, and journalists become an unpaid but highly credible sales force, reducing a company's expenses for promoting itself."[19]

Perhaps the biggest advantage of marketing through the expression of character is that it can be a company's greatest asset to building a loyal customer base. Why? Because unique character is difficult—if not downright impossible—for your competitors to emulate.

The Awesome Power of Perception

Whether you choose to project an image or a character, one thing is certain: Your efforts can succeed only if your products and services truly deliver what you communicate. Somebody once said that the ultimate definition of successful selling is "The Power to Persuade Plenty of Prospects to Purchase Your Product at a Profit." Marketing's role in this process is to zero in on those people who most need what you have to sell and then communicate a benefits-driven positioning that both differentiates it from the competition and answers for the prospect the "What's in it for me?" question.

When Big Isn't Better

In today's marketplace, many people are looking for a feeling of personal, intimate service rather than the large, "assembly line" type of aura. That need is especially acute in the funeral industry, from which people in grief-stricken circumstances seek comfort, understanding, and fairness. Nobody understands and has leveraged the principle better than Robert L. Waltrip, founder, chairman, and chief executive of Service Corporation International (SCI), which handles one in every eleven funerals nationwide at its 662 homes in thirty-nine states. Approaching $1 billion in annual sales, SCI has succeeded by standing the chain concept—perfected by restaurants, retailers, and hotels—on its head. Instead of using a common name to vouch for consistency, its funeral homes keep the local names that promise distinction and personal service.

SCI recognizes that while hamburger chains might benefit from customer perceptions of quick-serve efficiency and standardization, such an assembly line approach would offend most funeral home patrons. As one writer said, "Nobody wants a McFuneral."[20]

SCI has been successful by combining the local with the regional focus. It purchases a group of funeral homes with deep local roots in a particular area. Each home appears to be locally owned and operated, but the business structure allows centralized purchasing, training, finance, transportation, and embalming. Whereas in local funeral homes the vehicles sit idle waiting for a call, SCI uses hearses and other vehicles at more than one location, thus maximizing their value. By clustering homes in a region, SCI keeps staff and equipment consistently busy.

SCI as a corporate entity is essentially invisible. Instead, there are many local funeral homes that meet the needs of clients with efficiency and profitability. In New York City, where ethnic and economic groups all insist on their own funeral homes, SCI meets those needs by maintaining the local standards that established loyalty to the local company in the first place.

Campbell, the leading chiefly Christian funeral home, on Manhattan's East Side, and Riverside, the leading Jewish funeral home, on the West Side, proclaim their identities in bold lettering on sidewalk canopies and awnings. Plaques inside preserve the memory of their founders. At each home, SCI stays anonymous.

Your business may profit from positioning itself as a local suppliers as SCI has, or it may do better by declaring itself an exclusive market as Packard initially did. Whatever the particulars of your own business, your image must be clear to both your clients and your staff. Decide who you are and project that image clearly if you want to attract your target market.

Identifying High-Potential Prospects

At the beginning of this chapter, we identified three key marketing issues that needed to be addressed. We have examined the first two: targeting your market and creating the right positioning in the minds of potential customers. Let's consider the third of this marketing trilogy: identifying and separating out high-potential prospects for additional selling and marketing efforts in the future. We'll examine this step in two parts: (1) when you contact the suspect and (2) when the suspect calls you.

When You Contact the Suspect

When you take the initiative and contact suspects over the phone or in person, your initial objective is to get these potential customers to give you their attention and time so that you can qualify them. In today's business environment, people are conditioned to say no much more quickly than yes to a new purchase opportunity, so a careful strategy to overcome this resistance is important. Your "opener" is critical to a successful first contact, and there are three requirements for making this initial contact effective:

1. *Introduction.* Call the person by name and then pause for him or her to respond (e.g., "Mr. Jones?"). The more formal "Mr. Jones" is preferred to "Bill" when you are meeting this person for the first time. The formality sends a signal of respect.
2. *Statement of benefit.* Immediately provide a statement that summarizes what you do and what makes you unique. This statement must be simple and to the point, with well-chosen benefits that the suspect will find appealing.
3. *Permission to continue.* Ask a question that seeks permission to pursue the discussion.

Applying this three-part approach, consider the following:

[Introduction] Mr. Nunn? [Wait for his response] This is Jill Griffin with The Marketing Resource Center in Austin, Texas. [Benefit statement] We're specialists in helping companies like yours attract profitable customers and keep them loyal. [Permission to continue] Is now a good time to talk briefly?

Such an opener is designed to gain suspects' permission for you to spend more time with them once you have initiated the contact. Now let's look at the dynamics when suspects contact you. Remember, you first step is to qualify. You need cooperation to get the information you require.

When the Suspect Contacts You

Motivating potential customers to take an action that then identifies them as potential prospects is one strategy often used by marketers. For example, Renault, the automaker, sent watches with no movement in them to 300,000 German car buyers. Along with the watch was a note saying that the rest of the watch could be obtained by test-driving a Renault. One-third of the Germans—100,000—took the bait. Of those, 2,000 bought Renaults. How was the program's ultimate success determined? By the number of watches given away? By the number of people who test-drove the Renault? No. The program's success was evaluated by the number of cars actually sold.[21]

For many companies, the problem is not how to get potential buyers to contact them but how to move them toward a sale when they call. In his newsletter to furniture retailers, publisher Jerry Fried addresses this issue in a feature article aptly titled "Prospects Are Expensive, so Give a Damn." Fried begins his article with these questions: "What possible good is there in getting people into your store if you don't sell them anything? Do you have any idea how much it costs to deliver a warm, breathing prospect into your store?"[22]

Many companies, regardless of industry, operate as if getting the potential customer to contact them is the real feat. They fail to develop a system for qualifying these suspects as high-potential prospects and then converting the prospects into buyers.

Consider this real-life example. It was the afternoon of day two of Wayne Morgan's three-day sales seminar for residential real estate agents fulfilling classroom licensing training. Wayne brought a speakerphone into the training room and called, at random, homes listed for sale by realtors in the classified section of the newspaper. Wayne called six different realtors. On each call, he identified himself as a possible buyer and asked three questions:

- Will the house sell VA [loan for veterans]?
- Does the house have a large lot?
- What down payment is required?

In every case, the agent simply answered the question Wayne asked. Period. Finally, Wayne said, "Give me the address and I'll drive by. If I like it, I'll call you back."[23] Without any hesitancy, all six of the agents gave him the address and not one asked him for his telephone number. Only one even asked his name. "Wayne" was the answer, and the agent did not probe further to get his last name!

This example points out a common problem with marketing and sales programs. Oftentimes, more thought and preparation goes into how to get the telephone to ring (strategy) than what to do once it rings (execution and implementation). A company needs to have the staff members receiving these calls appropriately trained to handle them.

They must be trained to "shepherd" a suspect through the qualifying process and, once that suspect is qualified as a prospect, must have the sales skills for turning a qualified prospect into a first-time buyer. Otherwise, the effectiveness is greatly diminished.

In the case of these real estate ads, in addition to making the home seller feel that his or her house is being marketed, the ads are basically used to create a pool of suspects that can be qualified as prospects and ultimately sold a home. If this principle is not understood, then you get agents only answering questions, not asking them. Their options for qualifying people and then ultimately making a sale to them are dismally lost.

How to Qualify a Suspect

Whether you contact a suspect or a suspect contacts you, that person must be qualified as a prospect. To do that, several key questions need to be answered. These questions may vary depending on your particular industry, but the general concepts apply. Does the suspect

- have a problem you can help solve (i.e, Does the person have a need)?
- have the desire to solve the problem (i.e., What does the person want)?
- have the authority to buy?
- have the willingness and ability to pay for your products or services?
- have the authority to make a decision within a certain time period?

A yes to these questions can "graduate" a suspect into a prospect.

Let's revisit the question sequence from Wayne's training seminar and see how it could be changed.

NEEDS AND WANTS

To the question "Will the house sell VA?" the agent could have replied, "Yes. Is a VA loan important to you?" The realtor could use the same approach about the size of the lot: "Are you looking for a home with a large lot?" To the question "What down payment is required?" the agent could ask, "What size of down payment would you be comfortable in making?"

This questioning approach enables the agent to stay in control of the qualifying process and seek answers to key questions. A little-known fact is that very few homes are ever sold through classified ads. The ads are designed to generate prospects that can be matched to other homes more in keeping with the prospect's buying needs. You cannot match if you cannot graduate the suspect into the prospect stage, however.

Let's look at the request for an address. Giving out the address loses the suspect. In addition, many homes do not have particular "curb appeal" but are "grabbers" inside the front door. Wayne teaches this approach: Tell the caller that the owner has asked that all prospective buyers be accompanied to the house and that the agency is bound to this commitment. The agent would then offer to accompany the caller to the home at the caller's convenience. Finally, Wayne coaches the agents to request the name and telephone number of the caller. Only then can they possibly follow up.

Yes, the agents will get some resistance and some no's. But those responses are screening devices as well. Ask yourself this: If you were really interested in the house, would you let an agent's request to show you the property keep you from moving ahead? Experience says no.

AUTHORITY TO BUY

If you are not talking with the decision maker, you may be wasting your time. To determine if your suspect is the decision maker, pay close attention to how you ask the question. You do not want to ask, "Are you the decision maker?" Such a question can bruise and insult. Instead, ask such questions as "Before making your final decision, who else will you want to consult with?" and "Whose name will appear on the contract?" If another party is identified, you should try to speak to the decision makers together. In some cases, however, you may have to work through the decision influencer to sell yourself to the ultimate decision maker.

Sometimes you are faced with a totally unpredictable set of circumstances. Mark McCormick, chairman of International Management Group, a sports marketing company, tells of an experience with an automobile company that was introducing a new model and wanted to be identified with a major sport. For months, McCormick's company had bombarded a senior vice-president at the automaker's advertising agency with proposals—with no results. Yet the executive continued to encourage McCormick.

Just by chance, a friend at the auto company informed McCormick that he was talking to the wrong person. The automaker had moved sports promotion in-house. The advertising vice-president, whose ego may have been bruised, did not have the nerve to tell McCormick.

WILLINGNESS/ABILITY TO PAY FOR YOUR PRODUCTS OR SERVICES

Business consultant Nido Quebein uses a qualifying technique that is also the first step in his relationship with a suspect. Nido has a set fee for conducting a needs assessment for a prospective client. He reasons that if the prospective client is unwilling to pay for the needs assessment, he or she is probably unlikely to agree to the larger fees for the consulting project. Nido tests the "ability/willingness to pay" criteria early in the discussions with the suspect.

Many professionals become uncomfortable and often apologetic when the conversation turns to fees. The best approach is to confidently state, "Our fee for that service is $2,000," and then follow up the statement with the question "Is that in your budget?" The question will help you uncover any price resistance and, if it exists, to deal with it then and there.

TIME PERIOD

Is your suspect in a position to make a decision within a certain period of time? Several years ago, I was at a Parade of Homes, where community home builders showcase new homes in a subdivision over a two- to three-day period. Salespeople representing these builders are on hand to prospect for new business. It is imperative that the suspects are quickly separated from the prospects, and when the crowds are large, these salespeople must work smart, not just hard. I heard a savvy salesperson ask a zinger of a qualifying question to a woman who expressed interest in buying a custombuilt home. His first qualifying question to her was "Do you have your present home listed for sale?" I was struck by how profound this question was as a qualifier. In one singular question, the salesperson could get a good gauge of the woman's seriousness in changing homes. A response such as "Yes, our home is for sale with a realtor and we've had a couple of calls" says a lot about the likelihood that that this person is a qualified prospect for a custom-built home.

On the other hand, a response like "My husband refuses to even let a realtor appraise our house. We moved in a year ago, and he says he wants to stay at least three more years" would make the woman a less likely prospect. Understanding your suspect's buying cycle is important to the qualifying process.

With these questions answered, you have now determined that the person you are talking to has the authority to make the decision to hire you, has problems you can help solve, and has the resources to pay you. In essence, you have a qualified prospect. This person is truly deserving of additional investment of time and resources to convert him or her from a qualified prospect into a first-time customer.

Attracting plenty of high-potential prospects requires targeting, positioning, and qualifying. After you have gotten your own house in order by learning all you can about your market, have defined your target market, have created and refined your company's image, and have qualified prospects, you are ready to move on to the next step. Each step is essential if your business is to be successful in the long haul.

And while making the first sale is not necessarily the most important part of the process, it is definitely the most exciting and the sine qua non—if you don't make the sale, you won't develop the buyer into a loyal customer.

Summary

- A well-chosen target market dramatically increases your probability of successfully qualifying prospects and developing loyal customers.
- Market research, surveys, and segmentation are all vital tools to properly target your market.
- Customer service begins with the company's vision of the customer. Smart businesses carefully select their customers and then learn from them.

- Allow customers to know who you are and what you stand for. It helps them identify with you and can enhance your position in the market.
- Two key positioning tools are image and character. It is vital to choose the vehicle that will best support your positioning in the marketplace.
- The bottom line is that you must deliver what you communicate.
- In qualifying prospects, train your employees to ask the right questions. Too many marketing plans focus on strategy and fall short on execution.

5

Turning Qualified Prospects into First-Time Buyers

Turning qualified prospects into first-time customers requires the direct or indirect act of selling. Let's take a quick glance back at the history of selling in America.

Since before the beginning of recorded time, the art of salesmanship has been practiced and qualified prospects have been converted into first-time customers. Archaeological evidence supports the idea that Stone Age people traveled great distances to barter for goods unavailable in the area where they hunted and gathered food. In effect, "selling" has been taking place for thousands of years. For a very long time, there were no specialists who concentrated their efforts exclusively on selling. Generally, in those distant days, whoever had too much of one item and not enough of another simply took his or her leftovers and traded them for something else. In the early 1800s, all of that changed. It happened in Massachusetts, where some mill owners decided they wanted more business than they were getting. They found a man who would take samples of their work around the countryside and talk with potential customers about bringing their raw materials to the mill. He was, in fact, the first salesman. His only job was to get more orders. Although it is common practice today, in those days it was an innovative and revolutionary idea. But the idea took hold and worked for the mill. As a result, it caught on, and more and more manufacturers sent representatives out to find business. Selling has followed that pattern ever since.

For the past 200 years, American business has focused primarily on the mission of getting new customers, and sales forces across America were diligently trained to maximize sales. The zeal of customer acquisition and of "making the numbers" has done much to make American industry strong. Unfortunately, in the process, the same drive for sales and profits caused some buyers to be misinformed, misled, and high-pressured into buying things they later wished they hadn't. And that reality has left a negative perception about selling. When I taught marketing at the University of Texas, I included in my class lectures a section on selling. I always began that lecture by asking my business students to make a list of adjectives that best describe a salesperson. Words like *manipulative, insincere, untrustworthy, opportunistic,* and *evasive* were frequently heard. The emphasis on hard selling and acquisition marketing has taken its toll.

Now, almost 200 years after the early sales strategies were introduced in Massachusetts, a new breed of salesmanship is emerging. Today "value-added selling" and "consultive selling" are priorities across many industries. This new generation of selling suggests that companies are beginning to understand that the strategies of "making the sale" are not always compatible with the strategies of developing a customer.

Alfred Zeinen made it clear how his conception of a customer differed from the norm soon after he became CEO of The Gillette Company. When asked how his company's approach departed from his competitor's, Zeinen answered, "We capture customers. Remington sells shavers."[1]

The process of selling to a customer is an admirable, worthwhile pursuit. You will never have the loyal customer base you deserve without first mastering the principles of selling. This chapter will examine how to use selling principles to help lay the groundwork for long-term customer development and retention and, in doing so, how to turn qualified prospects into first-time customers.

The Ingredients of a Successful Sale

A recent sales force productivity study sponsored by *Sales & Marketing Management* magazine surveyed 192 companies representing a total of nearly 10,000 sales representatives. Survey respondents reported that it took an average of seven calls to close a first sale, compared with only three calls to close a subsequent sale.[2]

While recent statistics continue to prove the validity of the frequency of "seven," the concept has been recognized by some marketers for more than a half-century. The "rule of seven" can be traced back to the 1930s movie industry. The Great Depression made money scarce, and the studios quickly realized that despite the talents of film stars Charlie Chaplin, Gary Cooper, and Marlene Dietrich, a movie ticket was anything but a sought-after commodity. What's more, the movie marketers had a product with a short life span. The movie was viable only until the next feature movie came to the theater. Movie marketers had to find a way to entice the most people in the shortest length of time to spend their hard-earned money on a movie. The rule of seven offered the solution. The movie marketers found that a prospective moviegoer had to hear about a particular film at least seven times in a seventy-two-hour period in order to make the decision to buy a ticket.[3]

The objective here is to get a realistic picture of what it may take to turn your qualified prospect into a first-time buyer. Depending on your product or service, it may be unrealistic to expect to get a yes on your first, third, or even sixth visit with the prospect. You are building a relationship. And relationships take time to grow.

Perseverance Pays

Jerel Walters is a sales representative for Union Carbide Specialty Powders, selling industrial powders used in transportation systems. A year and a half ago, Walters qualified American Airlines as a potential new customer. Over the next eighteen months, Walters regularly called on the purchasing agent, discussing such benefits as price, quality, and service. The American Airlines purchasing agent was not particularly receptive. He had been in his position for a number of years and had strong loyalties to another company supplying specialty powder. Nevertheless, Walters continued to contact the buyer on a regular basis with updated proposals and new product information. With each contact, he learned more and more about his prospect's specialty powder needs.

Then something happened. Walters received a call from American

Airlines. The buyer had recently retired, and a new purchasing agent had replaced him. The new purchasing agent needed an emergency shipment of powder. Did Walters have this quantity on hand? Could it be at American Airlines in twenty-four hours? Walters and Union Carbide said yes to both.

Shortly after the shipment, the new purchasing agent contacted Jerel. The agent was ready to discuss a sizable contract with Union Carbide. He had reviewed his predecessor's files and was interested in exploring the cost-saving opportunities found in Jerel's proposals. End of story: Walters company got 27 percent of the American Airlines specialty powder business—representing $250,000 in annual sales.

How many contacts and follow-ups did Walters invest in this first-time sale? Ninety-two completed telephone calls, thirteen onsite meetings, and eighteen letters over a twenty-four-month period, according to Walters computerized sales activity tracking system. The reward for his efforts: a $250,000 annual contract. It's a fact: twenty percent of the sales representatives sell 80 percent of the products. The ones who keep working to build a good relationship with a prospect reap the biggest rewards.

The Required Investment May Be Rising

While seven contacts have been the closing norm in the past, experience is suggesting that the number may be rising. Why? At least three things appear to be contributing to the amount of time and contact required to convert a prospect into a first-time buyer.

First, customers and suppliers are forming deeper alliances. Product quality, consistency of service, and trust are key to these relationships. Price is frequently a secondary rather than a primary factor. These relationships, once formed, can be harder to infiltrate.

Second, in tough economies customers often have a different mental outlook. They avoid salespeople, thinking it is time to save money rather than spend it.

Third, cultural differences in global markets make relationship building key. Learning and adapting to different ways of doing business take time.

Consider the experience of The Stern Organization, an investment real estate brokerage in New York that has sold more than 2 million square feet of real estate in the past two years. One of Stern's brokers may meet with a potential investor a half-dozen times without presenting a property. It's a selling style that goes over well, particularly with the Japanese. "We talk about political views, social things, investment objectives. When we cease being strangers, then we may talk business," says Stern. "I believe in making long-term relationships instead of short-term, quick deals."[4]

Patience Is the New Watchword

The need to market internationally will demand a new level of patience from American marketers, one not encountered before. "Global markets are the thing from now until the end of time. That's true for small companies, many of which have extraordinary records overseas, as well as for the giant companies," says business analyst Tom Peters. Unlike the Western style of quick, overnight alliances and "Let's make a deal," Peters summarizes the key to a successful global marketing strategy in two statements: "Relationships are everything" and "We must learn to be patient."

Consider these statistics from Tom Peters. It took ARCO three and a half years to negotiate a tiny off-shore drilling contract with China. It took Rohm, the Silicon Valley telecommunications equipment maker, twenty visits over a multiyear period to land its first tiny order with a Japanese company. It took Coca-Cola ten years of investment and development of business in Japan before it turned its first profit. Relationships need time to develop.[5]

In his book *Thriving on Chaos*, Peters suggests that we'd be better off if we could pretend that all our customers are foreigners who do not speak our language. Peters maintains that we carry around a crippling disadvantage in being overconcerned about our products and services. Our customers, whether international or here in the United States, see the product through an entirely different set of lenses. Peters tells us, "Education is not the answer; listening and adapting is."

It's a Matter of Trust

Can the person and the company be trusted? That's the first thought most people have when they are considering dealing with someone they haven't done business with before. That issue of trust is translated into such thoughts as these:

- Is the person really knowledgeable?
- Can we trust his or her integrity?
- Is the salesperson concerned with our welfare or just making a sale?
- Will the company still be in business in two years?

"Actions speak louder than words," as the old saying goes, and when you think long-term, the willingness to invest in the relationship makes more sense. Rich Barsalou, a financial planner with John Hancock, realized that breaking into a new market would be difficult. He began by seeking out a reputable, well-known accountant in the area from whom he might be able to get some referrals to prospective clients. Instead of just asking for referrals, Barsalou hired the accountant to prepare his income tax return for him. He began to establish a relationship. Barsalou got to know the accountant on a personal level and, as time passed, gained his respect and trust. Eventually, the accountant gave him some names of prospective clients.

One of the referrals was a man who had recently purchased a local business and was in need of an employee benefits plan. Barsalou traveled to the plant at his own expense. To his disappointment, he discovered that the forty employees were well satisfied with the service and low cost of their existing plan. Barsalou soon concluded that his company could not offer a more competitive price, and so he offered to act as the company's negotiator in renewing the contract. What did Barsalou receive in return? No money, but lots of goodwill.

Soon after, that same client hired Barsalou to develop and launch a pension plan valued at $125,000 a year. The pension plan covered the local plant and another group in a different state that had traditionally faced high worker's compensation costs because of the nature of the research work the group did. Barsalou was able to persuade his company to offer lower rates if the members of the group passed a health examination.

To make sure the deal came through without any hitches, Barsalou wanted to close the sale quickly. He took an inspector and a nurse with him to the other state, and quickly had all the workers examined, the applications completed, and the sale made. Within a day, he had eighteen new disability plan members—most of whom later bought life insurance—and a happy client. The man who owned the business was so pleased with Barsalou's quick and satisfactory action that he bought $2 million worth of life insurance.

But the new business kept coming. After talking to his clients about Barsalou's performance, the accountant became a customer. He replaced his company's disability plan with one from Barsalou—and added $2 million in life insurance for his firm. "It started with my tax return," said Barsalou, "and I had no idea where it would take me."[6]

Barsalou's experience illustrates an important lesson: Trust is like credit. If you are reliable, pay your bills on time, and have a good work history and income, you can usually get credit. On the other hand, if you have a record of unpaid bills and a spotty work history, credit will be hard to get. In some circumstances, it takes only one mistake to permanently tarnish your record. We may not keep a running audit on each other's trustworthiness, but we do learn over time who we can count on and who's more likely to disappoint us. Whether we know it or not, we do have a trust account. When we show that we are trustworthy, our trust account builds.

When we are deciding whether or not to trust another person or situation, the most important information we have to help us make our decision is history. How has this person (or company) performed in the past? What's his or her record of trustworthiness? To get and keep any prospect's confidence and trust, you must first deserve it. Four key trust builders are outlined below:

Trust Builder 1: Appeal to a Prospect's Recognition Filter

A study on credibility found that when people hear about you, your company, or your product four or more times, they tend to perceive you as credible. That principle is what led sales management expert Rick Barrera to his cardinal rule of prospecting: Before you appeal to someone's need, first become familiar and recognizable. Barrera sends a prospect three or four different letters, one week apart, before making his first sales call. This way, he avoids making a totally "cold call."

Barrera explains, "Rather than having my prospects read the

content of my direct mail to decide whether my product or service fits their current need, I want them to recognize my name, and my company name, because of my direct mail. I don't care if they read it; I just want them to see it and recognize it."[7]

Experience has taught Barrera that a typical prospect reads mail as follows: The first letter gets glanced at and thrown away. By the second letter, the prospect says to himself or herself, "Didn't I get something from this person before?" With the third letter, the receiver says, "I know I got something else from this person, but what did I decide?" By the fourth letter, the prospect thinks, "I've heard lots about them—maybe I should give them a call."

When Barrera makes his first personal call on the prospect, he comes as a somewhat known quantity, and he usually gets an appointment right away. Through the use of direct mail, he has established a certain amount of credibility. His prospects have heard his name and his company name and are more willing to consider what he has to say. Using these mail contacts, Barrera has taken the first step to opening the door to a relationship.

Trust Builder 2: Consistently and Consciously Put the Customer's Interests Ahead of Your Own

Although your goal in business is to make your own business successful, the best way you can accomplish that goal is to make your customers happy and successful themselves. One way to ensure that both you and your customers are successful is by provding them with the information they need to make comfortable and informed decisions. Sharon Story learned this during her first experience as a salesperson.

Story was selling industrial filter bags, and during her visit to her new territory, she found that the client, a large steel company, was having a great many problems with its bags. The client asked many questions, and Story answered as well as she could, but both ended the meeting feeling dissatisfied.

A few weeks later, Story arranged for the general manager of her company to visit the executive and present him with the technical information he needed. By that time, however, an order had already been placed with another company.

Story was convinced that she had mishandled the account and that it was lost forever. But a few months later, the steel company executive called her. He was reviewing quotes for another bag order and realized Story's company was not on the bid list. At the executive's request, Story submitted a bid on another bag order. In this case, Story was successful. Her company got the $150,000 order. Story says, "If you go out of the way to try to help a prospect or customer, sooner or later one of them will go out of the way to help you."[8]

Trust Builder 3: Use Only Honest Facts and Figures to Back Up Claims

Inexperienced salespeople—as well as veterans—can fall into the trap of telling customers what they want to hear in order to keep them happy. Since "making the sale" is the goal, there is an incredible tendency for salespeople to do everything possible to get the order. This is often the case in the sales of long-distance services, according to Lenora Hyche, a top sales producer for American Telco, a long-distance company. For the past two years, Hyche has earned the distinction of being her company's most productive salesperson; she tripled the company average for individual sales in 1993 by bringing in 596 new accounts, for close to a $1 million in annual billings.

Hyche recalled a recent experience in which she and another long-distance carrier were in contention for a firm's business. Responding to the firm's request for specialized options, Hyche submitted a proposal that included the purchase of some additional equipment. Without the new equipment, Hyche reported, the capabilities could not be provided. The competitor's sales representative insisted that his company could meet the firm's requirements without new equipment, and he submitted a much lower bid. The firm accepted the competitor's proposal. Knowing the competitor had misrepresented the facts, Hyche graciously accepted the decision and took a "wait and see" attitude. Weeks later, the firm called Hyche with instructions to come and install the new equipment. The firm had dismissed the rival carrier. After misrepresentations and repeated delays, the sales representative conceded that he could not actually meet the firm's requirements without the purchase of new equipment. This unhappy experience resulted in the firm's staunch refusal to consider subsequent proposals from the competitive carrier as well as from its subsidiaries.

The tendency for salespeople to do everything to get the order can backfire, as evidenced by a story told me by a friend.

My friend was looking for a new car. She lives in a small town, and found a program car that she liked. This car had been driven for a short time by employees of the dealership. In discussing the car with the salesperson, she asked specifically about the warranty.

"Am I right in believing that the warranty is the same as on a new car?" she asked.

"Yes," the salesperson confirmed. "Just like a new car—three years or 30,000 miles."

"And that includes everything?" she pressed.

"Everything except normal maintenance—gas, oil, that sort of thing."

So my friend bought the car. She was pleased that she could buy from a local dealer, and the car suited her needs. A week or so later, however, she took the car in to the repair shop to fix a couple of small things that she'd found didn't work right.

The shop told her those things were not covered by the warranty. She wanted to know why not.

"Well, they were covered up to 3,000 miles, but since yours is a program car, it already has more miles on it than that. The salesperson should have made this clear."

The cost was minimal, but my friend had lost confidence in the dealership. A relationship that most likely would have lasted for years and through several automobile purchases was spoiled. She will not go back to buy her next car at that shop, simply because a salesperson was too eager to close the sale. Had she been told the facts to begin with, she probably would have bought the car anyway and expected to pay for minor repairs. But since that wasn't the case, she now has a bad feeling about the whole dealership.

Always tell the truth. False statements or even the inference of falsity can come back and haunt you, particularly when it's time to ask the customer to reorder.

Trust Builder 4: Promise Only What You Can Deliver

There exists no more critical time to build trust than during the initial encounter between prospect and salesperson. With no prior history, the prospect is often anxious and earnestly searching for "reasons to believe." Handled correctly, these early encounters can lay the foundation for a relationship and sales. Mishandled, these encounters can ruin any opportunity for business now or in the future.

Consider the letter in Figure 5–1, received by a travel agency that grossly mishandled the follow-up contact with a qualified prospect who had the potential to become a loyal, profitable corporate travel client.

As this prospect's words so vividly illustrate, trust is an all-important factor in converting a prospect into a first-time customer. At this stage, the prospect is looking for clues as to what he or she might expect as a customer and why he or she should trust this company. Nothing stifles trust more quickly with a prospect than poor follow-up. The travel agency demonstrated to the prospect by its actions (or lack of them) that it is not reliable. It flunked the prospect's first test of trust, confidence, and reliability.

Mismanagement of prospects is a common ailment in many industries. Consider the experience of Verne Newton, former international affairs consultant and author, and his personal account of mismanaged expectations and subsequent disappointments while car shopping:[9]

> Before entering the car market for the first time in 15 years, I resolved to buy American—a four door Oldsmobile Cutlass Supreme. After a broker and I expressed contempt for Americans who buy imports, I specified the features: anti-lock brakes, front-wheel drive, console gear shift, lumbar seats. I asked about an airbag.
>
> "Not possible," the dealer replied. He told me that I would have to go to a larger car but that I didn't want an airbag; they pop open for no reason, causing horrible accidents, and it costs $1,000 each to restuff them. He would call the next day, he said, and I could be driving by the weekend.
>
> After four days I called him. He was still looking for my car. Another call never came. That weekend, I went by his office. The car was at a

FIGURE 5–1

A "Lost" Prospect Speaks Out

Dear *(Name Withheld)*,

I received your business solicitation folder today–it is well done.

As a new businessman in town in December, I had no travel agent. I met your owner at a Chamber or Boy Scout meeting–I can't recall which. I told him I was looking for a good travel agent. I later called him back to remind him of my need and to ask for information on Barcelona for the Olympics. I called again in April asking for a visit. At that point I went with another agency, since no one from your agency appeared interested (after my three calls).

Since then: My son and I went to Barcelona, first class for the Olympics; my wife and I have visited Vancouver twice; I've been to meetings in Colorado Springs, first class; I took all 14 members of my family to Florida in May; I've taken three friends to Boston; and I've taken business trips to Phoenix, Washington, and Boca Raton.

There have been various other trips to sundry locations. I've been wondering if I'd ever hear from your agency, and I guess this mass mailing is it! Put down in your book that I sure tried to do business with you. I'm not mad, just curious to know that you're still there! My current agency says I'm a real good customer–like to go places and complain rarely. I went there since I met the owner in a barber shop and she was in my office the next day.

Why did I write this letter? Because I appreciate it when someone tells me how thoroughly we've screwed up a potential relationship."

Sincerely,

(Name Withheld)

---

dealership 40 minutes away. He said, "Why don't you go over and take it for a spin?" Features? It had a column shift, no lumbar seats and was a two door, not four.

Told by a car-maven friend that the Pontiac Grand Prix was nearly identical to the Cutlass Supreme, I went to see one. As I entered the showroom, salesmen jumped up and rushed toward the door. Although car sales were stagnant, I had not expected such a reception. Actually, the coffee wagon had arrived and they were heading for the doughnuts. No one remained for the prospect.

After I finally asked a saleman for help, he said they had nothing on the lot that met my needs. They could check with other dealers or could order from Detroit. How long would that take? "Could be six to eight weeks." [The dealership went under a few months later.]

Ford SHO [model] had nearly all the features I wanted, minus the airbag. I started talking lease versus purchase with an immaculately dressed, very personable salesman. Could he fax me the numbers? No problem. I never heard from him again.[10]

These events took their toll on Verne Newton, and his plea, "Stop me, I'm about to buy Japanese," went unanswered. He bought an Acura.

Listening: An Important Factor in Building Trust and Rapport

Golda Meir once said, "You cannot shake hands with a clenched fist." The secret to unlocking the "clenched fist" and developing a sense of trust and rapport with a new prospect is to learn to listen. Listening is key to building trust because of three important factors:

- I am much more inclined to trust a person who shows respect for me and for what I say.
- I am much more likely to trust you when you've listened carefully and helpfully to my problems than when you've tried to tell me what my problems are.
- The more I've told you, the more I trust you.

Key: Listening More and Talking Less

A recent survey of 432 corporate buyers found that 87 percent of the respondents said that salespeople don't ask enough questions about their needs, and 49 percent reported that salespeople just "talk too much." "Poor listening skills have a functional implication as well as a social implication," observes sales training executive Sean Carew. "You won't get the information, and you won't be able to relate to what your customer's needs are."[11]

Why Listening Is Hard Work

On the surface, listening seems simple. We all talk; we all listen. But it is not that simple. Why is listening hard? Why do so few people do it well? Basically, the problem is caused by the fact that we think much faster than we talk. For most Americans, the average rate of speech is around 125 words per minute.[12] This rate is very slow for the human brain, which is made up of more than 13 billion cells and operates in such a complicated manner that, in comparison, the great modern digital computers seem slow. As a result, most people find that because of the slow rate of speech, they have time to think of things other than the words being spoken. Subconsciously, they decide to sandwich a few thoughts of their own between the auditory ones that are arriving so slowly. But sooner or later, on one of the mental sidetracks, the listener is sure to stay away too long, and when he or she returns, the speaker is moving along ahead of the listener. At this point, it becomes harder for the listener to understand simply, because he or she has missed part of the oral message. The private mental sidetracks become more inviting than ever, and the listener slides off into several of them. Slowly, the listener misses more and more of what the speaker has to say.

Although the obvious solution is to slow thinking down to the speaking rate, that is almost impossible to do. Listening creates spare time in the brain that is almost automatically filled up by our own thoughts.

A major task in helping people listen better is teaching them to use their spare thinking time well. An extensive study of people's listening habits found that good listeners regularly engage in four mental activities during listening. They tend to direct a maximum amount of thought to the message being received, leaving a minimum amount of time for mental excursions or sidetracks that lead away from the talker's thought. In their book *Are You Listening*, authors Ralph Nichols and Leonard Stevens outline four processes used by good listeners:

1. The listener thinks ahead of the talker, trying to anticipate what the oral discourse is leading to and what conclusions will be drawn from the words spoken at the moment.
2. The listener weighs the evidence used by the talker to support

the points being made. "Is this evidence valid?" the listener asks himself or herself. "Is it complete evidence?"

3. Periodically, the listener reviews and mentally summarizes the points of the talk completed thus far.

4. Throughout the talk, the listener listens "between the lines," in search of meaning that is not necessarily put into spoken words. The listener pays attention to nonverbal communication (facial expressions, gestures, tone of voice) to see if it adds meaning to the spoken words. The listener asks himself or herself, "Is the talker purposely skirting some area of the subject? If so, why?"

Listening with an Open Mind

Although we often think that we listen carefully to what others say, in many cases we come to a conversation with certain expectations, certain goals, certain preset outcomes in mind. We listen selectively to what is being said, so that we hear only what fits into our preconceived notions of how the conversation should go. Often, if we are selling, we spend a lot of time thinking how to get the conversation over with and get on to closing the sale. Instead of paying attention to what the other person says, we listen for remarks that confirm what we already think is or should be the case. Rather than listening for information from an impartial point of view, too often our emotions are involved—we hear what we wish to hear rather than what is actually said.

"Hear the person out" is a phrase that describes an essential part of true listening. It requires giving up or setting aside one's own prejudices, frames of reference, and desires so as to experience as much as possible the speaker's world from his or her point of view. Here are some proven techniques for increasing the quality of listening:

THE "VISITOR FROM ANOTHER PLANET" TECHNIQUE

Communications specialist Elaine Zuker uses this method to become a better listener. She says that if you approach new people as if you had just landed on their planet and were trying to gain information, you will have fewer preconceived ideas about how the conversation will go. If you were on another planet, you would have no expectations. You would ask questions because you genuinely wanted information. Does this person speak as you do? Does this person talk about things the same way that you think of them? Simply gathering information without evaluating it makes for much better listening. If you avoid deciding in advance whether the information is good or bad, right or wrong, strange or familiar, you will be much better equipped to understand what is being said. If you continue the fantasy further, you can imagine that you must report on everything you learned when you return to your own planet. You will pay closer attention knowing that your information is important—and must be unbiased.

THE "LOOKING FOR NEGATIVE EVIDENCE" TECHNIQUE

Learning to be unbiased in your listening is important. Most of us automatically have an emotional reaction to another person and what that person says. Our inclination is to find evidence to support that emotional response, so we listen only for the words that confirm what we feel. Developing the technique that searches for evidence to dispute our emotional first reaction helps us hear more clearly what is being said. Initially, this is not an easy task. It is much easier and more instinctive to find confirmation for our beliefs. On the other hand, it can be done and it is helpful in understanding how another person perceives the situation differently. If we make up our minds to seek out the ideas that might prove us wrong, as well as those that might prove us right, we are less in danger of missing what people have to say.

LISTEN FOR IDEAS, NOT FACTS

Sometimes it is easier to listen to the surface of a conversation, rather than delving deeper to the essential ideas contained in the words. People want to communicate their ideas rather than a conglomeration of facts, but often we latch onto the facts and ignore the ideas behind them. Usually facts are given as examples of the main idea or as supporting evidence for the idea. When we listen specifically in order to understand the ideas, the facts become of secondary importance. Grasping ideas is the skill on which the good listener concentrates. The facts are important, but only peripherally. Once you understand the idea, the facts will come easily to mind.

Once you've trained yourself to listen more carefully, you'll see and hear things you would have overlooked before. You'll most likely find that people are more intriguing or interesting to you. If you can suspend judgment, you're apt to discover a better sense of rapport with them.

When It's Your Turn to Talk

Quality listening is an exchange process that requires quality *talking* as well. Robert Watson, director of advertising services at AT&T, recalls a memorable meeting with a media sales rep for *Puck the Comic Weekly*, a syndicated newspaper section. The salesman was trying to convince Robert to give him business for Clearasil and other "teen" brands in his media group at Benton & Bowles.[13]

The salesman introduced himself, sat down, and immediately began an obviously prepared sales pitch. He spoke quickly and without pause about facts, figures, and the details of his magazine. Watson realized that he was hearing very little of the information, because he was almost hypnotized by the manner of delivery. Soon he became impatient at the nonstop babble and interrupted the salesman to ask what all that had to do with his specific clientele.

The salesman continued to talk—twenty minutes in all—without ever addressing Watson's concerns or questions. At that point, he had finished his presentation and took his leave. Watson had no inclination to place ads with this representative. Nor did he ever hear from the salesman again.

Effective salespeople listen and ask questions. Only then can they start to understand the prospect's needs, problems, and way of thinking. Ineffective salespeople do just the opposite: They spew a flood of words, covering every benefit, every aspect, of the product, believing that sooner or later, the prospect will hear something positive and buy. As in Watson's case, he observed and heard things that turned him off and lost his patience rather than winning his attention.

Identify Your Customer's Buying Cycle

While the canned sales pitch can be disastrous in the development of a long-term customer, equally self-defeating is the salesperson who tries to close too soon.

Jan Ozer, an Atlanta-based marketing consultant, relates this experience:[14]

It was my first day with Barbara, our midwestern sales rep. The prospect was the Long Branch Inn, a resort recently purchased by a local businessman. Barbara had met with him twice before, once to interview and once to demo. She said the deal was ready to close.

We chatted briefly before Barbara summarized the benefits of the system and asked for the order.

Clearly surprised, the owner laughed and started in, "Place the order? What makes you think I'm ready to place the order? I haven't even started shopping yet!"

He pointed to the telephone on his desk. "You see that phone? It's part of a system I just paid thirty thousand dollars for. You know what I did before I bought it? First, I hired a consultant, because I don't know beans about telephones. He polled my staff to identify our needs. He arranged four product demonstrations. We visited sites and contacted references. We got proposals from all four companies. We selected two finalists and started negotiating. We got final offers from both and then we placed the order.

"I'm a businessman," he continued. "I don't make snap decisions. I'll be glad to speak with you next April, but I don't buy anything until I do my homework!"

Back in the car, I asked Barbara, "What made you think this deal would close today?" "Well," she replied, "at training they said deals close after the demonstration. I demo'd last time, so I thought it would close today. How was I to know he wouldn't buy until April?" Barbara retorted defensively. I responded, "You ask, Barbara, you ask!"

Barbara failed to distinguish between the seller's cycle and the buyer's cycle. In reality, companies buy at their own speed—they have their own selection process and timetable. It's important to uncover, understand, and confirm these needs before you begin to close.

Learn to Think Like a Sales Doctor

Selling is a process of satisfying needs. A truly effective salesperson is able to describe a product or service to someone in a way that allows that person to see how the product or service will satisfy his or her needs. To do this, you must first ask the right questions to learn what the prospect needs.

In considering how to proceed effectively, think of yourself as a "sales doctor." That's the approach Sharp Electronic Corporation adopted to train its dealers several years ago. As Morton Cohen, a national programs manager, related, "A doctor's job is to find the pain and help the patient—the prospect—understand that it's urgent he get treatment."[15] The key to this approach lies in getting prospects to discuss problems in their business, with specific emphasis on ones your product or service can fix.

Writing in *Success Magazine*, Brian Azar illustrates Sharp's sales doctor approach with the following dialogue:[16]

NEVER BEGIN WITH A PRESENTATION—ASK QUESTIONS

Prospect: I should tell you, our present copier works just fine.

Sales Doctor: Good. Can you tell me what you consider "fine"?

Prospect: I guess it jams sometimes, but overall, it gets the job done.

Sales Doctor: So if it didn't jam, you'd be completely happy with it?

Prospect: Well, no. After we fix the jam, the next twenty or so copies are smudged, so we do them all over again.

Sales Doctor: And that takes time?

Prospect: You bet it does.

Sales Doctor: How do you feel then?

Prospect: Terrible! Our real work isn't getting done, and we lose money.

PROBE DEEPER

Already the prospect's mind is on a problem the salesman can correct—with a copier that doesn't jam. But the sales doctor needs to define the pain better.

Sales Doctor: In your business, how important is a fast response to opportunity?

Prospect: Well, it's essential.

Sales Doctor: How much money a year do copier malfunctions at your company cost you in time and opportunity?

Prospect: I never added it up. . . .

Sales Doctor: $10,000? $20,000?

Prospect: Close to $20,000, I guess.

Sales Doctor: How does that lost $20,000 make you feel?

Prospect: Pretty awful. . . .

Sales Doctor: If you had a magic wand and money were no object, what would the solution be?

QUALIFY THE PATIENT

The sales doctor still has to establish that the prospect has "health insurance." He asks, "What kind of budget do you have for your problem?"

If the prospect says, "We don't really have a budget now," ask him when he will. If that doesn't elicit a reasonable timetable, it may be time to "go for NO"—to end the sales call. Don't avoid rejection. Often, your worst answer isn't "no"—it's "I'll think it over." That leaves you both in limbo.

NOW, PROPOSE THE CURE

If your prospect has the three key ingredients (pain, money to cure it, and authority to spend the money), you prescribe the cure—you make your presentation. Many salespeople want to present their whole routine anytime they see a prospect. The sales professional is willing to recognize that maybe the timing isn't right or that his product isn't a good fit and that there's no reason to go through the whole process:

Sales Doctor: As I understand it, these are the problems we're hoping I can solve.

Then, summarize the problems. Pause every so often to "take the patient's temperature": Ask summary questions like, "Do you see how that would solve your problem?"

Just when you think it's time to close—ask a question like, "What should we do next?" When the patient answers that kind of query, he has, in fact, closed the sale himself.

Jeff Thull of the P.R.I.M.E. Resource Group sales consulting firm says this about the sales doctor "diagnostic" selling technique: "Diagnostic selling means understanding the customer's situations, fears and concern—his 'pain.' No two customers are alike, even two people in the same company or decision-making process. It might sound basic, but the starting point is to realize that all customers are different and unique; and you tailor your sales 'prescription' to fit each of their needs as closely as possible."[17]

Use your dialogue with a prospect to build confidence and trust by practicing these guidelines:

- Avoid being a know-it-all. If you walk in the door with the attitude that you know everything, your credibility will already be suspect. People want someone who will help them find the answers to their problems, not someone who just tells them what to do.
- Help the prospect talk to you. If you are open and honest in your conversation with the prospect, it will encourage that person to be honest with you. Trust is a two-way street. You disclose something to someone; he or she discloses something to you. Sharing your own ideas and concerns will encourage your prospects to share theirs.

It's Not Just What You Say—It's How You Say It

Establishing rapport is more than providing information. It also involves verbal and body language resonance among people. Eye communication can be very important. Communications experts suggest spending more time looking at each person. Make contact three to five seconds with a person to truly achieve eye communication. Body language is also key to building rapport. Even when sitting down presenting to a single buyer, make sure you use gestures to communicate your excitement about your product or service.

Humor can also be a valuable tool for building rapport. A good example of how a sense of humor can make a sale comes from Mustang Engineering. Today Mustang employs 280 people and earns annual revenues of $30 million designing drilling platforms for clients all over the world. The company started out, however, at the very beginning of the oil slump and saw conditions in the industry worsen steadily. To keep afloat, the company took whatever business it could find that was in any way related to what it did. When things were looking as though the company was going to have to lay off key employees, the founder of the company heard about a new bus maintenance facility that was being planned. Mustang bid on the contract to provide engineering and drafting services. The trick would be to get the job—why would a transit commission pay attention to a company whose expertise was oil field engineering? Paul Redmon, one of the three cofounders of the company, describes their presentation:

> We knew we would be the last to present, just before lunchtime. We gave each guy a big Snickers bar, saying, "We don't want you thinking about lunch during our presentation." The last member of the board was a woman, and we knew from my friend that she was two months pregnant. So I gave her a big Snickers and a little one, too, for her baby. That a got a laugh—they could tell we had inside information—and it broke down the wall. Then we sang a takeoff on the Snickers jingle—you know, "Snickers will satisfy you." We sang, "Mustang Engineering will satisfy you."[18] Mustang got the job and managed to keep everyone working until the oil business began to generate enough to keep them busy and prospering.

Remember, feelings and emotions are usually far more persuasive than intellect. More energy is generated by feelings than facts. As someone once said, "Seeing's believing, but feeling's the truth."

Plan Your Return Call Before Your First Call

A McGraw-Hill survey reported that six out of ten customers will say no four times before they say yes. That makes repeat calls a virtual certainty. "Reasons to return" can play an important role in turning qualified prospects into first-time customers. Involving the buyer's interest is key to making these return encounters effective. Ten constructive reasons for returning are outlined below:

- To gather more information
- To add some important new data to your reply to a question the buyer asked last time
- To take a tour of the prospect's facility
- To explain a new or improved product or service
- To talk about a promotion the customer might run to increase sales on his or her (and your) product
- To follow up on literature sent
- To congratulate the customer on a promotion or award
- To accompany the prospect to a trade or professional meeting
- To introduce other prospective team members
- To entertain so as to show appreciation

Regardless of the "reason to return" by which the sales representative reconnects with the prospect, every sales contact should be planned with the objective of moving the prospect closer to a sale. Just because a salesperson isn't making a formal presentation doesn't mean that the call shouldn't be planned. In some cases, such planning takes only a few seconds before a call. But in every instance, it's vital for the sales representative to answer one simple question: For this call to be successful, what should result?

Patience, persistence, sales planning, and lots of reasons to return were what won Guy Anderson, Regional Vice President of Stockholder Systems, Inc. a $1.5 million account with E. I. du Pont de Nemours, beating out a field of four keen competitors. Du Pont decided to replace its stockholder record-keeping system and estimated the project would take about twenty-one months from the evaluation stage to installation and in-house operation. Du Pont was determined to find out everything about securities systems vendors and to make sure its own employees understood any new system that was considered. It was clear that making the sale would require patience, persistence, and serious involvement with the decision makers.

Anderson took advantage of the time involved in the analysis process to learn everything he could about du Pont. He got to know the people who would be working on the project. He spent time watching, listening, and learning. He made repeated contact with the people who were evaluating systems. Instead of simply touting his product, Anderson called to see how everything was going and offered to provide additional information and resources. He assumed the role of partner in the process, rather than outsider trying to sell the company something.

By planning to stay in constant touch, Anderson gained an important edge over the competition. He learned about the people—their personalities, their likes and dislikes, their working styles—and he learned about the various objectives the new system would have to satisfy. With his newfound information, Anderson was able to satisfy both corporate and personal concerns about the new system.

To reassure du Pont that his company would provide continued customer support, Anderson took its key people to visit some current satisfied customers and invited them to symposia where the product was demonstrated. Getting to know the system support people before buying the system reassured du Pont that help was available if it was needed. Seeing big customers who were satisfied with the system also allayed fears.

As it turned out, Anderson's presence and persistence paid off. He won the competition by being there, by being concerned and helpful, and by subtly selling his product again and again. By the time the planning stage was completed, Anderson had the contract in the bag. His own planning had paid off handsomely, and his four competitors were left waiting to give their big sales pitch.[19]

Rules for Ending Every Call

A critical aspect of every sales call is how the call is concluded. As we have discussed, the purpose of every sales call is to move systematically toward a completed sale, and there is no better place to ensure meeting that objective than to make sure you conclude your sales calls correctly. Consider these guidelines:

- Be sure you've uncovered the real points of interest about your product or service.
- Outline what you are going to do next.

- Tell the prospects what you need from them in order to provide the benefit they're interested in.
- Agree on the next contact. Get specific.

Throughout your conversation with the prospect, and particularly as you are concluding your call, beware of overpromising and building unrealistic expectations. Build your communication in a way that will influence prospective customers to expect a little less service than they will get. For example, if your company can routinely get a package door to door in eighteen hours, guarantee twenty-four-hour service. If you do this, you are promising something you know you can deliver, and your prospects will be delighted to have their expectations exceeded. As customer service consultant, Dr. Michael LeBoeuf says, "It's not the quality of service that you give but the quality of service that the customer perceives that causes him to buy and come back." Always keep in mind that as we convert prospects into first-time customers, we are not trying to merely make a sale. Instead, we are trying to develop a loyal customer.

Where There's a Will, There's a Way

Although many entrepreneurs and other professionals often feel that closing a sale is a life-or-death situation, in Sunny Graham's case this was no exaggeration. As a first-time salesperson, her commission-only salary was her sole hope to escape the likelihood of imprisonment by her government. With no time for sales training or lackluster beginnings, the neophyte salesperson had a short three months in which to make her money. Sound like an impossible task? Here's how she did it.

In the summer of 1971, Graham, a native Filipino living in Meycauayan in the Philippines, had just graduated from the University of the Philippines. Fearing martial law was near, Graham and her family were increasingly concerned that if she did not get out soon, she would be unable to leave the country at all. Graham had participated in the student movement on the University of the Philippines campus and was likely to be imprisoned for her activist work at the university.

In May 1971, upon receiving her college degree, Graham began looking for a job. She had three months to raise the necessary cash to finance her trip to the United States. Time was tight. She had to get to the States by the end of the summer in order to qualify for a student visa to get in school by the fall.

Through a friend, Graham found out that Compton's Encyclopedia (a division of Brittannica) was just entering the Philippines and was hiring local sales representatives. She applied and got the job.

Based on a commission of 200 pesos, or roughly $25, Graham determined she would have to sell, on average, seven sets of Compton's a day, five days a week, for three months to save the money she needed. Having no experience selling this product or any other, that seemed an enormous quota, but to achieve her goal of leaving the Philippines, she had no choice. She went to work.

Graham selected her target market: the upper-crust families in her community and in the neighboring city of Manila. She began by contacting families she knew. Her sales message stressed the benefits of Compton's as an important educational extension. There was no public library system in the Philippines, so Graham emphasized the merits of the encyclopedia to families in search of more education for their children. The fact that Sunny had successfully gotten a U.S. education (no one in her community had ever gone to the United States on scholarship) made her recommendation even more credible.

Graham's first sale was to the vice-mayor of her town. From that sale and others, she diligently ask for referrals. In addition, she also went door to door. On many calls, she went back two, three, and even four times before the sale was made.

Graham put in long hours and covered many miles. At first, sales were slow, but by the end of the summer, Graham had met her goal, averaging a remarkable seven sets a day! In fact, her average daily commission of $175 exceeded her brother's monthly salary as a long-time government official.

Graham returned to the United States in September 1971, four months before martial law was declared. As she had feared, professors, student leaders, and protesters were taken to prison. Four of her closest friends ultimately died in prison. Several others, who did not die in prison, were brutalized and beaten during their incarceration.

Upon returning to California, Graham did additional graduate work. She married the son of her "foster" parents, and they have been married for twenty-eight years. Graham and her husband now live in Dallas, Texas, where she heads an import-export business specializing in products from the Philippines.

What accounted for Sunny Graham's unlikely success? Was she a natural-born sales prodigy? Did she just experience beginner's luck? Was she at the right place at the right time? Perhaps the answer lies in a recent Harvard Business School study that identified the most common characteristics of top salespeople. According to the study's findings, most people can be top sellers if they are willing to study, concentrate, and focus on their performance. Here are eight attributes identified by the study as being key to successful salespeople:[20]

- Did not take "no" personally
- 100 percent acceptance of responsibility for results
- Above-average ambition
- High levels of empathy
- Intensely goal oriented
- Above-average willpower
- Impeccably honest with self and with the customer
- Ability to approach strangers

No doubt, Sunny Graham's unfortunate circumstances gave her lots of incentive to sell. But the good news is that this same level of success and more are available to anyone armed with a well-conceived product or service and equal measures of focus, diligence, common sense, and integrity.

Today, in her import-export business, Sunny Graham enjoys a luxury of time with her customers that she did not have when she sold encyclopedias. This enables her to focus less on making sales and more on developing customers. But Sunny's mastery of selling to first-time customers provides a distinct advantage. It's an important first step to a long, profitable, lasting relationship with a customer.

Learning from a Lost Sale

Let's face it. Despite your best efforts, you will never convert every qualified prospect into a new customer. But take heart. Even lost sales can provide you with valuable information about ways to build future sales and loyalty. Here's how one company made it happen.

Several years ago, Tom Tjelmeland of T&K Roofing Company was faced with a problem of fallen margins and lost bids. In 1988, profit margins had dropped from 5 to 1 percent on sales of $2.5 million, and the chief executive of the Ely, Iowa, roofing company was ready to do almost anything to halt the downward slide of retained earnings.

Tjelmeland and his son, Kurt, T&K's vice-president, decided to construct a form that would deliberately invite criticism from would-be customers who had awarded their roofing jobs to T&K's competitors. What emerged was the *Lost-Job Survey*, containing twenty-two quick-answer questions. Among the most important information that came back from the 1,000 surveys returned to T&K in a three-year period was that the respondents didn't want the indestructible, high-quality roofing that Tom thought they should buy. It was too expensive. "It forced us to ask prospects what they wanted, instead of offering them what we thought they needed," Tom said.[21]

The single question on the survey form that prompted the most changes in the way T&K sold its products was the one that asked customers if they had established a relationship with another roofing contractor. "If this was marked yes," Tjelmeland said, "it told me my people were out there slapping prices on jobs instead of developing relationships. Establishing a relationship takes time, but you learn more about what the customer wants besides a low price."[22]

T&K's *Lost-Job Survey* did more than show the company the way to make the difficult shift away from low-margin, low-bid contracts to the more lucrative, negotiated-bid contracts it had been losing before. The questionnaire provided the company with a revitalized sales philosophy that changed the emphasis to a "best solution for customers" approach. In the process, employees who couldn't change their methods quit; other were let go. Since it began using the survey, T&K's profit picture has improved and sales have grown to $4 million.

The experience of T&K Roofing illustrates a key fact: Even if a counted-on sale does not materialize, not all is lost. Valuable information can often be gleaned from the experience so as to identify problems and improve loyalty-building strategies.

Summary

- It takes an average of seven contacts to turn a prospect into a first-time buyer. Research suggests that this number may be rising, due to deeper alliances between buyers and sellers and a tougher economy.
- Canned sales pitches no longer work; customers want people who will listen to their needs, be honest and upfront, and diagnose problems and offer solutions.
- It takes patience and time to build trust in a customer—once trust is gained, there are many long-term benefits.
- Plan your return sales call before your first call. Develop a wide array of constructive reasons for recontacting your prospects.
- Feedback from lost sales provides valuable information about ways to make future sales and build customer loyalty.

6

Turning First-Time Buyers into Repeat Customers

When an American husband and wife purchased a faulty Sony compact disc player at a Tokyo department store, they received a lesson in customer loyalty that completely overwhelmed them and turned their anger into amazement.

The couple, who were staying with the husband's parents in the outlying city of Sagamihara, had tried to operate the disc player the morning after the purchase and were disappointed when it wouldn't run. Further investigation proved there was no motor or driving mechanism in the case.

Annoyed and perplexed, the husband had been practicing the scathing denunciation he planned to register by telephone with the manager of the Odakyu Department Store on the dot of 10:00 A.M., when the store opened.

But 9:59 A.M., the phone rang and was answered by the husband's mother, who had to hold the receiver away from her ear, so vehement was the barrage of Japanese honorifics that came from the other end of the line. The caller was none other than Odakyu's vice-president, who clamored effusively that he was on his way over with a new disc player.

In less than a hour, the vice-president of the company and a junior employee were standing on the doorstep. The younger man was laden down with packages and papers. As they met the customer at the door, both men began bowing enthusiastically.

Continuing to bow, the younger man began explaining to the

customer the steps they had taken to rectify their mistakes. On the day the customers had left the store, a salesclerk had discovered the problem and requested security guards to stop them at the door. Since they had already left, the clerk reported the error to his supervisor, who reported to his supervisor, and so on, until the vice-president learned of the error. Since the only identification the store personnel had was an American Express card number and name, they began there.

The clerk called thirty-two hotels in and around Tokyo to ask if the couple were registered. That turned up nothing, so a staff member was asked to stay late at the store, until 9:00 P.M., when the American Express headquarters in New York would be open. American Express gave him the couple's home phone number. When the employee called that number, at almost midnight Tokyo time, he reached the wife's parents, who were housesitting. He learned the couple's address in Tokyo from the wife's parents.

The young employee, breathless from his recitation, then began offering gifts to the customers: a new $280 disc player, a set of towels, a box of cakes, and a Chopin disc. In less than five minutes, the astonished couple watched the vice-president of the store and his employee climb back into a taxi—after profuse apologies for having made the customers wait while the salesclerk rewrote the sales slip. They sincerely hoped the couple would forgive the mistake.

While most stores would replace defective merchandise, how many would go to such lengths to make an unhappy customer a lifelong buyer? Certainly, top management would rarely even know that such a mistake had happened. It's this type of spirit to heroically preserve the good opinion and esteem of the customer that builds loyalty in first-time buyers.

Four Reasons Why First-Time Buyers Do Not Return

Consultant Richard Shapiro specializes in keeping management on track in the pursuit of customer retention. He reports that for many firms, first-year account attrition rates are often more than double those of older accounts. After performing a series of extensive "exit interviews" with a cross section of a software company's former customers, Shapiro discovered four key reasons why first-time buyer attrition can be so widespread:[1]

1. *Early Problems Sour Relationship.* If a problem develops during the first three to six months of a customer's life cycle, that customer assumes these situations will occur frequently and may feel buyer's remorse. Suspicion that there will always be problems can quickly sour the relationship and block any opportunity for future sales.

2. *No Formal Servicing System.* The same company that spends months or even years pursuing a new customer often fails to set up tight account management functions to ensure that orders are processed and fulfilled in a satisfactory manner.

3. *Communication Breakdown with Decision Makers.* Organizations rarely communicate on an ongoing basis with decision makers in the customer's business. They usually end up continuing their dialogue with users or technical buyers. Although these individuals may have been involved in the purchasing cycle, they are not usually solely responsible for retaining an organization as a supplier. As communications with decision makers weaken, the supplier is at risk. In addition, when an original decision maker leaves and new ones take over, the organization leaves itself vulnerable to competition if there is not consistent communication.

4. *Easy Return.* If the customer is still doing business with a former supplier, it is easy for the customer to return to that supplier if problems develop.

The Real Sale Begins After The "YES"

As the management at the Odakyu Department Store so aptly demonstrated, the real sale begins after the customer says yes. It's how you perform after the customer buys that determines whether you keep him or her as a loyal customer. Consider this short story.

> A man died and went to Heaven, where he was told he had a choice between Heaven and Hell. He decided to take this unusual offer and checked out both opportunities. Heaven was very serene, bathed in a pleasing white light. A lot of people were walking around in white robes and singing hymns. Nice, but a tad boring for eternity, the visitor reasoned. On his visit to Hell, he was surprised to find people having fun. They were playing golf, they were playing cards, and it wasn't at all hot. He had an easy decision, he told the angels at the Pearly Gates, and headed back to Hell.

But when he got there, everything was different from his first visit. It was hot and terrible, and people were miserable—a lot like his original expectations.

"What happened?" he worriedly asked the Devil. "This isn't at all what I saw when I visited."

"When you visited, you were a prospect," the Devil told him. "Now you're a customer."[2]

This humorous account provides a sad but true commentary about how businesses operate. The rapport and trust established during the selling process can quickly fade when a new customer's needs are not met. An article in the *Wall Street Journal* illustrated how tenuous the period is right after an initial sale and how easily goodwill can be lost. The story appeared shortly after the introduction of IBM's new Ambra PC, with the headline "Ordering IBM Ambra PC Can Be a Hassle." Three new buyers were profiled:

David Harrison, a Washington lawyer, says he eagerly ordered an Ambra on Aug. 3, the day it began advertising, and was told to expect his machine in three to five days. He says he never received the PC and, despite 50 phone calls over the ensuing weeks, could never find out the status of his order.[3]

Mark Lewis, a Trumball, Connecticut, computer consultant who ordered an Ambra PC, called three days later to make sure it was shipped. "They said, 'We don't have any system in place to say where your order is.'" A week later, he canceled his order. He says he made repeat follow-up calls, but no one ever confirmed his cancellation.

Tom Gresham of Natchitoches, La., a freelance writer, ordered an Ambra but changed his mind the next day and called to cancel. After a week of calls, he too had a clerk tell him that the Ambra order system couldn't confirm his cancellation.

The article went on to quote an Ambra spokesman, who said the company's computers do track orders and the three callers who had trouble must have been unusual cases. "Unusual" or not, Ambra's poor performance is representative of a simple truth: Every customer's experience is greatly determined by how his or her particular order is processed.

Follow the Order

In the movie *All the President's Men*, which chronicles the Watergate scandal, journalists Carl Bernstein and Bob Woodward receive inside information from an unidentified contact called Deep Throat. Deep Throat's most frequent advice is "Follow the money." To anyone interested in developing loyal customers, the advice could easily be "Follow the order." Why? Because every customer's experience is greatly determined by a company's order management cycle (OMC).

Writing in the *Harvard Business Review*, professors Benson Shapiro, Kastari Rangan, and John Sviokla encourage managers to track each step of the OMC by working their way though the company from the customer's point of view rather than their own. Say the authors, "In the course of the order management cycle, every time the order is handled, the customer is handled, [and] every time the order sits unattended, the customer sits unattended. Paradoxically, the best way to be customer-oriented is to go beyond customers and products to the order; the moment of truth occurs at every step of the OMC, and every employee in the company who affects the OMC is the equivalent of a front line worker."[4] It is the order, say the authors, that connects the customer to the company in a systematic and companywide fashion.

The ten steps, from planning to postsales service, that define a company's OMC are outlined below. Opportunities for improving overall operations and creating new competitive advantages can be found in these ten steps:[5]

1. Order planning
2. Order generation
3. Cost estimation
4. Order receipt
5. Order selection
6. Scheduling
7. Fulfillment
8. Billing
9. Returns and claims
10. Postsales service

"Follow the order" is an apt description of what General Mc-Dermott did when he assumed the position of chief executive of USAA in 1968. (As you will recall from earlier chapters, USAA provides insurance services to military officers.) McDermott describes the situation he found:

> There was paper everywhere. We had 650,000 members at that time and 3,000 employees. Every desk in the building was covered with stacks of paper—files, claim forms, applications, correspondence. You can't imagine how much paper. Stacks and piles and trays and baskets of it. And of course a lot of it got lost. On any given day, the chances were only 50–50 that we'd be able to put our hands on any particular file. When I first started, I would often stay late and go around putting little marks on papers and files, then I'd check the next night to see if they'd been moved. A lot of people moved no paper at all.[6]
>
> We constantly got letters and phone calls about poor service. Most of our members were sticking with us because our premiums were lower than anyone else's and because we were good on claims. It certainly wasn't because of our prompt and dependable service in any other area.
>
> There were 55 steps associated with every new insurance policy USAA processed. The first person would open the envelope, remove the paper clips, and pass it to the second person, who would check addresses on big Rolodexes and write in corrections with a pen, then pass it to the third person, and the fourth person, and so on—55 steps. The average employee stayed with the company for 11 months. We were giving terrible service and boring our employees.

Contrast that with the company today and the transformation is truly remarkable. With 14,000 employees, the nation's fifth largest insurer serves more than 2 million customers and policyholders and manages $20.7 billion in assets. The company's retention rate is a remarkable 98 percent.

Twenty-five years later, USAA, under General McDermott's leadership, is still "following the order." Over a six-year period, the company created an AIE (an automated insurance environment) that includes policy writing, service, claims, billing, customer accounting—all aspects of the OMC.

McDermott explains, Now when you want to buy a new car, get it insured, add a driver, and change your coverage and address, you can make one phone call—average time, five minutes—and nothing else is necessary. One stop, on-line, the policy goes out the door the next morning about 4:00 A.M. In one five-minute phone call, you and our service representative have done all the work that used to take 55 steps, umpteen people, two weeks and a lot of money.

We get about 150,000 pieces of mail every morning, of which 60% to 65% are checks. Of the remainder, less than half ever leaves the mailroom. All of our policy-service correspondence is imaged, indexed, prioritized; it's then instantly available anywhere the company.[7]

General McDermott illustrates:

Suppose Colonel Smith has sent us a letter asking for a change in his homeowner's insurance, and he calls and wants to know if we've received it. The service representative says, "Yes, sir, I've got it right here." "You do?" he says. "Yes," the rep says, "I have it right in front of me. What can I do for you?"[11] The colonel's impressed. We received his letter only that morning, but it's already been imaged, so it's instantly available to every service representative in the building. Now let's say Colonel Smith calls back the next day with some additional information we've asked him for and talks to a different service rep, who also has his letter "right here in front of me." Now the colonel's impressed and amazed.

Let's say the service rep, who has not only Colonel Smith's letter but his entire file available on the screen, goes on to explain how the change Smith wants to make in his homeowner's coverage may reduce his need for umbrella liability and thus lower the cost of that policy. Now the colonel's impressed and amazed and very pleased. And so are we, because the whole transaction's taken five minutes.[8]

Giving Employees the Tools to Perform

USAA has identified and championed a key element of customer loyalty that other companies are now just beginning to understand: that the key to "growing" loyal customers rests first in creating effective employees. To succeed in the 1990s, service companies must transform their internal operating systems into structures that empower rather than impede front line success with customers. As Ron Zemke, president of Performance Research Associates, says, "An organization's reputation for quality customer service is indeed built one customer and one contact at a time. Most frequently, that contact is a face-to-face, living, breathing, human contact."

Successful management realizes it is essential that the employees who deal directly with customers have the necessary time, tools, and training and the complete support of the company. It is the performance of those front line employees on which judgments of the entire company are made—and future sales made or lost. No sharp advertising campaign, no glossy packaging, can make up for poor relationships between the customer and the company's representative who deals directly with him or her.

In many businesses, the practice has been to put customers first and employees last. This is a mistake from every perspective. Disgruntled employees can lead only to dissatisfied customers. We realize today that employees who are committed to their jobs, who are well provided for by their employers, and who feel valued are much more likely to serve customers well and to help the business succeed. The new model gives priority to front line workers and designs the customer delivery system around them. According to Harvard professors Leonard Schlesinger and James Heskett, companies that follow this model

- value investments in people more than investments in machines;
- use technology to support the efforts of employees on the front line, not to monitor or replace them;
- make recruiting and training as crucial for salesclerks and maintenance workers as for managers and senior executives; and
- link compensation to performance for employees at every level, not just for those at the top.

Federal Express is a company designed along these lines. Incorporated in 1973, the company has captured an impressive 42.5 percent share of the total air cargo market, armed with a corporate philosophy that simply states "People, Service, Profit." James Perkins, senior vice-president of personnel, says, "We believe that if we put employees first, they in turn will deliver the impeccable service demanded by our customers, who will reward us with the profitability necessary to secure our future."[9]

Federal Express incorporates the four principles of the new model throughout its organization. For example, state-of-the art technology includes interactive video, which combines computer technology and audiovisual capabilities so that employees can train themselves with little or no supervision. Couriers use hand-held computers to relay all package information to a centralized computer, enabling fast retrieval of information on all shipments. The importance of specific job training skills are emphasized in all groups of hourly employees. Hub package handlers receive 40 hours of training; new couriers, 160 hours; and new customer service agents, 200 hours. All pay groups are eligible for special compensation programs. Federal Express's pay-for-performance program rewards domestic customer-contact hourly employees for experience and knowledge of the job. Known as "Propay," this lump-sum bonus is available to 50,000-plus customer-contact and package-handling employees.

In addition to its impressive sales and profit performance, what other indication exists within Federal Express that the new model works? In the company's most recent annual survey of all Federal Express U.S. employees, 85 percent said they are proud to work for the company. And how about its customers? The company's most recent customer survey, conducted by an independent agency, reported that 95 percent of the company's customers are completely satisfied with the company's service.

Federal Express's system obviously works—customers are happy, employees are happy, and business is booming. The emphasis on providing employees with the necessary tools to satisfy their customers and make them loyal has resulted in a business that is the leader in its field.

A Closer Look at First-Time Buyers

Every purchase entails consequences for a buyer. These consequences occur as a result of what consumer behaviorists call post-decision reevaluation. Every customer brings to a purchase a certain set of expectations. Following a purchase, the buyer compares what he or she received with what he or she expected. If the comparison is favorable, the buyer is said to be satisfied. If the comparison is unfavorable, the buyer is said to be dissatisfied.

First-time buyers are in effect "triers." They are trying the new product or service, and their perception of quality and their resulting level of satisfaction will influence their desire to buy again. A feeling of satisfaction from the first-time purchase improves the likelihood that these persons will buy again. Their second purchase is significant, because it represents a change from the first. This time, the buyers make their purchase decision based on a new set of criteria, what consumer behaviorists call nonrandom purchase behavior. This means that the buyers go into the repeat purchase process with a substantiated preference about what and from whom to buy. This preference has been at least partly earned through the positive first-time purchase experience.

On the other hand, when a purchase expectation is not met, dissatisfaction will result. Dissatisfaction is defined as "the degree of disparity between expectations and perceived product performance." When a disparity between performance and expectancy exists, the new buyer experiences a state of psychological inconsistency, or dissonance. The degree of postpurchase dissonance is a function of several factors:[10]

- The more important the decision, the greater the dissonance.
- The greater the number of alternatives considered before the purchase decision, the greater the dissonance.
- The more attractive the rejected alternative, the greater the dissonance.
- The more frequently the product or brand is purchased, the less the degree of dissonance.
- The more irrevocable the purchase, the greater the dissonance.

A state of dissonance is uncomfortable for the purchaser and, if not appropriately handled, can lead to increased dissatisfaction. This increased dissatisfaction can in turn lead to lost sales, as seen in the case of US West Cellular.

How US West Cellular Fights Postpurchase Dissonance

US West Cellular had a problem: The company invests at least $700 to recruit a new customer, with a payback on this investment of at least seven months. US West discovered that many accounts were canceling their service before this payback period was complete. In fact, 50 percent of all new accounts never made it to long-term status. Financial analysis indicated that if the monthly cancellation rate could be cut by just one-tenth of 1 percent, approximately $1 million could be added to US West Cellular's bottom line.

Unlike many firms that regard past-due accounts as simply collection problems, US West Cellular determined that 75 percent of all overdue payment disputes were actually customer service problems. Dissatisfied customers are not as prompt in paying their bills as satisfied customers. Recognizing this fact, the company merged its financial service and customer service departments and made John Suhm, a company accountant, head of customer service.

Suhm and his staff soon discovered that a large percentage of the company's new customers were canceling service soon after receiving their first bill. Why? The first bill includes a charge for the first month's service, long-distance charges for all calls placed that first month, and charges for the next month's service. As a result, the total bill is usually two times more than the customer expects.

To help cycle customers through this first "buying" period, the service reps on Suhm's team place "welcome new customer" calls with the purpose of thanking them for their business, answering questions, and, most important, reassuring them that future bills will be considerably less. Through company research, US West Cellular found an interesting link between customer contact and customer satisfaction. It seemed that when customer representatives called customers periodically, those customers developed a perception that their cellular service was of a higher quality (less static, etc.) than that perceived by customers who did not receive calls.

Another team of company employees, called the "Retention Group," focuses exclusively on handling customers who wish to disconnect their service. With a brass ship's bell hanging prominently in the group's work area, a rep earns the right to ring the bell whenever he or she "saves" a customer from canceling. Moreover, US West Cellular created a companywide bonus plan that encourages every employee to take actions to reduce customer losses. Referred to by Suhm as the "churn" bonus, even a file clerk receives a monthly bonus of $50 when company disconnect goals are achieved.

US West Cellular has seen dramatic results from these measures.

The save rate has increased by 150 percent, monthly attrition has dropped by 30 percent, and, according to Suhm, the bottom line has improved by $8 million.[11]

The Right Information at the Right Time

Carefully selecting the means by which information is fed to new buyers can help reduce postpurchase dissonance. One study that attempted to reduce dissonance among people who had just bought refrigerators obtained mixed results: Letters to the new customers appeared to get a favorable response, but telephone calls did not.

One-third of all customer complaints come from customers who do not know how to use the product, according to John Goodman, president of Technical Assistance Research Programs, a customer service consulting organization. Service visits, mailings, and other forms of active communication can educate customers about product use and help keep them satisfied. For example, Armstrong found that many purchasers of its no-wax floors cared for them improperly and complained when they deteriorated. In response, Armstrong prominently stamped an 800 number on the surface of each floor with the message "Call for instructions on how to remove this number." The number comes off with water, but callers also receive instructions on how to care for the floor. The result? A significant increase in repeat purchase from satisfied customers.[12]

Even doctor-patient relationships can improve with the right information, according to the findings from a test by two cancer specialists in Sydney, Australia, who were looking for ways to increase patients' satisfaction with their care. The study showed that doctors who write letters to their patients repeating what they told the patients in the office feel a higher level of satisfaction with their medical care. The researchers reported that they tested the idea on forty-eight cancer patients who came in to see one of the specialists, M. H. N. Tattersall, for follow-up consultations after treatment. Half of the patients were randomly chosen to receive a letter dictated by Dr. Tattersall immediately after the patient's visit. The letter summarized what had been discussed during the visit.

In the ensuing three weeks, all forty-eight patients were interviewed and asked how satisfied they were with the visit, on a scale of one to five. The patients who received the letters expressed a higher degree of satisfaction than those who didn't receive a letter. Of the twenty-four letter recipients, thirteen reported "complete satisfaction" with their visit, while only four of those who didn't get a letter reported complete satisfaction.[13]

What Service Means in the 1990s

As we saw in Chapter 1, customers increasingly want more than just a one-night stand with the businesses from which they buy. Consumers are becoming more concerned about service and how they are treated when they purchase something than they are about the price alone. Nurturing customer relationships is the cornerstone of a growing number of companies new customer marketing strategies, as reflected in the increased offering of long-term guarantees on products, service packages, investments, and other similar incentives. What kind of service will turn first-time buyers into repeat customers? Perhaps part of the answer can be found in how customers of the 1990s perceive the concept of service after the sale.

The five dimensions of service quality were first identified through a model developed by researchers from Texas A&M University in 1988 and then validated again four years later in a 1992 study by The Forum Corporation. In comparing customers' expectations of service quality with their actual experiences, both studies identified five key dimensions of service most important to a buyer:[14]

1. *Reliability*—the ability to provide what was promised, dependably and accurately
2. *Assurance*—the knowledge and courtesy of employees and their ability to convey trust and confidence
3. *Tangibles*—the physical facilities and equipment and the appearance of personnel
4. *Empathy*—the degree of caring and individual attention provided to customers
5. *Responsiveness*—the willingness to help customers and provide prompt service

Let's take a closer look at two critical dimensions: on reliability and responsiveness.

Reliability

Customers put "reliability" first in assessing service, yet salespeople and sales managers still perceive that customers regard "responsiveness" as more important. One possible reason for this disparity is that, unlike reliability which is a wider organizational issue and takes an investment of time and money, responsiveness is most often provided by sales and service people and therefore is an easier dimension for them to provide and control. Research reveals that salespeople and sales managers even make references about reliability less often than their customers.

Research has also shown that honesty plays an important role in reliability, according to Forum Senior Vice-President Jennifer Potter-Brotman. Explains Brotman, "If a customer requests a product on a Monday, yet reality dictates a Wednesday delivery, being open with the customer significantly increases the chances of earning his or her trust and establishing a long-term relationship. Customers have considerable empathy for the seller's position, yet they have little patience for sellers who overpromise, don't establish the proper expectations, or bring the customer in on a problem when it's too late for them to contribute to its solution."[15]

Responsiveness

Since the late 1980s, a customer's perception of responsiveness has also grown in scope. Buyers used to look for a quick reaction to a request or a problem. Now, reports Brotman, "Customers want companies to anticipate problems before they happen and to be honest about potential problems. In short, responsiveness now begins before the point of purchase. Rather than fixing a problem quickly, companies must make sure that the problem doesn't occur in the first place. When a certain photocopy company is called to fix one of their customers' many copy machines, the repair person checks every other copy machine in the company to make sure they're all working properly. They also ask users how the machines are operating and if they need additional service or training on how to use the features. In this way, they build the organization's confidence—through proactive service and maintenance."[16]

The other three factors—assurance, tangibles, and empathy—are closely tied to these two. Demonstrations of responsiveness and reliability confirm that the company is knowledgeable and empathetic with the customer's needs, and, over time, the tangibles become less important and more acceptable. Once the customer is convinced that he or she can rely on the product and the responsiveness of the employees, there is a good probability that that customer will become a loyal repeat buyer.

Fourteen Actions That Encourage First-Time Customers to Return

Listed below are a number of steps businesses can take to help get customers to return. Consider each of the following in light of your business's particular needs, and choose those most appropriate for your specific situation.

1. Say Thank You for the Purchase

Thanking the customer after a purchase is overlooked as a loyalty-building marketing technique by many companies. A customer can be a first-time buyer only once. Passing up the chance to thank the customer for his or her purchase—especially the first one—is a big opportunity lost on the road to building loyalty. Retail consultant and business colleague Murray Raphel shares this personal experience:[17]

> Within the past few months I bought a $5,000 air conditioner, a $600 TV set, a $7,000 car and a $50 pair of shoes. Following these sales, I heard from none of the businesses—except my shoe salesman. He thanked me for coming in to buy and hoped I would "receive much comfort" and remember him the next time I wanted another pair of shoes.
>
> There's something wrong here.
>
> I called each of the retailers (except the shoe store) and asked if they ever thought of writing thank-you letters after the sale. These are the actual answers:
>
> *The air-conditioner dealer:* "I don't think we ever did that. Well, once in a while our financing company writes a letter to all the people they carry on their books." (What for? He wasn't sure.) "Listen, we

know it's a good idea and I know you're going to ask why we don't do it, and the answer is, I guess we just never got around to it. There's so much to do in this business."

The television dealer: "Sending a thank-you letter is the best thing we ever did. Absolutely. We stopped about eight or nine months ago. We're so backed up with all the paperwork in warranties and finance deals that we just don't have the time anymore. But I'll tell you something—from the customer's point of view, it was terrific. We used to get a big response. We have to get back to that sometime."

The automobile dealer: "Are you kidding? Why that's the first thing we do. The day the car is delivered, the salesman sits downs and writes a thank-you letter right away. Positively."

Well, that was a month ago. No letter yet.

A simple thank-you letter is an easy and inexpensive way to help reassure new buyers that they have made a good choice by shopping at your business. All it takes is a couple of sentences that say "Thank you for your recent purchase. Hope you enjoy using your [name of product]. If you have any questions or need more information on [name of product], please call me." Do not fall into the trap of sending a generic letter addressed "Dear Valued Customer." That approach, though often used today, can do more harm than good. If a customer is worth having, then all written communication should appear personalized.

A letter of thanks can go a long way toward sowing the seeds of loyalty in a new customer. Since so few marketers do it, it can set you apart and allow you to connect with the customer on a more personal basis. As Stan Rapp, CEO of the international marketing firm Rapp & Collins so aptly describes marketing in the 1990s, "Winning share of mind is giving way to winning share of heart." Thank-you letters can be an effective first step for doing just that.

2. Seek Customer Feedback Early and Respond Quickly

An enterprising sales director for the AmeriSuites Hotel in Dallas found client follow-up to be an important way to anchor loyalty in both the traveler and the secretary who made the travel arrangements.

The key was to call the secretary and inquire about the visit during the guest's stay. Most travelers communicated with their office daily, so the strategy worked nicely. In the event there was a problem, the sales director could help remedy the situation while the guest was still in the hotel. In one instance, the guest, informed by his secretary that the hotel had called, came out of his room, searched out the sales director, and said, "I want to shake your hand and thank you for following up with my secretary before I even leave to make sure that everything is OK. I'm impressed!" This follow-up technique helped the hotel sales director forge relationships with both customers—the secretary/travel arranger and the hotel guest.

A first-time customer must be satisfied with his or her purchase. Would you buy a second Acme widget if the first one did not work? Of course not. In order for your customers to buy from you again, they must perceive your product as having solved their problem. Follow up the first sale with some form of customer contact soon after the sale. Ask your customers if they are pleased with the product or service. If they have a problem with the product, correct it. Make this follow-up strictly for evaluating satisfaction. With the customer's satisfaction assured, you are better positioned to start to win a repeat purchase.

3. Use Indoctrination Mailings

Another reason why a first-time customer may not repurchase is that the customer fails to use the product or service. For example, how many home computers have you seen family and friends buy that now sit, dust-covered, in a back room? If a customer does not use your product or service, he or she will probably lose interest in continuing a business relationship with you.

The indoctrination mailing—a mailing sent after a purchase that tells the new owner in painstaking detail how to use the product or service—helps motivate your customer to use the product. The mailing tells the customer why his or her decision to buy was a wise one and how to get the most out of what was bought. Design your mailing to draw the first-time customer's attention back to the product and to reinforce the person's original interest in it. Send the mailing out to your customer immediately after he or she receives the product or uses the service. Along with the letter to your first-time customer, provide an offer that will encourage him or her to use the new purchase. For example, a computer retailer could offer free introductory word processing lessons to new computer owners, or give them half off their next printer cartridge replacement if they bring it in within six months.

4. Constantly Reinforce Your Value in the Eyes of Your Customer

Good service is not enough. It counts only when your customers recognize it. One company that understands the importance of reminding customers of its value-added service is Allcounty Plumbing and Heating Corporation in Brooklyn, New York. The competition among plumbers in the Brooklyn market is fierce, with twenty pages of yellow page advertisements to prove it. A customer has plenty of opportunity to go elsewhere. To help keep customers loyal, Allcounty sends thank-you letters to customers after a service to help build and reinforce that perception of quality. In the following passage from one such letter, notice how Allcounty presents a generic offering in an exceptional, customer-driven light: "Our effort to please you started with the carefully considered selection of each and every employee, from receptionist and dispatcher to servicemen and supervisory staff. It continued with the commitment to be there seven days a week, day or night, should you ever need us." The letter continues: "You probably have noticed our one-year guarantee, proof of our commitment to your satisfaction. Should you ever need help or have a question, we have a customer service number: (718) 856–8700."[18]

Office Depot operates the nation's largest chain of office products warehouse stores, with more than 290 stores in thirty-two states. From its 3-store start-up in 1986 to its almost 300 stores by 1992, the company has won loyal customers among small-and medium-size businesses with its wide selection of brand-name office products at everyday low prices. The company does not use a central warehouse, but maintains its inventory on the sales floor of its no-frills stores. Office Depot is able to offer its customers a broad in-stock selection at prices generally 40 to 60 percent below manufacturers' suggested retail prices.

Recognizing that its everyday low prices are what its customers value most, Office Depot provides a unique pricing comparison at two important points during the customer's shopping trip: at the shelf during selection and on every customer's receipt. I recently stopped in at Office Depot in Austin to buy a flip chart pad for an upcoming presentation. My sales receipt had a series of lines that read:

> Catalog list price would have cost you $15.75.
> Office Depot's low everyday price $8.29.
> You saved $7.46.
> Thank you for saving at Office Depot.

How about adding value each time you communicate with your customer? Consider this strategy: Every time you call your client, have a bit of interesting news at hand that will help him or her run the business better. It could be something you read in a trade magazine or newspaper or heard from a colleague. For example, when you call your client, you could say, "Pat, I'm calling today for a couple of reasons. First, I want to share some information I read in the *Harvard Business Review* that could have an impact on your business. Second, I'd like to tell you about a new product that might be of interest to you."

The value-added strategy can help businesses earn future contracts and orders. Says People's Bank vice-president Ken Weinsten, "We try to make sure than we are building a relationship instead of forcing a relationship. You want customers to use more of your services, but you have to earn it. Customers are looking for value."

5. Develop a Customer Database and Use It

Fischer Florist in Atlantic City, New Jersey, understands the importance of repeat customers. Founded in 1876 and one of the top one hundred FTD florists in the United States, this veteran retailer sends its customers who have bought flowers on "repetitive" occasions, like birthdays, anniversaries, and holidays, reminders in the mail. If our president, Bill Clinton, was a Fischer Florist customer, his 1995 reminder letter sent in early June might read as follows: "On June 14, 1994, you remembered Hillary on her birthday. Remember this important occasion this year by giving us a call at Fischer Florist. We have enclosed a selection guide of gift ideas appropriate for the occasion." The florist encloses a brochure for easy gift selection along with the letter.

The program was originally administered by hand with a card file, but, thanks to modern technology, the process is now computerized. Fischer owner and CEO Charles Fischer, Jr., reports that the reminder program is a mainstay of the company and is a very cost-effective method of producing repeat purchases. Fischer adds that customers have grown to see the reminder as a service, and once, when the florist missed a mailing, several customers called, annoyed because they'd failed to receive their reminder!

Fischer Florist is only one of the thousands of retailers, service companies, manufacturers, and distributors that are discovering the benefits of database marketing. As discussed in Chapter 3, database marketing is a fancy name for a simple concept—collecting information about prospects or customers, then using the database to make specially targeted direct mail or telemarketing pitches.

In its first pilot program with database marketing, Saab Cars U.S.A., the importer of luxury automobiles from Sweden, undertook an ambitious program to use database marketing to sell models like the 900 CS and CSE sports sedans to American drivers.

Approximately 200,000 owners of new and used Saabs were mailed brochures, letters, and fanciful offers like a $2,000-off coupon. The result? Spending $200,000 to mail letters expressing "appreciation of our customers' loyalty to the Saab marque" was one of the key factors that helped generate sales of an estimated $62 million worth of Saabs. "To build sales, you have to build a relationship with the customer," said Holly Pvlika, executive vice-president and creative director of Fox Pavlika, the agency handling Saab's direct response programs. "You have to create a sense of value, a sense of trust, and reinforce the fact the customer has made an intelligent decision."[19]

The customer database is helping aggressive pizza delivery companies win the "pizza wars" around university campuses. One of my marketing students at the University of Texas, Steve Lassister, shared this "repeat buyer" experience with me. Steve was in his apartment near campus one weekday evening around 9:00 P.M. (just about the time the Burger King "Aren't You Hungry?" ads begin to appear on TV). A Pizza Hut representative called and said, "Steve, we're calling to tell you that when you place your next order with Pizza Hut, you will receive a $2 savings." The Pizza Hut representative continued, "If you'd like to order now, we'll get a hot pizza right out to you." Steve thought for a second, decided a pizza sounded good, and said yes. The next question for Steve was "Do you want your usual large with pepperoni and extra cheese?" Think about it. Pizza Hut already had all the information required to get the next purchase—even down to what the customer ordered last time. Now it simply put the information to use. Right customer, right time.

The database can serve as an easy tracker of who your customers are and of what they are and—equally important—are not buying from you. Brad Hale, who runs a lawn maintenance company with annual gross sales of about $150,000, uses his database to "cross-sell" lawn care services that his current customers aren't already getting.

George Watts, proprietor of George Watts & Sons crystal and china store in Milwaukee, uses his database of more than 43,000 customers to target-mail flyers to groups of 500 to 600 people interested in sought-after sterling patterns, notifying them of upcoming sales. He also lets customers know when their particular china patterns are being discontinued, tipping them off to potential clearance bargains.

As useful and effective as database marketing can be, it takes time and effort to implement. The collection of customer information must be carefully planned, and the data must be easily retrievable and kept up to date. This takes a commitment of company resources and people to make it happen. Businesses, however, that organize a plan and carry through with it find that database marketing offers a big advantage over competitors using the shotgun approach to marketing. The key is to start collecting the customer information with the buyer's very first purchase.

6. Continually Communicate Your Full Range of Services

Business consultant Howard Upton tells of a recent experience of being in the office of the president of a petroleum equipment company. The firm stocked and sold pumps, valves, and other such equipment used in service stations. In recent years, the company had been heavily engaged in the installation of underground storage tanks. As Upton and the president were conversing, the company's service manager stopped by briefly and said, "You're not going to believe this, but I've just been talking with the executive vice president of K-Plus and it turns out he didn't know we do tank installations."[20]

Upton explains, "K-Plus [not the real name] owns and operates 400 service stations [and] is one of the principal customers of the equipment company whose president I was visiting. Yet, here was the company's service manager reporting that the top operations executives at K-Plus had been unaware of one of the major services offered by this company."[21]

"Oh, you must be mistaken," the equipment company president responded. "Everyone knows we do tank installations."[22]

This experience demonstrates an important fact: In an increasingly complex business environment, customers and prospective customers rarely comprehend the full range of services offered by any company until those services are spelled out for them. Even then, customers have short memories and must be reminded. Company brochures, newsletters, direct mail letters, and sales calls are some of the ways companies can keep reinforcing to customers their range of services. "The most serious marketing mistake management can make is to assume that 'Everybody knows what we do,'" says Upton. "In subtle ways each company differs from all similar companies in the industry. These unique differences must be continually communicated to clients and prospective clients."[23]

7. Paint a Picture of Future Possession

A friend of mine has been quite successful as an independent interior designer. She works with clients in redecorating existing homes and furnishing new ones. Her ability to turn first-time buyers into long-lasting clients is evident from the many client relationships originating from her first year in business. One of her keen abilities is to "paint a picture of possession" with new customers. It's rare that a new customer can completely refurnish a home or even a room all at one time. Recognizing that, my friend provides a master design plan, complete with specifics on major furniture pieces, accessories, color swatches, and even artwork. She then guides the customer through initial purchases based on her available budget. Using the master plan as her guide, she touches base with each customer periodically to encourage and support the person on their next acquisition. Comments like "I'll be going to the High Point market next month. Why don't we talk before the trip and decide what kind of rug you would like me to look for" sound less like a sales pitch and more like a service call. The master plan concept has also helped to inspire anniversary, birthday, and Christmas gifts within her client families.

The concept of painting a picture of possession has application across a wide range of industries. From residential landscaping to computers to hair care to antique cars—many companies can benefit from painting a picture of possession with first-time buyers well beyond that first purchase and then assisting those buyers in achieving that vision over time.

8. Turn Repeat Purchasing into a Service

The dispenser containing the black gooey makeup that women use on their eyelashes can be a haven for bacteria if not replaced on a regular basis. If this bacteria-infested mascara gets in the eye, serious eye disorders may result, including blindness. Jana Beatty is a cosmetic specialist in Waco. Recognizing the awareness that many women have about the hazards of mascara, Jana identified a way to help them practice a safe make-up routine and at the same time turn first-time mascara buyers into regular customers. Here's how she did it:

When Jana sells a tube of mascara to a new buyer, she explains the importance of replacing the tube every three months and how, as a member of her "mascara club," the buyer can receive fresh mascara delivered to her home four times a year. Jana provides a sticker on the tube with the date of the purchase. She then sends a fresh tube of mascara to the buyer in the mail before the three-month period is over. Jana tells me that before she mails the mascara, she will call her customer and ask whether there is any other makeup item she needs. Jana says that, more often than not, she will also receive requests for other products.

How does Jana Beatty convert first-time buyers into repeat customers? By identifying a specific need and then filling it.

9. Treat Customer Service Costs as a Worthwhile Investment

Expenditures made to help strengthen customer loyalty can be cheap when compared with the cost of losing a customer. Recognizing the possible future income from repeat business and favorable referrals, Ford authorizes its dealers to spend up to $250 per customer of "goodwill" money to correct, without charge, problems the customers sees as the fault of either the dealer or the company. Ford considers the $250 well spent to protect profits from future sales.

One extraordinary act can earn a customer's loyalty forever. When a ride in Disney World broke down, the part manufacturer Premier Industrial Corporation found a replacement part in Chicago and had an employee fly and drive it to the Florida amusement park within five hours, for a charge of $14. Disney executives were embarrassed by the low fee and offered to pay more, but Premier refused. Premier CEO Mort Mandel sees it this way: Exceptional service really is not costly, because it is needed only once every couple of years per customer. But the loyalty it generates among customers, says Mandel, drops right to the bottom line.[24]

10. Nurture and Protect Communication with Decision Makers

When a company is selling to a large organization, several individuals can be involved in the final decision to purchase its services. These purchasing professionals often form what can be called a "buying center." The parties can include any or all of the following: the user (the person using the service), the influencer (the individual who determines the specifications), the buyer (the person who has formal authority to select the vendor), the decision maker (the one who has final authority for vendor selection and terms), and the gatekeeper (the person who controls the information into the buying center).

Once the initial purchase decision is made, a fatal mistake often follows: Sales and service personnel and even senior management often end up dealing with the day-to-day users in a customer's organization, not the decision maker. According to Richard Shapiro, President of the consulting firm, MJ Associates, "When relationships are built with users and not decision makers, employees feel less comfortable approaching senior management within the customer's organization. This may occur because they have lost touch with their customer's organizational structure and strategic direction. All the while, competition is continuing to reach decision makers within the customer's organization and informing them of newer technologies, better approaches or more cost-effective ways of providing services."[25]

This situation can be prevented, says Shapiro, by initiating a program of collecting direct feedback through a structured interview process. This process provides a sales or service representative with a legitimate reason to schedule an appointment with the decision maker to review how the organization is meeting the customer's needs. Explains Shapiro, "This formalized process will also provide an opportunity [for the sales representative] to communicate improvements currently being planned and explain new policies or procedures that may have been recently implemented."[26]

Shapiro suggests the following questions as effective ways to open dialogue with a decision maker as well as provide valuable input to an organization:

- What do you like best about dealing with our organization?
- If you could change anything about the relationship you have with our organization that would reduce frustrations and make it more effective, what would it be?
- How does our organization stack up against our competitors?
- What additional products/services should our organization provide as part of our overall offerings?
- If you were president of our organization, how would you go about retaining customers?

To benefit from the customer feedback you will want to determine when first-time customer data will be collected and who will be analyzing it. Additionally, you will want to decide how this information will be processed and disseminated within your organization.

11. Develop Customer Reward Programs

Beginning with the first purchase, many companies are developing programs to anchor the relationship. Over the past five years, Mitchell's auto dealerships in Simsbury, Connecticut, have offered a "Mitchell Preferred Customer" card to new customers purchasing a vehicle. Free car washes in the first year, a loaner car or shuttle service during repairs, and discounts on certain auto accessories are part of the privileges of the holder. "We are trying to say that it is more than just the price. We want to offer you a relationship," said David Tefft, general sales manager of Mitchell's Pontiac, Dodge, Volvo, Volkswagen, and Subaru dealerships. "We have to spend money on our customers to maintain them."

One specific type of customer reward program is the "family promotion." These are special events or happenings that only customers and clients are notified about. Family promotions are an effective way to make customers feel they are getting an opportunity reserved only for those people who have earned it with their patronage. Direct mail postcards, letters, and telephone calls are good ways to communicate these family specials.

12. Develop "New Customer Welcome" Promotions

A "new customer welcome" kit can be an effective way to help motivate first-time customers to return. A hair salon in my neighborhood designed such a kit for its new customers. The kit contains a "Salon Sampler" card that provides special introductory savings on a variety of products and services throughout the salon. These savings are redeemable on the second, third, fourth, and fifth visits. (In the hair care industry, five consecutive visits is the average number required to turn first-time buyers into solid, repeat customers.)

The kit also provides a brochure outlining the salon's unique services, like the "emergency haircut" for busy customers who may need a spur-of-the-moment haircut to look their best for an important meeting. A comprehensive list of the salon's services and prices is also included as part of the brochure.

Finally, the kit contains a "Recommend a Friend" card, outlining how the new customer can enjoy special gifts and treats by referring friends to the salon.

These three pieces are delivered to new customers by the receptionist upon "checkout" in an oversize envelope printed on the front with the words "We Want You Back Pack." The receptionist acknowledges the customer as a first-timer, thanks him or her for the visit, presents the customer with the kit as a token of the salon's appreciation, and invites him or her to return.

13. Offer Product Guarantees

The Bombay Company is one of the hottest retail chains in North America. The company sells replicas of eighteenth- and nineteenth-century English furniture in roughly 400 mall stores throughout the United States and Canada. Using a worldwide network of supply channels, the company manufacturers its own lines. The company's prices are 30 to 60 percent below competitors', and no item in the stores costs more than $500. With sales of $232 million, Bombay's average sales per foot is $340, well above the industry average of $110.

An unconditional guarantee is a primary component of the company's customer support policies. Explaining that the best time to capture a customer for life is when he or she needs a refund, President and CEO Robert Nourse says, "We'll take the thing back with no hassle, no questions, no guff about 'Where's the receipt?' The cost of that is peanuts compared with what you gain in customer loyalty. Too many retailers have forgotten what service means. When you treat customers like a million dollars, they'll come back."[27]

Product guarantees are moving to the forefront of Procter and Gamble's customer support programs as well. In September 1993, the company launched a national newspaper and television campaign offering consumers a six-month guarantee for two of its toothpaste brands—Crest Regular for children and Tartar Control Crest for adults. The company guarantees you will be refunded the full cost of six months' worth of Crest ($15) if you use Crest for six months and are not satisfied with the results. Consumers enroll in the program by calling a toll-free number or writing the company. Respondents then receive an enrollment card to be filled out by a dentist with the details of the condition of the teeth before the use of the toothpaste. At a six-month check-up, satisfied or dissatisfied responses are recorded by the dentist, who then returns the enrollment card to the company. This program reinforces Procter and Gamble's desire to expand and maintain its customer base by emphasizing quality and value. With thousands of consumers signing up, the company is capturing customer names and addresses as well as dentist names. Both types of information are rich in follow-up opportunity for the future.

For guarantees to truly assist in winning customer loyalty, execution is critical. When customers encounter difficulty in getting a guarantee honored, the trust and goodwill felt toward the organization can be greatly damaged.

14. Develop Value-Added Promotions

When Leo Spellman, director of advertising for Steinway and Sons in New York City, talks about customer relationships, he thinks thirty years into the future. "We are trying to engage our customers in not just a one-purchase deal, but in building a relationship," says the maker of pianos. "We think of things that will add value, or perceived value, to the purchase."[46] This very philosophy is what led Spellman and Steinway in 1991 to begin giving its dealers an option of offering zero-coupon bonds of ten-, twenty- or thirty-year maturities as buyer incentives.

During the month-long promotion period, anyone who purchased a Steinway and Sons piano received a zero-coupon bond equal to the piano's purchase price. Zero-coupon bonds are bought at a discount to their face value. No interest is paid on the bonds until they mature, at which time they pay their face value. For example, the buyer of a Steinway with a $20,000 purchase price would receive a zero-coupon bond for the same amount. After thirty years, the $20,000 zero-coupon bond could be redeemed for $20,000.

Clinton's of Hartford, a piano retailer and one of Steinway's one hundred dealers, participated in the recent bond promotion. Clinton's manager, Harold E. Niver, was attracted to the promotion for one key reason: Customers who typically purchase Steinway pianos—which vary in price from $10,000 to $70,000—consider their purchase an investment and often hand down their pianos as family heirlooms. Says Niver, "If [customers] held [the bond] to maturity, they would realize the price of the piano," and when the bond does reach maturity, customers "still have the product, which has actually appreciated in value." Niver's instincts proved correct. The promotion helped boost the store's Steinway sales to about $100,000 for the month, representing a 50 percent increase over normal sales for that period. What's more, the promotion helps ensure that the name Steinway is kept alive in the minds of the purchaser's family for years to come, further increasing the likelihood that any future piano bought by a family member will also be a Steinway.

In his book *Winning through Enlightenment*, Dr. Ron Smothermon offers his observation about relationships and loyalty: "There is something curious about loyalty. There is something that must be in order for loyalty to endure: it must be noticed. If you simply remember that no owes you anything, loyalty will be easy for you to notice and acknowledge. If you begin to think 'they' owe you loyalty, you are in trouble."[28]

There is no more important place to start noticing patronage and nurturing its beginnings than with the first-time customer. Turning the first-time customer into a repeat customer is a major passage on the journey to earning the customer's long-term loyalty.

Summary

- First-time buyer attrition is often double that of older accounts. Turning first-time buyers into repeat customers requires the constant attention of the seller.
- In every company, the order is a surrogate for the customer. When the order sits unattended, so does the customer. The best way to be customer oriented is to go beyond customers and products to the order.
- Judgments about an entire company are made by the performance of front line employees. These employees must have the time, tools, and training to perform.
- Customer database technology can be extremely helpful in building strong relationships with customers and turning new buyers into repeat customers.
- Steps should be taken to help reduce the amount of dissonance experienced by first-time customers.

- To help keep accounts loyal, nurture relationships with the users of your products and services as well as with the account's decison makers.
- Indoctrination mailings, "new customer welcome" promotions, and customer reward programs are a few of the marketing tools proved to be effective at turning new buyers into repeat customers.
- Never take a customer's loyalty for granted. For loyalty to endure, it must be noticed and acknowledged.

7

Turning Repeat Customers into Loyal Clients

There is a mom-and-pop store in Coon Rapids, Minnesota, that competes with chains like 7-Eleven and is prosperous despite economic predictions that small independent stores are doomed. According to a 1989 *Reader's Digest* article written by Ralph Brauer, "Millie's stays around because people keep coming to her store for more than things like soda pop, snack foods, cereal, and hot dogs. They come because Millie doesn't ask for your ID when you cash a check or food stamps, and if you happen to be short a dollar, Millie would tell you it's OK to pay later."

To Millie, the old slogan "The customer is always right" still means something, and for that reason her way of doing business is close to a lost art. "Everyone who walks in the door is treated with the same courtesy and respect—from those who drive Mercedees to men in flannel work shirts who drive old pickups," Brauer writes.

Millie is successfully bucking a trend. What is it about her company that is different? The answer is deceptively simple: At Millie's, there are no invisible customers—everybody is important.

The same philosophy drives Tom Carns of Las Vegas, Nevada, whose PDQ Quick Printing business annually grosses nineteen times the industry average because he understands that customers come before any other consideration in the planning of his printing services. He points out that it is not hard to understand how "60 percent of all printing done in America is either screwed up or late because of attitudes reflected by a sign in the window of a Las Vegas printer that says 'This is not Burger King. Here you get it my way, or you don't get it at all.'"

While Millie and Tom operate dissimilar kinds of enterprises, both are well aware that businesses in the 1990s that fail to show strong appreciation for their customers and instead take them for granted are businesses with a short future. The fact of the matter is that loyal customers are an increasingly precious commodity. No longer can they be regarded as an endless stream of convenient cash machines that buy the products offered to them without complaint about poor service, failed promises, arrogant or inattentive sales-people, or company policies that place more emphasis on profit than on customer satisfaction. Economists are predicting tough competition ahead, reflected in the slower growth rate of the population, of income, and of retail sales.

As we have seen from earlier chapters, analysts who study business profiles to determine who will remain successful in tougher competitive times have discovered the following:

- Most businesses get their profits from their long-term customers. Says business consultant Frederick F. Reichfeld, director of Bain & Co., "New customers are actually money losers. Much money is spent to attract them, but many do not make it past the first-time customer stage."
- The average business invests six times more money in acquiring new customers than it does in retaining customers. Yet it is estimated that customer loyalty is worth ten times the value of a single purchase.
- Customer retention produces profits, since long-term customers are cheaper to deal with. They know a company's personnel and procedures, and the company knows their tastes.

How can a business, as a matter of policy, upgrade repeat customers into loyal clients and keep them loyal? The answer is quite simple: The company must deliver value—as defined by the customer—by changing, enhancing, or improving the basic product or service to increase its payoff to the customer.

The importance of value and the role it plays at this later stage in loyalty development is partly illustrated by Steven Covey's concept of a person's emotional bank account. Covey describes a person's emotional bank account as operating on deposits and withdrawals just as an actual bank account does. We get "overdrawn" with others when, in their eyes, we've "withdrawn" from them more than we have "deposited." The same concept applies to our customers. To upgrade our customers to loyal clients and to keep them loyal, we must deliver value so that they continue to feel we have deposited more in their account than we have withdrawn. In other words, in their eyes, we have given more value to them than they have given to us.

While the concept of delivering value is not new, how customers define it is. Historically, customers have viewed value as being a combination of price and quality. The customers of the 1990s have enlarged their definition of value to include such factors as reliability, purchase convenience, and after-sale service.

Three Types of Value

The companies who have attained leadership positions over the last ten years have achieved their success by narrowing their business focus and delivering value in one of three categories of value: operational excellence, customer intimacy, or product leadership.[1] Operational excellence means providing customers with reliable products at competitive prices and with minimum purchase difficulty. When college student Michael Dell began selling computers out of his dorm room at the University of Texas, he based his business on operational excellence. His approach was a radical departure from market leaders Compaq and IBM, both of which embraced dealer distribution and "king of the hill" technology. Dell pioneered a telemarketing system that bypassed dealers and sold to customers directly. In doing so, he created a low-cost corporate culture that enabled PC buyers to buy state-of-the-art technology both easily and affordably. From such sparse beginnings, operational excellence has helped drive Dell Computer's revenues to a remarkable $1.7 billion in less than ten years. IBM, in contrast, has been forced to lower prices and overhead.

The second value category, customer intimacy, means segmenting and targeting markets with exact precision and then customizing offerings to meet the demands of these niches. Two factors are critical for companies excelling in customer intimacy: detailed customer knowledge and flexible operations. Combined, these two factors make it possible to respond quickly to customer needs and special requests. Unlike operational excellence, which depends on a lean and efficient operation, customer intimacy requires that a company look beyond the value of a single transaction to the customer's lifetime value and do whatever it takes to ensure that the customer gets exactly what he or she truly wants.

Home Depot, the $5 billion Atlanta-based retailer, has established the customer intimacy gold standard within the home improvement and hardware industry. Throughout the company's 140 stores, knowledgeable salespeople, frequently recruited from the ranks of electricians and carpenters, are urged to spend lots of time with customers to determine what product is required to solve his or her particular home repair problem. Home Depot also routinely offers free demos on everything from installing complete bathrooms to simple installations of home lighting fixtures. Made-to-order service is the way Home Depot delivers value. Customers whose overriding concern is price are outside the corporation's target market. The company's approach has struck a cord with homeowners, as evidenced by Home Depot's healthy earnings and 25 percent annual growth rate.

In the third category, product leadership, a company makes its value contribution by providing customers with leading-edge products and services that make competitors' goods obsolete. For example, in the sport shoe category, Nike has product leadership; in eye care products, it's Johnson and Johnson; in computer software, Microsoft excels. With product leadership, a company must continually challenge itself to pursue new solutions and make its own technology obsolete. Otherwise, a competitor will do it.

In determining how to best deliver value, a company must take into account its capabilities and strengths as well as those of its competitors. For example, both Dell Computer and Home Depot chose their particular type of value by carefully analyzing market conditions as well as their own resources and capabilities. Through analysis, planning, and in-market experience, these companies have determined how to best deliver value so that repeat customers become loyal clients. The same can be true for you. But to lock in loyalty, you must determine what your repeat customers value most and how to best give it to them.

As discussed in Chapter 1, the loyal client stage is the most critical in regard to potential profit payoff. At the repeat customer stage, the customer's momentum is in your favor. The customer has bought from you at least two times. Now is the opportunity to "lock in" the customer to a consistent pattern of buying from you. The key here is to firmly anchor the customer's loyalty rather than let it wane.

Whether it's operational excellence, customer intimacy, or product leadership, value delivery can take a number of forms, depending on the nature of the firm's products and services, its competitors, and its customers. Nonetheless, there are five factors that should be considered in the formulation of any strategy for transforming repeat customers into loyal clients: (1) researching your customer, (2) constructing barriers to switching, (3) hiring and training for loyalty, (4) motivating your staff for loyalty, and (5) marketing for loyalty. We'll examine the importance of each of these in the remainder of this chapter.

Researching Your Customer

True loyalty is not measured by what a customer says; it is measured by his or her buying habits as they relate to your products or services. The objective of customer research is to discover who the largest customers are, what they are buying, and why they are loyal. This information is critical to any plan for upgrading loyalty. Most companies don't know the answers to these pertinent questions, yet the answers can be gotten without a great deal of digging. You can review a customer's buying habits by going back to purchase records and evaluating such patterns as customer visits per year, spending per visit, year-on-year comparisons of units shipped, and products and services purchased.

Who Are Your Best Customers, and What Do They Buy?

Rank your customers by sales dollars and unit volume. Look carefully at who is at the top of the list. As a rule, the people at the top third of your list truly represent the source of your profits. These are the people who contribute cash to your bottom line in a reliable, repeating fashion. Typically, your return is usually highest with the customers who buy the most and who have been associated with you for the longest time. They are one of the few appreciating assets in your company. Next, evaluate what products and services your best customers are buying. Identifying the products or services your customers are buying most can give you valuable clues on how to increase future sales.

Joan V. Silver, president of Reeves Audio Visual Systems, discovered that her secret weapon for identifying ways to build sales and loyalty were found in a surprising place: her sales receipts. Silver directs an industrial audiovisual equipment company in New York City, providing both sales and service. Silver's marketing breakthrough came when she wanted to increase sales of a new $16,000 Sony video projection system she had recently added to her offerings. Silver began going through her receipts to determine which of her clients could not afford the system. Most could, she reasoned, since she believed that 90 percent came from Fortune 500 companies. But Silver got a big surprise. Receipts revealed that just 58 percent of revenues came from these large corporations. The remainder came from smaller companies, many with less than $1 million in sales.[2]

Silver analyzed the receipts (including invoices and purchase orders) in more detail and established a ranking of her top twenty customers by sales. Next she identified what they were buying most. More surprises were in store. Many of her larger accounts had disappeared due to mergers and cutbacks. Advertising agencies and insurance companies had taken their place. Ad agencies were buying custom-designed turnkey editing systems. Rather than subcontracting out the work, they were setting up their own editing suites. Insurance companies were buying TV production equipment to make in-house training tapes.

Armed with this information, Silver adopted a new strategy: She searched through her receipts for ad agencies and insurance companies that had not yet bought such equipment. She sent out personalized letters with a very simple sales message: "Your competitors are bringing their production work in-house. Shouldn't you?" She conclude her letters by outlining Reeve's full-service audiovisual capabilities.

As for her smaller accounts, her analysis showed that because such accounts usually need service on the spur of the moment, they rarely have the luxury to bid out the work. Since they do not have in-house support, they often need both support and service. This makes profits on such accounts higher. To accommodate that business, Silver enlarged her product lines and provided three-hour delivery. Silver has now replaced her larger, unfocused quarterly mailings of the past with smaller monthly mailings targeted to these smaller identified markets. Since launching this new strategy, the company's response rate has jumped 10 percent.

Closely tracking customer purchases can also give you insights into the loyalty of a customer who has been buying steadily from you and then shows signs of faltering. The loss of steady customers can indicate a failing of your products or services or new marketing, pricing, or technical innovations among your competitors. Sudden increases in sales can also reveal opportunities. One company I know about noticed that one of its clients was buying unusually large quantities of its product. Upon investigation, the company learned that its client was reselling the product to a third organization that was buying the shipments, and thus an entirely new application for its product was opened.

Why Do Your Customers Buy?

Another vital part of customer research is for a company to carefully evaluate what makes its customers loyal. In other words, what particular aspects of the company's products and services create the loyalty? Is it the attitude of the employees? Are customers impressed by the company's policies regarding guarantees, returns, or exchanges? What exactly does the company do that engenders loyalty? Many companies make mistakes by assuming they know the answer.

When Mac McConnell, owner of the Artful Framer Gallery in Plantation, Florida, conducted a poll of 300 of his customers six years ago, he got the surprise of his life.[3] Price, which he believed was the factor that ensured customer patronage, was last on the list of his customers' priorities. Until the survey, McConnell had always competed on price and believed he had no choice. Now he discovered that the customers' first requirement was quality, followed by uniqueness.

The same survey indicated that word of mouth brought in a

third of his customers. So McConnell set about reinventing his business to give people more reason to tell their friends about his shop. Because repeat customers wanted quality, McConnell abandoned his low-end framing options. "We made museum framing the standard," said McConnell. He answered the need for more creative framing options by stocking 1,800 frame samples. He began providing a lifetime guarantee on all work and started calling customers a month after purchase to see if they were satisfied. When he knows an order might be delayed, he calls customers and gives them plenty of notice.

He taught his salespeople to take a more consultive selling approach–by talking first about where the customer plans to hang the art, followed by a discussion of price.

The results of McConnell's changes? The store's average invoice increased from $67 to $167. Over four years, sales tripled, to $600,000, with net profits up 26 percent. Reports McConnell, "When we changed our focus to making great frames, the money came."

After determining what creates the loyalty, the next step is to determine what you can do to increase and extend it. One way is to pay close attention to customer service during peak demand. Have you ever noticed in fast-food restaurants that order takers often come out to take orders from waiting customers when the line is long? Slow checkouts are a huge cause of lost sales in restaurants, discount stores, and supermarkets. One study showed that when more than four people are in line at a checkout, there's a high probability the fifth will just leave. To speed shoppers through the checkout lines, hundreds of thousands of stores now rely on scanners that automatically read bar codes, record prices, and print out an itemized bill. Kmart's new satellite system takes seconds to approve credit card purchases, vs. minutes for phoning in a credit check. With the old approach, "You would discourage exactly those customers you wanted to encourage," says David Carlson, Kmart manager of information.

To discover what his customers valued, Steve Glenn, CEO of Executive Travel, a six-year-old travel agency in Lincoln, Nebraska, started holding regular review sessions with his corporate accounts. Intuitively, Steve began asking the question "What is the most important thing we do that makes you continue to use us?" Expecting to hear such reasons as competitive airfares and hotel rates, Steve was surprised by the most frequent answer: "You are here meeting with us."

After nine successive new product failures, Techsonic Industries, a manufacturer of sonar devices for fishermen, decided to listen to customers. But the next decision was the toughest. With profits on a steep decline, would the company commit the $20,000 necessary to do the necessary focus group interviews among prospects and customers? Despite an industry with revenues of roughly $55 million, market research was simply not done, and Techsonic Chairman Jim Balkcom wasn't sure he wanted to be any different. Said Balkcom, "If you're going to invest money, you think about what you'll have when you you're through. Spending money on this [research], all you have is a folder with some stuff in it. It's not an asset, like a [design] mold."[4]

Balkcom was even more uncomfortable when he saw the results: $20,000 for a single sheet of paper with phrases, each with a ranking, numbering one through forty-five. "Sunlight" was the number one problem consumers had with their depth finders, according to the sheet and its ninety-four pages of support data.

From the focus group findings, a more quantitative telephone survey was conducted. More than 1,800 fisherman were surveyed to determine a ranking of problems consumers had with their depth finders. The findings were surprising, to say the least. "Sunlight" reigned as the number one complaint reflecting fishermen's problem with reading fish finders in bright sunlight.

"We really had no idea how important that was," said Balkcom. Complaint number two? Fishermen generally found fish finders too complicated. Once again, Balkcom was shocked: "Our conventional wisdom was that fishermen liked to press buttons."[5]

Long story made short: Focus group feedback, combined with the quantitative research, enabled the company to identify a gap in the industry and fill it with a new fish-identifying technology called LCR (Liquid Crystal Recorders). The result? The company sold more than 100,000 units of the product its debut year, an impressive number given that 96,280 units was the record for the company's biggest seller in its best year.

This experience with market research made a believer out of

Techsonic, which was out in the marketplace with its LCR soon after introduction, seeking feedback for future upgrades.

Each of the businesses mentioned above is practicing the art and profiting from a key customer loyalty principle: Probe customers to find out what is creating loyalty and what the company can do to increase and extend it. The most successful companies know that this is a never-ending process. It's human nature and a fact of business that customers' expectations rise in relation to their satisfaction with a company. The better a company satisfies, the more the customer comes to expect. Companies must continue to ask the questions "How are we doing?" and "What can we do better?"

Constructing Barriers to Switching

Understanding who your customers are, what they buy, and why they buy can provide you with valuable insights into using another loyalty-building tool: barriers to switching. This tool can enable you to upgrade repeat customers into loyal clients by creating "barriers" that discourage them from not doing business with you. There are at least three types of barriers that can help keep customers loyal: physical, psychological, and economic. Let's consider each one separately.

The physical barrier is something you establish with the customer that visibly adds value, from the customer's perspective, to the relationship. For example, Tramex Travel in Austin, Texas, specializes in corporate travel. For its larger volume accounts, Tramex places a full-time agent on the customer's site as soon as the customer's travel expenditures are large enough to warrant it. Says Margo Portillo, Tramex co-owner, "Using an on-site agent does two things. First, it gets our agency more fully integrated with our client. By being on-site, we are more accessible and, in turn, can serve them better. Second, our on-site agent begins to be perceived as a staff member with the client's company—not ours—and that's good for us. We like to set up on-site services as soon as it's financially feasible."

Another bonus to Tramex is the fact that when a competitive travel agency calls the client, the caller is usually routed first to the Tramex on-site agent. As a result, at all times Tramex has a good idea of which competitors are knocking on its client's door.

The second type of exit barrier that keeps customers loyal is the economic barrier. Both financial incentives and disincentives for terminating business can help keep customers loyal. For example, a company that purchased an extensive data processing system from IBM may be very reluctant to switch to a competitor's system, due to the costs of retraining personnel, the capital requirements for the changeover, and the expense of acquiring new equipment.

The third type of exit barrier is the psychological one—creating the perception in the customer's mind that he or she depends on your products or services. One industry that encourages customer loyalty based on this premise is the hair care industry. Statistics show that a customer who is a regular user of chemical services such as perms and colors is more loyal to the stylist who performs the service than she would be to a stylist who simply gives her a haircut. Why? Because of the perception of risk. The customer feels that a haircut can be repaired easier and faster than a bad perm or the wrong hair color. Salons learn to build to this advantage two ways: first, by converting every possible salon customer into a user of chemical services, and second, by reminding the perm or color customer that the salon has her formula on file for dependable and easy reference when these services are again needed. The loyalty/risk relationship is illustrated in Figure 7–1.

Another example of a company who uses the psychological barrier to its advantage is Pearson Automotive Services. This first-class service center uses a central computer to keep detailed records of a customer's repeat purchase history and then references this history at each repair. Pearson's staff use this benefit when talking with repeat customers by saying, "Let's pull your service history up on our computer. We have all the details recorded." To new customers, the attendant will say, "Have you been in before? If so, we can pull up your record." For customers who care about their cars, the message is clear: Come to Pearson and you'll get first-class care.

Hiring and Training for Loyalty

To make any loyalty plan truly work, employers first have to realize that their employees, the people on the front line, are the ones in direct contact with customers. They represent the company's prod-

FIGURE 7–1

The Loyalty/Risk Relationship For Haircare Customers: The Higher the Customer Perception of Risk the Greater the Loyalty Potential

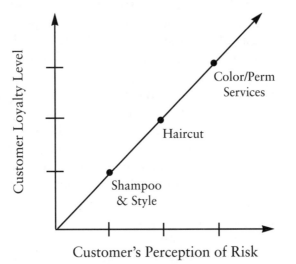

Customer Loyalty Level

Color/Perm
Services

Haircut

Shampoo
& Style

Customer's Perception of Risk

ucts or services for better or worse and can win loyalty for a company or turn customers away.

Management must deal with the fact that it is not in charge of satisfying the customer. Rather, it is the employee who talks to the customer. Many companies lack an effective program for hiring and training employees. A few companies have pioneered especially strong training programs that have reinforced their customer loyalty culture.

Employee teamwork and empowerment are key concerns for companies building loyalty-focused cultures. Disneyland interviews prospective employees or "cast members" in groups of three so it can watch how they interact. Do they show respect, for example, by paying attention when the other employees speak? At the Four Seasons, it takes four or five rigorous interviews to sort out applicants with a friendly nature and a sense of teamwork. When the chain opened its Los Angeles hotel in 1987, it interviewed 14,000 candidates for 350 slots. More and more, companies are realizing that it takes employees empowered with know-how and initiative to build loyal customers. As a result, these companies are giving employees the authority to resolve complaints from customers on the spot, in a way that's bound to satisfy. Companies with empowerment programs are making empowerment potential a factor in the selection process: If you aren't willing to empower this employee, then do not hire him.

"We have thousands [of guests] who stay with us more than seventy-five nights per year," said Roger Dow, vice-president of sales and marketing services for Marriott.[6] By estimating that one such customer will spend about $125,000 during ten years, Dow suggested that if just eight of those guests turned to competitors, Marriott would lose $1 million in sales. To retain customers, Marriott began testing an empowerment program in 1988; since then, it has introduced formal training that stresses how much money could be lost if steady customers decided to check in at competitors' properties.

Empowerment training is producing loyalty-building behavior in Marriott staff. Each employee feels a sense of responsibility for the satisfaction of the customers. In one case, a bellman accidentally damaged a customer's electronic typewriter. Faced with the possibility of an angry guest taking his business somewhere else, the bellman and other employees found a solution and replaced the typewriter with a new, undamaged machine. On another occasion, a guest who was leaving the hotel mentioned to the staff member carrying his luggage that his breakfast had been improperly prepared. The staffer immediately escorted the guest back to the desk, where his breakfast charges were completely refunded.[7]

Companies that develop strong customer loyalty have at least three things in common:

1. The management has a clear understanding about what builds loyalty for a company and trains its staff members to encourage customer loyalty.
2. The required behaviors are written in clear, straightforward, easy-to-understand guidelines. The behavior is measurable.
3. The company has a written credo that is reinforced constantly to staff members at staff meetings, in memos, and in clever displays.

Customer retention consultant Frederick F. Reichfeld put the importance of employee training in sharp perspective when he said, "In a service business knowledge and information are the raw materials and the assets are loyal customers and employees. Accounting systems don't measure these."[8]

Nissan Motor Company has gained a reputation for having some of the most customer-oriented dealers in the business, and it's largely the result of innovative training and customer service systems. The company operates a six-day boot camp for dealers of its luxury automobile, Infiniti. All dealer employees must attend, including clerks and receptionists. "The receptionist probably talks to more customers than any other person in the showroom," says instructor Ken Petty. "Our receptionists can tell you how the cars handle on the track and they have driven the Lexus, Infiniti's key competitor, too."[9]

That's part of the plan to equip every employee at a dealership to answer any question about the Infiniti lineup. These same people are taught buyer demographics, or how to pitch an Infiniti to various age-groups and people of different lifestyles, and they can even compare the merits between their car and competitors. This training is paying dividends. The result of a J. D. Powers & Associates 1993 customer satisfaction survey found Infiniti number one in customer sales satisfaction among car buyers.

Once employees are well trained, a company must retain them. Before you can have a loyal customers, you must first have loyal employees. Says Republic National Bank treasurer Thomas F. Robards, "The most explicit quality technique is to get good staff and retain them."

One of the most common reasons for losing good employees is that companies set high customer loyalty standards without giving employees the capability and tools to perform to those expectations. In today's competitive marketplace, customer loyalty systems may require hefty spending on technology to ensure that front line employees have the tools they need to be loyalty-driven. A leading financial brokerage firm understands that not all customers require the same service level or generate the same revenues. The company recently installed a telephone-computer system that recognizes individual clients by their telephone numbers when they call. Large accounts and callers who make frequent transactions are automatically routed to their own senior account representative. Those customers who place only an occasional order may be routed to a more junior representative. In either situation, the customer's record appears on the representative's screen before the call is taken.

Such a system provides a host of service benefits for the company and its customers. For example, similar accounts can be grouped under one rep who specializes in that instrument, removing the need to train every rep on every financial tool. In addition, the company can direct certain value-added services or products to only those clients it knows would be interested.

Another example of technology playing a major role in a customer loyalty system is United Parcel Service, which has outfitted its drivers with electronic clipboards that include a stylus and a pressure-sensitive receipt pad. Consignee signatures are downloaded overnight, and by the next day, volume senders who subscribe to a special service can log on to UPS's database from their PC to check on the status of key packages.

Motivating Your Staff for Loyalty

American business is suffering today from a "hyped out" employee. The techniques for inspiring the work force with things like compensation and benefits plans and motivational seminars aren't as effective as they used to be. It's hard to get anyone excited about simply generating profits for someone else. The key is to encourage employees to be part of the building process. They will be more cooperative if they can see some of their own ideas put into action. If you really want to build customer loyalty, put your staff in charge of building it and give them the autonomy, training, information, support, and rewards they need to do what is already natural to them. Your employees are just like your customers. Treat them with respect and allow them to make their own decisions and they will treat your customers in the same manner. But equally important, don't tolerate in employees a casual regard for loyalty.

This sharing of corporate goals by employees at every level is similar in spirit to the labor methods that operate plants owned by Applied Energy Services (AES). The energy-producing company has a clear corporate philosophy that places responsibility for job effectiveness in the individual rather than in a policy manual. There is no personnel department at AES ("It's too important to be left to experts."); there are no legal, finance, public relations, or engineering departments. Instead, the 413 staff members of AES group themselves in multidiscipline teams designed for specific tasks.

Said Dennis Bakke, president of AES, "Economists have done us a major disservice by seeing people as labor, as machines. And engineers have stressed the notion of efficient organizations, which I reject. It may be effective in some areas, but not in a company like ours. But don't get me wrong; people have to be accountable."

Accountability at AES causes job leveling in the interest of the company's combined production and altruistic objectives, and it facilitates communication from the top down. All senior executives are expected to spend at least one week each year working alongside technicians at the plant level. "I spent my first night in the plant on my hands and knees, trying to clear clinkers from the bottom of the furnace," Roger Naill, vice-president, remembered. It was during a graveyard shift one night that Naill, with the help of those in the mechanic shop, worked out the company's generous performance incentive scheme, which his group at the head office had been wrestling with for months.

Marketing for Loyalty

The goal of marketing for loyalty is to use well-conceived marketing programs to create intrinsic value for a company and its products and services in the eyes of the customer. As we've already established, loyalty will increase in direct proportion to the value the customer perceives. Using loyalty programs will help increase this perceived value. Following are three key loyalty marketing programs:

1. Relationship marketing
2. Frequency marketing
3. Membership marketing

Obviously, marketing programs that effectively anchor loyalty must be designed from the point of view of the customer. Those that are effective create a positive response from the customer, one that might go like this, if the customer were to put his or her thoughts into words: I'm glad to buy from you because you let me know you know who I am. You recognize in dozens of small ways the fact that I have been doing business with you for a long time. That makes me feel appreciated, and I keep coming back because the experience is pleasant and satisfying.

Relationship Marketing

Taking a newly developed relationship with a customer and anchoring his or her loyalty with services that grow a personal bond is the goal of relationship marketing. Sherwin-Williams, Inc., the big paint company, recently let executives from Sears, Roebuck and Company, help select the Sherwin-Williams staff members who would service the Sears account. "We already had joint sales and product turnover goals, so it made sense to jointly select the people who can make those goals happen," said T. Scott King, vice-president of sales for Sherwin-Williams.[10]

Digital Equipment Corporation often helps its smaller customers put together corporate image programs in their communities. "They are buying our product, so anything we do to help them be successful makes sense," said Joseph Codispoti, Digital's media relations manager.[11]

Xerox Corporation and General Electric Company, which buy from each other, send people to each other's in-house training sessions. "To really focus on customer needs, you must understand more about them than how they use your product," said Waylon Hicks, Xerox's executive vice-president for marketing and customer relations.[12]

One of the signposts of the 1990s is the willingness of companies to devise different and exciting ways to deliver relationship marketing to customers. The key is first to study and discern the customer's real, intrinsic needs and then to determine how to provide the products and services that will satisfy those needs. In many industries, this challenge requires a change in thinking from product to customer. *The customer must come first*! What does the customer want? Find this answer, and then produce and deliver in a fashion that will create a lasting bond.

Frequency Marketing

Frequency marketing is a strong loyalty builder. Here the goal is simple: Build loyalty and increase business by rewarding customers for their cumulative purchases through targeted communications, incentives, and performance tracking. The computer is making this doable for almost any size business. This technique is a way to say thank you on a regular basis. One good example of frequency marketing is the frequent-flyer program pioneered by American Airlines. The success of the program and its translation to countless other industries are testimony to the fact that the program is built on a very important principle: It rewards the company's best customers and, by so doing, helps insulate them from competitive offers and awards.

A personal example of the effectiveness of frequency marketing is worthwhile relating: In 1987, I developed the AmeriClub frequent traveler program for AmeriSuites Hotels. Targeted to independent business travelers (those travelers who make their own travel choices—not tied to corporate dictates), this program rewarded frequent hotel stays with a $50 U.S. Savings Bond. Eight years later, the same program is still a mainstay of the chain's marketing program and is universally viewed as the key marketing weapon for keeping travelers loyal.

Some businesses are better suited than others for frequency marketing programs. Consider these questions in determining whether frequency marketing programs make senses for your company:

- *Does your product or service have a frequent and regular repeat purchase cycle?* The most successful programs are those that occur when customers have an ongoing need for your product or service.
- *Do your customers perceive little differentiation between your product or service and your competitors'?* If your customers perceive your product as replaceable and if they can be persuaded to buy from a competitor, then a frequency marketing program may be useful.
- *Will your customers perceive the rewards as valuable?* Your customers must consider your frequent buyer benefits to be valuable and definitely worth working for.
- *Are both you and your staff willing to commit to the program*

long-term? Frequent buyer programs are not short-term. They require a long-term commitment in order to work.

- *Will you communicate with these customers on a frequent and ongoing basis in order to build a long-term relationship?* A monthly statement by which you report to your customer is one way to accomplish this.
- *Does your product or service lend itself to easy collection of proofs of purchase?* Either the company or the customer must track purchases. The easier you make it for the customer, the better.
- *Can you afford the program?* The rewards, tracking, regular communication, and customer inquiries associated with the program require significant time and monetary resources.
- *Do your competitors offer a frequency marketing program?* If they do but you do not, you may want to give serious consideration to a program.

Membership Marketing

Organizing customers into membership groups or clubs is a way to strengthen repeat purchase and build loyalty. Consider Staples, the office supply giant, which has created a staunch loyalty among companies that employ fewer than fifty people. The company induces shoppers to complete a membership application—membership is free—by charging higher prices to nonmembers. Members get at least a 5 percent discount on the fastest-moving items. To get the discount, customers must show their club card, which means Staples can track sales by customer, and these data give the company all kinds of information on products that this customer would be most interested in. Staples then targets club members by direct mail with tantalizing offers, customized specifically for them, to keep them coming back.

A successful twist on membership marketing has given MCI Communications Corporation a larger share of the long-distance telephone service market as a result of a program that reduces rates to subscribers who place frequent calls to relatives or friends. Since March 1991, when "Friends and Family" was launched, MCI has doubled its market share from 1 to 2 percent, taking its increase directly from telephone giant AT&T.

MCI's strategy is simple and savvy. It asks a customer to form a circle of up to twenty family members or friends who want to sign up for discounted calls—discounts some months are as high as 40 percent off the base cost of the long-distance charge. The program has proved so popular—because it relies on the power of personal persuasion (one member recruiting another)—that MCI added 5 million new subscribers in a twelve-month period. This telecommunication maverick has found an ingenious way to effectively upgrade clients into advocates.

As we discussed in Chapter 3, membership marketing is one factor in the success of legendary motorcycle maker Harley-Davidson. HOG (Harley-Davidson Owners Group) launched in 1983, helps keep Harley owners loyal. Buyers of Harleys receive a club membership for the first year. Subsequent yearly memberships are only $35. Membership privileges include a bimonthly newspaper, cycle rental options, and road safety instruction. HOG gatherings are frequent and help reinforce for buyers the "mystique" of the Harley as the powerful American road machine. Today HOG has a remarkable membership of 140,000.

Creating and giving customers value—as they define it—is the secret to customer loyalty. Nowhere is value more important than in transforming repeat customers into loyal clients. Smart companies will build programs that support this process. Customer research, corporate policies, staff training and motivation, and marketing programs all support the organization's overall objective of providing value and building a loyal customer base.

The transformation of the customer from a person who does repeat business with a company to a loyal one who has an emotional attachment to the company is critical to the whole system of managing customer loyalty. Companies that fail to realize the importance of the loyalty-bonding process are going to be the ones that fall by the wayside in the future.

Summary

- In terms of potential profit payoff, the loyal client stage is the most critical.
- Successful companies deliver value in one of three categories:

operational excellence, customer intimacy, or product leadership.

- In developing any plan for upgrading repeat customers into loyal clients, five factors should be considered: (1) researching your customer, (2) constructing barriers to switching, (3) hiring and training for loyalty, (4) motivating your staff for loyalty, and (5) marketing for loyalty.
- Customers have valuable information and are willing to share it if you are willing to commit financially and organizationally to capture feedback.
- Providing key services increases your customers' reluctance to switch to competitors—physically, economically, and psychologically.
- Before you can gain loyal customers, you must have loyal, empowered employees.
- Marketing plans should be tailored to maximize customer loyalty through relationship, frequency, and membership plans.

8

Turning Loyal Clients into Advocates

Once, *The Road Less Traveled* by psychiatrist M. Scott Peck was just another psychology/relationships book languishing on bookstore shelves. Then a few people read it, told their friends, and started a chain reaction that's still going on. Today there are millions of copies in print, and the book has been on the *New York Times* best-seller list for more than nine years.

Initial sales of the book were generated by two people who became convinced that it offered an outstanding message. One was the publisher's sales representative, who was so impressed that he insisted book buyers at stores read the book. The other was a teacher in Buffalo, New York, who gave copies to colleagues and ministers she knew. Word of mouth created demand for the book. Two churches invited the author to speak, and the local Buffalo bookstore began selling hundreds of copies. Impressed by what was happening, the publisher, Simon & Schuster, took another look at the book. A promotional tour boosted sales, which continued to rise. The author has now published a teaching guide to the original book and a new book expanding on the ideas in *The Road Less Traveled*.

When customers become advocates for your products or services, you have achieved a relationship of great closeness and trust. This is the most valued and sought-after level of bonding, where word-of-mouth advertising can flourish. This chapter will examine why it is not enough for a loyal customer or client to buy exclusive-

159

ly from an organization. To fully leverage its opportunity with a customer or client, a company needs to recruit new prospects and customers through him or her.

We'll examine word-of-mouth or third-party endorsements and why they are so powerful. We'll then consider proven strategies for "getting the word out" and "keeping the word out" through client advocates.

Blitzed and Deceived?

As discussed in Chapter 4, it is estimated that each American is exposed to well over 3,000 marketing messages per day. This continual assault of advertising and marketing messages has had a pronounced effect on American buyers: They remember advertising less and less. For example, the market researcher Video Storyboard Tests says viewer retention of television commercials has dropped significantly since the mid-1980s. In 1986, 64 percent of those surveyed could name a TV commercial they had seen in the previous four weeks, while in 1990, only 48 percent could do so. Moreover, even when consumers remember advertising, their retention is scarred by cynicism or, at best, indifference.

Reports Silicon Valley marketing consultant and author Regis McKenna, "Increasingly, people are skeptical of what they read or see in advertisements. I often tell clients that advertising has a built-in 'discount factor.' People are deluged with promotional information, and they are beginning to distrust it. People are more likely to make decisions based on what they hear directly from other people—friends, experts, or even salespeople. . . . Advertising, therefore, should be one of the last parts of a marketing strategy, not the first."[1]

If there's any doubt about the awesome power of word of mouth, consider the movie industry, one that rises and falls on word-of-mouth marketing. "Seen any good movies lately?" is that oft-asked question among friends that every movie executive knows can make or break a newly released film. Positive word of mouth can take a low-budget movie that has little or no advertising support and turn it into a multimillion-dollar hit. "Word of mouth is like wildfire," says Marvin Antonowsky, head of marketing for four Universal Pictures.[2] For example, *Home Alone* seemed to sneak into theaters one Thanksgiving as just another children's movie. But word of mouth made it a wild success. Likewise, *Wayne's World* was a low-budget, 1992 summer movie that earned a high talk factor and stunned everybody by becoming a hit. And how about *The Crying Game*? Miramax Films was the only distributor willing to gamble on the success of this film. As a result of a much-talked-about plot twist, the film catapulted to national prominence and Miramax executives were soon crying all the way to the bank.

Just as good word of mouth can help a movie gross millions, bad word of mouth can move the needle in the opposite direction. *Harper's Magazine* recently interviewed some of the movie industry's marketing whizzes, and their comments were quite revealing. For example, the talk factor is so powerful that movie marketers concede that soon after a movie is released, the influence of studio marketing quickly evaporates. Says Joe Nimziki, executive vice-president of a Hollywood advertising agency, "After about two weeks [from the date of release], it's mostly word-of-mouth. Our job is pretty much over."[3]

Commenting about the gratification of getting enough people to see a bad film on the opening weekend before reviews and word of mouth dissuade other people from spending their money on it, Mark Gill, senior vice-president of publicity and promotion for Columbia Pictures, says, "If [a movie] opens big and then crashes, that's when you know that the marketing campaign was absolute perfection."[4]

While negative word of mouth can destroy a business, positive talk can make one thrive. Let's examine the factors that make word of mouth such a powerful force in the marketplace.

Why Word of Mouth Can Be So Powerful

Referral is the most powerful pathway for any business to recruit new customers successfully. Referrals are so effective because they come from an objective second party. The words come from someone who knows you and your products and services, is confident of your ability and reputation to follow through, and has no financial motive for touting your product. Many times your products are "sold" before you even meet the new customer or client. When a new prospect comes to you through a second-party endorsement, you have three distinct selling advantages:

1. *Less Selling Time Is Required.* Sales statistics indicate that you'll spend half the time selling the referred prospect as you will selling the nonreferred prospect. Why? Because much of the selling has already been accomplished by your referral source. Think about Chapter 5 and its discussion of how to turn qualified prospects into first-time buyers. There I established that trust and believability are key factors in making the first sale. And winning trust and believability takes time. These important factors become almost "nonissues" when people get a referral from someone they know and respect.

2. *These Prospects Have Greater Loyalty Potential.* People who buy because of a personal referral tend to be more loyal than those who buy because of an advertisement. Consider the experience of Laura Peck. Laura Peck used to advertise her workshops, but due to financial problems she discontinued the ads and instead began cultivating her own network of friends and acquaintances for clients. Now, two years later, her business is thriving. She says, "When I advertised, I seemed to attract people who came because of the discount I offered. These clients often did not return, would cancel sessions and generally were not repeaters. The people who were most enthusiastic, most loyal, and continued with their sessions were almost always clients who had been personally referred. Had it not been for the economics involved, I would probably not have learned this important lesson; personal recommendation is the best advertising there is."[5]

3. *People Come Ready to Buy.* An industry that evokes mistrust and fear is the auto repair industry. Who hasn't heard a horror story of an auto repair that was unjustified or was never done right? So why does a customer who comes back to Direct Tire in Watertown, Massachusetts, spend $173 during an average visit and new customers who have been referred by someone else spend $224?

According to Direct Tire President Barry Steinberg, the answer is quite simple. These big spenders have usually been putting off a major repair or purchase until they can find a repair shop they can trust. Once they hear about Direct Tire's service, they come in and spend.[6]

A reputation of trust, reliability, and terrific service has made Direct Tire a profitable, flourishing business. The nearby Goodyear outlet sells tires for a Ford Taurus for $50 to $100 apiece, while Direct Tire sells the same tire for $60 to $120. Steinberg, who has spent his entire adult life in the tire business, says, "On average, we are consistently 10 to 12 percent higher than just about everybody else." Direct Tire does not sell on price—it sells on service. This formula works, as evidenced by Direct Tire's profit margins, which are twice the industry average, and its loyal client base. From this base, about 75 percent of the company's monthly sales are recorded from repeat customers.

Earn Word of Mouth: Four Proven Strategies

1. Give 'em Something to Talk About

Bonnie Raitt, the popular blues/country cross-over artist, had a *Billboard* Chart hit in 1992 entitled "Let's Give Them Something to Talk About" that told how a good story travels fast. That same philosophy is key to creating a high talk factor between customers and their friends. Two companies that have given their customers something to talk about are Windham Hill Records and Direct Tire. Here's how they did it.

William Ackerman literally learned the record business from the ground up. In the late 1970s, as a contractor and carpenter, Ackerman operated a Palo Alto contracting business called Windham Hill. Ackerman was hired to build warehouses for two small, folk-oriented record companies in the San Francisco area. In between his sawing and hammering, he got a bird's-eye view of the companies' daily operations and got to ask a lot of questions. During work breaks, Ackerman and his friends played guitar on the back of their pickup trucks.

In his spare time, Ackerman played guitar on campus at Stanford University. Although lacking only a few credits to graduate (including a course in Chaucer taught by his father), Ackerman had dropped out of the university, but he still got requests to perform. People were constantly asking to record his music into their cassettes. With $5 each from some sixty people and a small loan from his friend and eventual partner, Anne Robinson, Ackerman recorded *In Search of the Turtle's Navel*, an album of guitar solos.

"The sum total of my ambitions consisted of selling 300 records, which was the minimum order the record pressing plant demanded," said Ackerman. "I fully envisioned a closet in my house laden with at least 100 extra records for the rest of my life."[7]

After selling approximately sixty copies to friends, Ackerman gave some extra records to ten FM radio stations and listeners began calling the stations to inquire about his music. Soon a few record stores contacted him, and orders began to slowly flow in.

Today the company sells about $30 million worth of records a year wholesale. Robinson and Ackerman attribute word of mouth in the early years as fundamental to their success. Robinson explained, "We found there were a lot of people who became evangelistic about our music. We got letters from people who said that they went to their friend's house for dinner and heard our music. Then they had to have it because it spoke to them, so they went out and bought it and then played it for their friends."[8]

It was by accident that Windham Hill moved into an audiophile line in 1976. It happened through a chance meeting at an engineers' convention. Ackerman's engineer ended up sitting next to Stan Ricker, the premier half-speed-mastering engineer in America. At that time, few people had heard of half-speed mastering or its deeply enhanced sonics. As a result of the meeting, Ackerman's company adopted Ricker's recommendations of using quality pressings on high-quality imported vinyl, double-laminated covers, plastic inner sleeves, and superb graphics.

"'Quality begets quality' is the summary," Ackerman insists. "You need to be economically viable to be able to do any work in this society, but there are so many people whose principal desire is to see quality fostered in the marketplace that if you stand for that, people will come to you."[9]

Rod Watts, an early Windham Hill convert, observes, "In a record store, Windham Hill is the first place I head for. I'd much rather buy one of these albums, even if I haven't heard it, than buy some other musician or label cold."[10]

Explaining his company's strong commitment to customer satisfaction, Ackerman says, "You haven't made the sale just in selling the record. You've made the sale when somebody gets home and feels utterly happy with the record. I did that when I was building houses, too. The last handshake when you walked out of the house was when you sold the house, not when you signed the contract to build it; it's leaving them happy with what they've bought. In the long run, it brings about an audience loyalty that can't be overemphasized as an element of our success."[11]

Direct Tire President Barry Steinberg sees the whole purpose of customer service very simply: to keep customers coming back and to get satisfied customers telling others. Virtually everything that takes place at Direct Tire is directed to that objective. Need to buy some tires and be in and out in an hour? Direct Tire will schedule an appointment whenever it's convenient for you. Need transportation immediately? Direct Tire offers one of the company's seven loaners to use. You can pick up your car on the way home. What if those new tires blow out after 30,000 miles or if for some reason you are simply not satisfied? Direct Tire guarantees the tires as well as any service work the shop does—forever.

How does Steinberg know these services are important and worth the necessary expense? Consider his large loaner fleet. Says Steinberg, "Three years ago, before I had the loaners, I was doing $50,000 to $55,000 a month in service work. Today I'm averaging $120,000 a month and the gross margins on service work are 30% higher than on tires. People will call up and say, 'I understand you have a free car I can use while you work on mine.' We'll say, 'Yes, that's right,' and they'll schedule an appointment right then. A lot of them don't even bother to ask what the work will cost. I'm going to add more cars."[12]

Typical of the length to which Direct Tire will go to keep a customer happy and loyal was the case of the customer whose car was sitting on a lift for front-end alignment. The customer had called in ahead of time to make certain there would be no delay for him to get to work. But Bobby Binnall, an employee who transports passengers to and from work, was delayed in a car that had stalled. The customer was getting edgy, and Steinberg had an inspiration: "I called the local taxi company, and in five minutes they were here and took the guy over to his office. The cab fare was $17, but can you imagine how many people he's going to tell this story to? It was the best $17 I ever spent."[13]

It is this kind of reasoning that has allowed Steinberg to maintain his high net margin, even as he has increased his investment in customer service. But he measures his return on that investment with a satisfying fiscal picture that shows how effective he has been in turning one-time buyers into regular customers. Direct Tire's revenues continue to increase steadily, as they have every year since its founding in 1974, despite generally flat sales for the industry as a whole—all because he wins over customers who tell other people about their positive experience at Direct Tire.

2. Continually Search for New Ways to Earn the Talk Factor

A computer check-writing program called *Quicken* has become the most successful personal finance program ever written, holding an impressive 60 percent market share. Says Jeffrey Tarter, editor of the industry publication *Softletter*, "It has become the brand-name product in what would otherwise be a commodity business. It's the Kleenex or Xerox of its market."[14] Sales have continued to explode. The company now generates annual sales of more than $33 million and sells close to 1 million units annually.

Quicken is carried by Target, Wal-Mart, and other retailers and computer chains nationwide. And how large is the company's sales force? It comprises exactly two people. But Scott Cook, CEO of Intuit, the maker of *Quicken*, sees it differently: "Really, we have hundreds of thousands of salespeople. They're our customers." Scott speaks of his customers as "apostles" and states that Intuit's mission is to "make the customer feel so good about the product they'll go and tell five friends to buy it."[15]

But things weren't always so rosy. According to Cook, May 1, 1985, was the worst day of his life. His company, Intuit, was less than two years old and he had to tell his seven employees that, because he could no longer pay their salaries, he had to let them go.

Cook's flagship product, an easy-to-use check-writing program for personal computers, had plenty of potential. What he lacked was money. Cook had started the company with $350,000, a sum raised from a combination of family loans, his life savings, credit cards, and home-equity credit. Attempts to interest venture capitalists got him nowhere. And now his start-up capital was nearly gone.

By the summer of 1986, the little company had just $125,000, generated primarily from Intuit sales in bank lobbies. If he wanted to catch the all-important Christmas selling season, Scott had to roll the dice on a make-or-break ad campaign. He wrote the ad himself and spent all of the $125,000 on the campaign. It worked. Scott's all-or-nothing ad campaign, coupled with his uncompromising efforts to create a product that truly satisfied its buyers, paid off.

To create this phenomenal word of mouth with such potential mass-market appeal, the *Quicken* program had to be fast, cheap, hassle free, and, above all, easy to use—so easy that anyone as a first-time user could sit down at the computer and start writing checks. And Intuit is on a constant crusade to meet these objectives. One such example is Intuit's Follow-Me-Home program, in which *Quicken* buyers from local stores are asked to let an Intuit representative observe them when they first use *Quicken*. This way, Intuit gets continual feedback on how the product might be made just a tiny bit easier for first-time users. "If people don't use the product," says Tom LeFevre, chief programmer, "they won't tell their friends to use it, either."[16]

3. Get Your Product in the Hands of Influencers

Conventional wisdom says that in order to get a group of "opinion leaders" to earnestly spread the word about a new product, its maker must first give the product away.

Not so with Approach Software, a start-up in Redwood City, California, which found a way to earn initial sales from opinion leaders and then *triple* the number of people who purchased its product on the advice of friends or associates in the six months following the product's launch. How did the company do it? By offering a low introductory price and a ninety-day, money-back guarantee. The target of the offer was carefully selected, influential users, who were asked to try the company's first product, a database software program designed for nontechies.

Approach's limited-time offer of $149 for *Approach 1.0 for Windows*, plus free technical support, quickly got the innovative software into the hands of thousands of small-company CEOs and other targeted customers. The price was hard to beat, given the software's appealing characteristics—less than a half-hour to learn the program and seamless integration with other database software. Competing products cost as much as $799.

4. Turn Centers of Influence into Full-Time Advocates

One unique application of word-of-mouth advertising in the Deep South proved how effective this form of prestige recommendation can be. Fifteen years ago, Jay Stein decided to expand the department store in Greenville, Mississippi, that his grandfather had founded in 1908. As a stroke of luck, several well-to-do women from Greenville volunteered to help out during the stores's liquidation sales of some designer clothing. Commenting for the *Wall Street Journal*, Stein said, "They had firsthand knowledge of this better merchandise, because they had worn it for years." The experience convinced Stein that the concept was worth replicating. When Stein Mart opened its second store, this time in Memphis, he created a designer boutique department in the store and he and his wife recruited socialite friends to operate it.

Today, to be hired as a Stein Mart "boutique lady" is a bit of a status symbol, as indicated by the waiting lists for the job at all fifty-one Stein Mart stores. "As soon as I heard they had an opening, I called to put my name in," reports Gay Kemp, who is married to an international marketing executive. "Everybody I knew was doing it and they kept talking about how fun it was. When you look at the women who are doing it—doctors' wives, women who have mansions on the river—well, it's a neat association."[17]

"The boutique ladies are our secret weapon" says Jay Stein. These women work one day a week, earn $7 an hour, and are excused from cash register responsibility and evening shifts. Instead, their activities are focused on "spreading the word" about designer merchandise. For example, when a shipment of $39 designer silk separates arrived at the Jacksonville Stein Mart, boutique lady Joy Abney, the wife of a former managing partner of Coopers and Lybrand, hit the phones. She called fellow board members at Wolfson Children's Hospital and "told them to get over here." Joy's friends obliged by spending $2,000 in her department that same day.

For many boutique ladies, it's gratifying to learn that women of a certain age and without a résumé are still welcomed in the work force. Many compare the job to volunteer work, since, as Kemp sees it, "you are busy helping people." The pay is a bonus. "It's fun to get a paycheck that's mine," says Kemp, who also adds that the employee discount of 25 percent is more important to her than her

$40 paycheck. "I don't care who you are or how much you have, everybody likes a discount," she says.[18]

In return, Stein Mart enjoys a polished, loyal sales force of advocates. Joyce de la Houssaye of New Orleans wedges her boutique duties into a full schedule of Junior League, golf, and four grandchildren. She brings flowers from her award-winning garden to decorate her boutique department. After organizing a special store reception, she took off in her golf cart to deliver flyers to neighbors about the upcoming event.

Getting the Word out about You

Once you have developed a loyal client, you then have the opportunity to multiply that one client by a factor of two, three, five, or more. Each person you sell to can be multiplied by the number of his or her associates who are prospects for your offerings. It all depends on getting the word out through your client advocates. Let's examine the tools you need to maximize your talk factor.

What's in It for Your Endorser?

An advocate, or endorser, is someone who goes out and advocates your cause. Is this a totally selfless move on the part of your endorser? Not entirely. To an advocate, you are the best in the business, and his or her selfish motivation is to keep you in business. The advocate wants to keep you going so you'll always be able to continue doing business with him or her. Moreover, when you perform well for the new customer and he or she is satisfied, you make the endorser look good. In some ways, the new customer now "owes one" to the endorser. So the next time you are shy about asking for an endorsement, take into consideration the fact that the giving of an endorsement is not a totally selfless act on the part of your advocate. There is something in it for the advocate as well.

The Satisfied Customer File

One invaluable sales aid is to keep a satisfied customer file. Make a point of adding a satisfied customer story every week. Write it up, including the names, addresses, and phone numbers of the satisfied customers. Ask each one, in advance, for permission to use his or her name as a reference. When you're trying to win over a tough prospect, scan your file, identify a success story that nearly matches the prospect's situation, and invite the prospect to contact the customer directly for a reference. Among sales professionals, this technique is known as reference selling.

Reference selling is so effective that it can overcome hurdles that seem insurmountable, as Lynn Green, a sales engineer at Data I/O Corporation in New Hampshire, discovered. She was able to overcome legitimate price objections from a prospect by referring him to loyal customers. Though her company is the market leader, she says, "Our pricing is usually the main stumbling block with a new customer who has used competitive products."

In one situation, she was selling a product for $15,000, against a competitor who was offering something similar for only $2,000. Lynn remembers that the prospect "called and asked why he should pay $15,000 when he could buy seven of the competitor's products for less money."

That was when she asked him to seek the advice of her own customers who had used the competitor's products in the past but had switched back to hers.

"At the time," she says, "I didn't think I would get the sale because of the wide difference in price. But, once again, my existing customers made the sale for me."

Green stresses the importance of developing good rapport with your existing customer base. And she found out that her customers enjoy assisting her. "If you and your company have a customer's loyalty, it can pay off in more ways than one," she states.

The Testimonial Letter

Another approach to reference selling is by using the testimonial letter. Such a letter can be used in a number of ways. It can be part of marketing materials given to a prospective customer, for example, or an excerpt from the letter can be used in brochures.

Ask your satisfied customers and clients to write you a letter on their company letterhead outlining how your products or services helped their organizations. Encourage your clients to identify concrete benefits they derived from you. Make these benefits as specific as possible. Ideally, you should ask for letters from as many customers and clients as possible. Prospective customers like to see testimonials from companies in their industries and from their regions of the country.

Often a client is happy to write a letter but asks for assistance in what to say. Show the person examples of other testimonial letters. Ask him or her questions about what he or she found most beneficial from your products or services. From the resultant description, you can suggest the thrust of what the person can say.

- How long did he or she use your product?
- How does yours compare with others he or she has used?
- What was the scope of the project or sale?
- What were the tangible results?

Remember the customer advantage section discussed earlier and the benefits of comparing the "after" with the "before"? A statement of specific results can be very powerful in building credibility. Excerpts from testimonial letters in my files that refer to specific results include one from a hotel client: "Jill created a marketing and sales system for each of our five AmeriSuites hotel properties. The result has been a 19 percent increase in corporate business this past year." From a distributor of a syndicated radio series came this one: "Jill's direct mail and telemarketing programs increased our response rate among prospective radio affiliates from 16 to 40 percent."

Perhaps you provide products or services whose use is not so easily quantified. Get as specific as possible regarding outcomes. From a state agency whose annual planning retreat I facilitated came this testimonial: "Not only were a large number of 'big ideas' conceived for next year's marketing plan but, as a result of the deliberations, our two groups have become even more effective in working together as a team. Your ability to keep a large group focused and motivated, and insistence that the discussions be interesting and fun—all contributed to the success of our retreat."

Make the testimonial letter development process as easy as possible for the client. I've had several clients who have suggested that I write the letter for them. I love it when this happens. They review it and may make some changes. From the draft, they finalize the letter.

The Preheat Letter

Juanell Teague, who operates a successful consulting business for established and aspiring speakers, suggests an approach called the "preheat letter" to turn satisfied clients into advocates. Ask your satisfied clients, she says, to write a preheat letter to between five and forty of their personal contacts. You get your clients to provide you with names, addresses, and phone numbers, along with their letterhead and envelopes. You prepare the mailing, including postage, and return the letters to them for signatures and mailing. About a week later, you make follow-up calls. Obviously, the preheat letter is a warmup before you make a call on your customer's referral.

Juanell advises that the most successful preheat letters accomplish four objectives:

- Explain the client's requirements that you filled
- Describe how he or she found you
- Outline the work you accomplished
- Recommend you

An example of a preheat letter from one of my clients is shown below. This letter was instrumental in helping me get several new assignments.

Dear Mr. Randall:

The first of a three-part seminar series on marketing and profitability in the salon was presented recently by Peel's Beauty Supply. The "Sharpen the Edge" seminar was created to address some of today's most pertinent salon issues.

To meet this need, we compiled some dynamic educators. Michael Cole and Jill Griffin were two of the participants. Jill Griffin was brought to my attention by Michael Cole after he heard her speak at Sebastian's Turning Point Conference in Las Vegas last November. Michael described Jill as a high-content, high-energy speaker with an in-depth understanding of salon marketing. The "Sharpen the Edge" audiences were extremely excited and enthusiastic about Jill's presentations also.

Jill presented a one-day course in "Power Promotions: Twenty-one Ways to Increase Salon Sales," and "Cash Comebacks: How to Turn

Customer Service into Customer Sales." Using colored slides, audience participation, and attention-getting props, Jill effectively illustrated each presentation. Responses to Jill's presentation: "I got some fresh new solutions" and "Quickest two hours I've experienced in a long time." Our sales consultants were equally energized.

I would recommend Jill Griffin for any future educational programs your company may be considering. Jill's presentation was a straightforward, yet entertaining, attention-keeping approach to salon marketing.

For more information on Jill's marketing education programs, please direct correspondence to:

> Jill Griffin
> The Marketing Resource Center
> 2729 Exposition Boulevard, Suite 420
> Austin, TX 78703
> (512) 469–1757

Sincerely,

William C. Peel
President

Perhaps the simplest way to use the endorsement for selling is by asking your client for referrals and then promptly following up. Asking for referrals should be a natural part of your interaction with your client. As we discussed earlier, satisfied clients benefit by giving your referrals. Don't be shy. Just ask.

There is a right way and a wrong way to ask for referrals:

Wrong: You don't know anyone else who might be interested in my product, do you?

Reason: Based on a negative supposition. Leads the client to say no.

Wrong: Do you know someone who might need my product?

Reason: Provides the client with the opportunity to just say no.

Right: Who do you know that might appreciate knowing about my services?

Reason: Takes a more positive, proactive approach that implies "I'm a problem solver."

Once you have been given the first name, ask, "Who else do you know?" and repeat the process until your client runs out of referrals.

Ask permission to use the referrer's name with the question "May I use your name as a reference when I contact them?" and then abide by his or her wishes.

Recommend-a-Friend Rewards

One of the most profitable yet overlooked methods for stimulating word of mouth and referrals is recommend-a-friend promotions. The basic technique is to offer an incentive to a customer in exchange for the favor of referral. At Indy Lube, customers who send friends to the $3.6 million quick-lube chain get a $10 certificate toward their next oil change. It's a way to thank customers who take the time to fill out an Indy Lube referral card and give it to a friend. The new customer uses the card to get $5 off his or her first oil change. The Indianapolis company won thirty-five new customers that way in one month alone. When Indy runs a contest among its fifteen locations for most customer referrals in a month, CEO Jim Sapp says, he redeems as many as fifty referral cards per store.

Another twist on the recommend-a-friend promotion is the recommend-a-friend card, whereby a customer receives a special reward for providing referrals. Experience has shown that you can expect a larger number of friends' names if your customers are guaranteed that their name will not be used in soliciting their friends. Response from friends will be higher, however, if you are allowed to reference the name of the friend who provided the name. Therefore, you may want to give the customer a choice of whether his or her name will be used in solicitation by using this question: "May we use your name as our referral source?"

Response decreases in proportion to the number of names provided by the customer. Thus, response from three names provided by one customer will most likely be greater than the total response from six names provided by another. Additionally, experience has shown that people list names according to likelihood of interest. Therefore, contact the names provided in the order of their listing, giving priority to those listed first.

Companies that have acquired names through customers have

found that the people listed are, with few exceptions, more responsive and ripe for conversion than those on most any list the company can rent or buy.

Learn to Say Thank You Every Time

Any action on anyone's part in referring a prospect to you deserves a thank-you. The rule is simple: Thank the person in writing. Thank the person right away. Whether or not you convert the referral into a customer or client, the source for the referral deserves recognition. A thank-you message from a realtor might read, "Thank you for suggesting that Paul and Brenda Logan call me regarding their real estate needs. I met with Paul and Brenda on Tuesday and enjoyed talking with them. The Logans mentioned how enthusiastic and complimentary you were in giving them my name. I truly appreciate your confidence in my abilities." Notice what the note does *not* say: It does not say "I got the Logans' listing. Thank you." If the realtor did receive the listing, then that piece of information could be incorporated into the thank-you note. But the most important thing about the communication is that the client is properly thanked for the referral. Period.

Keeping the Word out about You

Have you had the experience of being out of touch with a colleague or client and then running into him or her unexpectedly and learning something to the effect that "I was just in need of someone with your know-how" or "My neighbor was just asking about . . . I completely forgot that you provide that service."

The key is to keep yourself visible and top of mind with those people by creating a simple yet effective system for staying in touch.

Blueprint for Staying in Touch Long-Term

Maintaining a network of clients and market influencers who are likely to provide you with contacts and leads for future business is essential to business success. The secret to a strong network is constant contact. Consider this system for staying in touch:[19]

Written Notes: Five a Day

Have some type of stationery with you at all times. This is important, because it's during those moments while you are unexpectedly waiting that you use the time to keep in touch. Note cards are great for this purpose. If you write five notes a day and you are in business 250 days a year, that's more than 1,200 extra contacts.

With five notes a day, you can create friendships from business contacts by simply taking the two minutes necessary to jot down a thought. Two to three sentences is all it takes to say to someone "I was thinking of you." While birthdays, anniversaries, and promotions are a reason to write, do not wait for special events. A note that simply says "Hello" and "How are you?" can do the trick. Mailing a copy of an article you think may be of interest to a customer can be an added bonus.

The key to this tool is to maintain a good mailing list of clients and addresses; doing so is crucial to your ability to stay in touch.

Phone Calls: Five a Week

Make a minimum of five calls a week. Keeps the calls brief. Two brief calls are better than one long call. You become the source. You are generating the communication, and you are building the network. Take the opportunity to ask the persons you call their opinion on something you are undertaking. William James once said, "The greatest need of every human being is the need for appreciation." Let them know you respect their opinion.

In-Person Contacts: Five a Month

Make five personal contacts a month. Practice the "out to lunch" method by calling and inviting three clients to lunch. Pick a popular lunch spot. Mix new clients with long-term clients. Make it a social affair that can pay you business dividends.

THE NUMBERS SPEAK FOR THEMSELVES

250 days x 5 notes/day = 1,250 contacts
50 weeks x 5 calls/week = 250 contacts
12 months x 5 contacts/month = 60 contacts

TOTAL CONTACTS. . . ..1560 CONTACTS PER YEAR

WHAT THIS MEANS TO YOU IS. . . ...

- You can reach 260 people 6 times a year
- You can reach 390 people 4 times a year
- You can reach 780 people 2 times a year

CONSIDER THE IMPACT OF 1,560 ADDITIONAL CONTACTS TO YOUR BUSINESS!

Putting Newsletters to Work

An effective way to stay in touch with customers and clients and in doing so to create camaraderie among a customer's customers is to publish a newsletter. A newsletter can help establish a "club" feeling, giving customers a sense of belonging, of being special.

Any restaurateur will tell you that the secret to longevity in the restaurant business does not lie in getting customers in the door. The real task is getting them to return. The newsletter has become the weapon of choice for many restaurants in meeting this important objective.

Back in 1981, Jim Lark was searching for a means to let his customers know about the special monthly theme dinners he and his wife, Mary, were serving at their exclusive restaurant, The Lark, in West Bloomfield, Mississippi. A newsletter seemed like a logical choice. So Jim created a newsletter with a masthead that proudly proclaimed itself "American's first monthly restaurant newsletter," and it contained prose that read like a letter to family and friends. The communication did the trick, and the special theme dinners, with the help of the customer newsletter, continue to be sell-outs a decade later.

With the exception of an occasional tombstone ad in a charity program, the newsletter is Jim Lark's primary way of letting customers know what's going on. The newsletter helps The Lark enjoy a healthy loyal clientele. Says Lark, "About 85% of our business is repeat business."[20]

Consider this newsletter sampling: "Mary and I have just returned from safari. The African setting, the wildlife and the camaraderie of the friends who accompanied us were all that we hoped for. What we did not expect was the exceptional cuisine, which took full advantage not only of the best wild game in the world, but the bounty of extensive orchards and vineyards of the surrounding area."[21]

Jim Lark's experience has taught him what companies in a wide cross section of industries have discovered: A well-conceived newsletter that provides a payoff to the reader in terms of education and information can help a company to

- maintain contact with customers
- foster long-term relationships
- provide product information
- establish the company as an expert in the field, and
- cultivate future sales

Technology has enabled other vehicles, such as audio and video cassettes, computer disks, and e-mail, to convey the information provided by a newsletter. But all these other vehicles require some sort of support equipment. The printed newsletter is still the most versatile of these information pieces.

Recent increases in the volume of direct mail, however, make high quality and professional execution of a newsletter critical to break through the clutter. Writing in the Financial Services edition of *Life & Health*, John Graham says, "It takes time and effort to create an effective company newsletter. Yet the investment is invaluable when it comes to building solid relationships with your customers." Graham warns not to make a newsletter an "ad" for your company: "It won't get read. Use the newsletter as an opportunity to pass along helpful information. Be sure to feature your customers too. This will go a long way toward strengthening the ties with your firm."

Jim Lark's newsletter savvy has grown with the years. If a patron has not been to The Lark for five months, Lark places a gold sticker on the newsletter that goes out on the sixth month. The sticker says "We miss you." If after being stickered several times the customer still does not return, the customer is usually dropped from the list. Aware of what the the sticker implies and not wanting to be dropped from the list, The Lark customers refer to them as "the dreaded sticker" and visit the bistro soon in order to stay in good stead.

Suppose you are a printer specializing in high-resolution color printing and you consider promoting your company by means of a newsletter. Face it, for the newsletter to be effective, it must be good. Very good. That was reality for Hemlock Printers, based in Burnaby, British Columbia. The company is the largest sheet-fed printer in the region and considers its market to be almost every prime buyer of sheet-fed printing in western Canada.

It was not a decision made lightly, according to Marketing Manager Steve McElroy, as he traced the development of *Inklings*, Hemlock's quarterly newsletter. Reflects McElroy, "Accept the seriousness of the decision to publish. If one's newsletter is bland, uninteresting, or obviously an afterthought, it can do more harm than good. Prospects and customers alike are unforgiving of a bad, boring, or stupid newsletter. They associate the sponsor with the newsletter. A printing firm's newsletter must be a good example of what the firm can do. The decision to publish should be a top-level decision, and the resulting house publication should be excellent, with virtually no production compromises."

Steve McElroy reported, "One of the chief objectives of *Inklings* was to nurture present clients and nudge them toward greater volume, while impressing prospects and ultimately making them customers. Our first step in developing this publication was to formulate a statement of purpose and objectives, as follows: '*Inklings* will focus firmly on the reader, his or her interests, problems, goals and aspirations, and thus will achieve its selling purpose through value rendered rather than overt persuasion and self-serving "advertorials." The reader will recognize *Inklings* for its excellence. As the avalanche of information competing for attention continues to rise, he/she will favor *Inklings* for its topical and incisive editorial content, its lively writing and dynamic graphics and its innovative ideas and superior reproduction quality.'"[22]

McElroy and his staff then collected many samples, and spoke to writing and design professionals to help sharpen the editorial and visual focus.

Says McElroy, "I advise [other] firms to think of their newsletter program as a service they could very well charge for. In all fields there are scrawny four-page newsletters that demand annual subscription rates higher than most magazines. Fashion your newsletter as if it were going to subscribers who pay, say, two dollars or more per issue. Then, it seems, the whole creative attitude toward the venture changes for the better."[23]

While few firms would require the scrutiny to quality that a newsletter from a color printer specialist demands, before you jump in with a newsletter, remember Steve McElroy's final words of advice: "The bottom line is this—your publication should be really worth something to the recipient. If it is essentially worthless, it will hit the circular file faster than you can say 'advertising strategy.'"[24]

Be Ready for More Customers

Think twice before you launch a plan to encourage personal recommendation referrals. Properly executed, it can produce dynamic results. But when a business is not ready for expansion, having a lot of new customers can threaten quality by reducing standards in order to meet demand. The result can be disastrous: disillusioned prospects, dissatisfied customers, low employee morale, and general frustration at not being able to provide good service. When this happens, unhappy prospects and customers will tell their friends, and a downward business spiral begins.

Summary

- Word of mouth is the most powerful advertising your business can have.
- Referred customers require less selling time and are more loyal than other customers. They come ready to buy because in effect they have already been sold.
- Always remember to thank your customers, and realize that where they buy is a choice they make.

- Use testimonials, customer files, and reward programs to increase the loyalty of customers and to build a strong reputation.
- Continually strive to increase and improve your long-term contacts—they directly and indirectly increase your sales. As few as five notes a day, five calls a week, and five meetings a month with your network can provide a substantial boost to your business.
- Be ready for more customers. Launch an aggressive plan for encouraging referrals once you have the systems in place to effectively handle them.

9

Customer Inactivity

How to Prevent It and What to Do When It Strikes

I got a phone call today from one of our oldest customers.
He fired us.
After 20 years. He fired us.
Said he didn't know us anymore.
I think I know why.
We used to do business with a handshake, face to face. . . .
Now it's "I'll get back to you later."
Well, folks, some things gotta change.
That's the reason we're gonna set out today with a face-to-face
chat with every customer we have.

—*United Airlines commercial*

The Real Cost of Losing a Customer

When a long-term client stops doing business with you, when in effect he or she goes "inactive," it's an expensive loss. As we saw in Chapter 1, in terms of profit contribution, it is the long-term client who contributes most to a company's bottom line. When such a client goes inactive—stops buying from you—you lose a higher proportion of profits than when a first-time customer stops purchasing.

And the loss is not a simple short-term loss. You also forfeit future profits as well. For example, a grocery shopper who spends approximately $100 weekly on groceries for the family represents roughly $50,000 over a decade of purchases. The average lifetime value of a car buyer, excluding repairs, is around $150,000. The customer and his or her future buying potential represent a power-

183

ful appreciating asset for any business. So when a customer stops buying, the loss is far greater than simply one missed purchase.

In *Thriving on Chaos*, author Tom Peters states, "When the Federal Express courier enters my office, she should see $180,000 stamped on the forehead of our receptionist. My little twenty-five-person firm runs about a $1500 a month Fed Ex bill. Over ten years, that will add up to $180,000. I suggest that this simple device, calculating the ten-year value of a customer, can be very powerful."[1]

But the losses are greater still. When a customer leaves, you lose more than just the person's buying power. You also lose his or her referrals and word-of-mouth advertising. For example, if an auto dealer's customer sells just one friend on doing business with the dealership, that customer's value appreciates from $150,000 to $300,000. With two referrals, the customer's value increases to $600,000.

Customers who leave you are a double-edged sword: Not only do you lose their specific business, but also you jeopardize gaining future business with new customers because of the negative word of mouth. A typical dissatisfied customer will tell eight to ten people about his or her experience. One in five will tell twenty. And if you're Dr. Robert Leone, you may tell even more.

What if you hired a national moving company to transport your household possessions to your new home halfway across the country and the truck, the driver, and your possessions were "lost" for three months? That's precisely the predicament Dr. Robert Leone found himself in during the late 1970s when he moved from Minneapolis to Austin to join the marketing faculty at the University of Texas.

Dr. Leone hired an attorney, took his case to court, and won. In the end, the moving company met all of Dr. Leone's requirements for settlement but one: It refused to give him a letter of apology.

What was next for Dr. Leone? He began exhibiting the classic symptom of a dissatisfied customer. He told people—lots of people—about his experience. In fact, Bob Leone made a point of telling his story to each of his introductory marketing classes at the university. And each year at Christmas, Dr. Leone would send a Christmas card to the president of the moving company, and include a "running total" of how many people he had told thus far. Dr. Leone continued this tradition for ten years. Four years ago, Dr. Leone sent his last Christmas greeting to the moving company president. The number on the card: 3,503.

The Lost Customer Dilemma: A Closer Look

This very minute, your best customers and clients are your competitors' most sought-after prospects. No one understands this reality better than Browning Ferris Industries, the nation's number two trash hauler, which, like others in this industry, loses about 14 percent of its customer base annually to competitors. Competitors can easily spot the company's clients by simply touring streets and alleys looking for the blue Browning Ferris dumpsters.

In 1992, Browning Ferris managed a net gain of 33,000 U.S. commercial and industrial hauling customers, increasing its total to 570,000. But that meant actually having to find 103,000 new customers, because 70,000 old ones were lost. The company's chairman and CEO, William D. Ruckelshaus, called the phenomenon a "tremendous customer churn" and, in an effort to stop the attrition, has embarked on a multimillion-dollar research effort to understand why people become unhappy.

Simply undercutting price is often enough to take away the business unless good service has created loyal customers. Browning Ferris's research is providing understanding of what customers really want from their garbage collector. Customers frequently mention price when threatening to switch haulers, but they're usually angry about something else, too. Says Ruckelshaus, "If you solve that problem for them, the price issue goes away."[2]

Executives in other industries concur. At a recent roundtable session on customer service at *Inc. Magazine*'s conference for the fastest-growing small companies, American Teleconferencing Services COO Michael Twomey explained the effect the loss of a major client had on the Overland Park, Kansas, company: "We'll make up the sales loss, but it's devastating for the sales and support staff, who went all out." Says Twomey, "The client gave us high scores on customer service, but we lost out to a competitor that gave the equipment away."[3]

The advice from some of the twenty-two participating executives: "You probably lost the customer six months before. The relationship has usually soured by the time price becomes the issue."[4]

The Slow Leak

A longtime customer or client is yours to keep or yours to lose. By the time an account has gotten to the repeat customer or client stage, there is a history and both parties have invested a lot. After selling to this person over a period of time, you know his or her staff and his or her needs, just as this client knows you, your staff, and your company. A considerable investment has been made by both parties.

Why, then, will a client leave? What prompts the decision to defect? In most cases, it's a feeling of dissatisfaction that develops progressively over time. The client leaves you when he or she finally feels that the cost of sustaining such lower levels of satisfaction has gotten too high.

Like a car tire, most businesses don't dissolve because of a "blow-out." Instead, it's the slow leak that kills them over time. Most businesses don't fail because of a huge mistake or gigantic blunder. Most fail because they slowly lose touch with their customers. In return, these customers become indifferent and become open to the possibility of giving their business to new suppliers. And as we saw above with Browning Ferris, competitors are everywhere, waiting to capitalize on such indifference.

A Rockefeller Foundation study on lost customers found these reasons for why customers leave:

- 14 percent left because of complaints that were not handled.
- 9 percent left because of the competition.
- 9 percent left because of relocation.
- 68 percent left because of no special reason.

If you look past "no special reason," you'll usually find customers leaving because of benign neglect. As the United Airlines commercial points out, many customers leave because they feel no particular connection with your company. You failed to tell them you cared. You failed to keep in touch. You took them for granted. The bottom line: You made it easy for them to walk away.

Reading Between the Lines

"Clients are funny," observed Ira Gottfried, vice-president at Coopers and Lybrand in Los Angeles. "You'll suddenly find that the work stops and you don't get any new work. You seldom know why. It's a very rare client who will let you know they are having a problem. . . . [T]he Christian ethic says you don't nail somebody; you just walk away."[5]

Indeed, statistics support what Gottfried has learned from experience. Only a small percentage of customers will complain. A typical business hears from only 4 percent of its dissatisfied customers. The remaining 96 percent go away, and, on average, 91 percent never come back.

The old saying "Actions speak louder than words" is an apt description of most customers. They will not voluntarily tell you they are unhappy, but their actions can. Unhappy customers often exhibit one or more of these purchase behaviors—each increasingly creating more distance between you and your customer:

- Customer approval of your proposals come slower.
- Access to upper-level management decreases.
- The flow of customer data slows down.
- Plans for future work become progressively shorter-term.
- One or more of your products or services are discontinued.
- The volume of business they are doing with you is reduced.

These signs are often symptoms of a developing dissatisfaction. When they are, it is useless to attack them directly. Instead, you must discover and address the customer's underlying dissatisfaction.

The Origins of Dissatisfaction

In many cases, dissatisfaction is a result of misunderstanding what is important to your customers. Although you meet the customer's general needs, you don't understand or deliver what is of primary importance to the person. For example, let's say your customer, Joe, wants blue widgets and you respond with yellow ones, assuming that what he really needs is simply widgets, the customer may feel general dissatisfaction—because blue is his favorite color and distinguishes his machine from everyone else's. In other words, you have been concentrating on the wrong things, satisfying the customer in general but overlooking what counts most for the person. The other possibility is that you accurately perceive what is important to the customer but do not deliver quickly enough. You have blue widgets custom made for the person, but it takes six months for them to be delivered, and he or she counted on two. Time is money to this customer, whose dissatisfaction grows with every day that finds him or her behind in reaching objectives. Finally, the waiting becomes unaffordable and the customer severs the relationship with you.

Understanding Where You Stand

Identifying and continually assessing a client's "must list" and then delivering those things in a timely way is the key to Granite Rock's success. This construction materials company has established itself as the high-end producer in an industry that all but defines the term *commodity business*.

Based in Watsonville, California, the hundred-year-old family-owned company, which has a dozen locations between San Francisco and Monterey, quarries granite and produces concrete, asphalt, sand, and gravel. In addition, the company buys and resells cinder block, drywall, and brick and masonry tools. Competing in an industry where customers are conditioned to take the low bid under the mistaken assumption that "all loads of stone are created equal," Granite Rock has taken the high road and chosen to provide high-quality rock supported by high-quality service. In return, Granite Rock customers pay, on average, up to 6 percent more than they would be charged by the competition.

Charging a premium and positioning itself as providing the best value in the industry put a real burden on Granite Rock to deliver. The company must continually prove to customers that its products and services are worth the premium they pay. This means that Granite Rock employees must provide the kind of value customers are willing to pay for. How does the company accomplish this? With a three-pronged strategy: first, by understanding how its customers define quality and service (i.e., the customer's "must list"); second, by regularly gauging customers' opinions about Granite Rock's performance in comparison to its competitors'; and third, by communicating all this information to its employees.

The company accomplishes the first step of the strategy by conducting, every three to four years, a lengthy customer survey in which its customer needs and wants related to each of the company's product lines are extensively probed. In this survey, customers are also asked to rank the most important factors related to choosing a construction materials supplier. This survey is important because it helps the company determine whether it is concentrating on the right things—those the customers value the most.

The second and third steps of the strategy are where Granite Rock really shines by creating a report card of its performance vs. that of the competition. Every year, the company conducts an opinion survey that compares its performance with competitors'. All of Granite Rock's customers receive a survey in which they are asked to grade their top three suppliers on areas related to product quality and customer service.

Combining the long-survey data and the short-survey information, Granite Rock produces "report card" graphs that are posted on bulletin boards throughout the company. Through these graphs, employees can see how they measure up when compared with their competition. Says Dave Franceschi of Granite Rock's quality planning department, "We have a strong belief that if something is worth doing, it's probably worth measuring." Adds Wes Clark, general manager of the company's three northern concrete plants, "We believe that you don't stress a negative—you chart it. Our people are competitive. They will look at that negative and want to do something about it."[6]

In this increasingly competitive world market, a company keeps its customers by providing value every day. As business veterans Mark Hanan and Peter Karp explain, "Whether you are doing the wrong thing or doing the right things cost-ineffectively, the customer who is losing opportunities for enhancing his value will do you in. He cannot help it. He has no choice but to maximize his opportunities."[7]

No one understands that reality more than General Electric's Claudi Santiago. When he started in the General Electric Information Services (GEIS) office in Barcelona back in 1980, the company had local "help desks" to troubleshoot problems around the world. Customers would call the company via telephone, talk with someone in their own language, and get help on the software or network problem they were encountering. The electronic age and a dramatically shortened response time have changed all that. As recent as the late 1980s, GE clients like Chrysler, Caterpillar, and Chemical Bank would accept two-hour maintenance delays when a system "crashed." No longer. Today a ten-minute delay time is all it takes to lose a client to a competitor.

"Customers are getting more and more demanding, and they are putting a lot of pressure on us," says Santiago. "They use our system to order raw materials or parts or to trade stocks and bonds. If an order gets lost or delayed, we can literally stop a manufacturing facility. Our clients' tolerance level for problems is close to zero. That's the reality."[8]

In 1991, GE created Santiago's position. Today he leads a staff of 200 people worldwide who anticipate user problems; fix them rapidly, if and when they do occur; and prevent them from reoccurring in the future. To help meet these objectives, GEIS has created an innovative system for soliciting user feedback. The users respond to an electronic report card, grading the company daily on such areas as response time and service, with zero for "outstanding" all the way up to five for "disastrous." Results are tallied, and an overall grade is determined at the end of each week and each month. These monthly averages are compared against a target set by a client advisory council, and if they meet the target, predetermined percentage bonuses are rewarded to all GEIS employees.

One of GEIS's most successful products is e-mail, so "ClientTalk," a special e-mail system on which customers can send and receive messages about the company's services, was a natural spin-off service. The newest Client-Talk innovation enables customers to flag their messages for readership by GEIS management. These messages are then republished in the president's and vice-presidents' daily reports. Another important Client-Talk improvement is the ability to inform clients about user complaints elsewhere in their company. Explains Santiago, "Sometimes a client can have a distributor in Singapore who had a problem with an order and the client didn't know about it because we fixed it so quickly. Now they can see on a daily, weekly or monthly basis all the Client-Talk problems that come up for them on a worldwide basis and how long it takes GEIS to fix them."[9]

It is clear that keeping clients loyal—and keeping them happy—depends on a company's ability to identify dissatisfaction quickly and respond immediately. If you don't know a client is having a problem with your company, chances are slim that the problem can be corrected before the client defects to a competitor. Constant monitoring and solicitation of customer feedback are essential to maintaining loyal customers.

Complaints as Loyalty Builders

Life in the real world means things don't always go according to plan. Problems are inevitable in any continuing business relationship. Hotel reservations get lost; a car breaks down; a customer experiences difficulty in operating a new office machine. What's important is the way the company responds to these problems. Some research suggests that people whose complaints are properly dealt with may become more loyal customers than those people who have never experienced problems.

The company's eagerness to solve a problem and improve performance is what builds the customer's trust and translates into future business. Consider these statistics from McKinsey and Company:

- Customers who have major problems but don't complain about them have a repurchase intention rate of about 9 percent.
- Those who do complain, regardless of the outcome, have a repurchase intention rate of approximately 19 percent.
- Customers who have their complaint resolved have a repurchase intention rate of 54 percent.
- Customers who have complaints quickly resolved have a repurchase intention rate of 82 percent.

Notice that, in this study, the customer's intention to repurchase doubled (from 9 to 19 percent) by simply having a forum by which to complain. The large gains in intention to repurchase (54 and 82 percent) can take place only if the company is first aware of the problem.

No News Is Bad News

"One of the sure signs of a bad or declining relationship is the absence of complaints from the customer," says Harvard Professor Theodore Levitt, writing in the *Harvard Business Review*. "Nobody is ever that satisfied, especially not over an extended period of time. The customer either is not being candid or is not being contacted."

If you are not receiving complaints from customers, something is wrong. Don't be fooled into thinking there are no unhappy customers. Instead, it means that rather than complaining, your customers are probably leaving or, at best, reducing the amount of business they are doing with you. Moreover, the "iceberg effect" is alive and well when it comes to complaints. According to the Consumer Affairs Department, if one customer complains to a business, there are usually twenty-five additional customers with the same complaint that haven't been heard from.

Four Ways to Keep Your Customers from Leaving

1. MAKE IT EASY FOR CUSTOMERS TO GIVE YOU FEEDBACK

One of the most profitable activities a business can engage in is to seek out customer complaints, making it easy for the customer to give feedback. Ask customers on a regular basis about their most recent purchase. Did it meet their needs? Was it what they expected? How could it be improved? Here's how one start-up company facilitated feedback from customers.

Restek Marketing Director Neil Mosesman knew customer calls were getting out of hand when he was taking them even while he was away at trade shows. Like any company that suddenly experiences an acceleration in growth, Restek, a manufacturer of lab equipment parts in Bellefonte, Pennsylvania, found itself bombarded with customer questions, comments, and complaints. To effectively deal with these calls, Restek adopted an unconventional solution. Rather than delegating call handling to a "customer service" department, Restek spreads the responsibility throughout the company by providing employees with service training and incentives.

All employees are continually updated on Restek's product applications, big customers, and primary competition. Job candidates are screened for their ability to converse with customers. Even a candidate for an R&D job must be comfortable in this role. Handling irate customers is a key part of the training received by Restek's technical staff.

To encourage employees to be concerned about customer satisfaction, Restek provides a bonus program that includes a customer service component. Employees call 200 to 300 customers each month just to check in and make sure everything is going well. Many of these customers are first-time buyers. Employees ask if the product arrived on time, if the customer is having any problems, and if there are new ways the company can meet the customer's needs—through new or different products, for example. Restek's employees also contact customers who are showing signs of discontent—those who have returned a product or have not ordered within a year.

The callback program gives Restek the direct word on why customers don't come back and hard feedback on new products. "When customers complain about a product, the follow-up call might be made by the person who manufactured it or tested it," explains Mosesman, "so they really want to know why something didn't work. And they feel like they have to bend over backward to fix the problem. They can't say, 'Oh, that customer doesn't know what he's talking about.'"[10]

The callback program has helped fuel Restek's continued growth. In the two years the program has been in place, the company has grown more than 50 percent, from $6.4 million in 1991 sales to 10.95. Nearly $11 million for 1993.

At IBM Rochester, the Customer Partnership Call process thanks customers for purchasing AS/400 systems. Calls are made ninety days after systems are shipped, and customers are asked what they like about the system, what they dislike about it, and what suggestions they might have for improvement. These comments are then compiled into a database, analyzed, and distributed regularly to engineering, programming, marketing, manufacturing, and service teams to guide them in their work.

Federal Express has a toll-free number for the hearing impaired and an automated call distribution system for smoothing out demand peaks, relaying calls to the first available agent at any one of its eighteen call centers. Cadillac has twenty-one different toll-free numbers that customers and dealers can use. All employees are invited to listen to recorded calls so as to acquire a sensitivity to what customers are telling the company about its products.

Here are some other ways companies encourage customer feedback:

- *Surveys.* Whether in writing, face to face, or by phone, a survey can be an excellent way to get customer feedback. Each year, Whirlpool mails its Standardized Appliance Measurement Survey (SAMS) to 180,000 households, requesting people to rate all their appliances on a variety of attributes. When consumers rank a competitor's products higher, Whirlpool engineers go to work, ripping the competitor's product apart, to understand why.
- *Order forms.* American Supply International gets customer feedback from a comment section incorporated directly into its order form. The mail-order company, located in Bryans Road, Maryland, provides overseas Americans with hard-to-get U.S. products. Among its biggest sellers are 9 Lives Cat Food and canned chili. The comment form, according to cofounder Steve Reed, has provided the company with new service ideas and contributed to the company's impressive 85 percent customer retention rate.
- *Newsletters.* Printing letters from readers is the key to motivating customer feedback through newsletters. That's the word from Paul de Benedictis, communications director for Opcode Systems Inc. Using newsletters has enabled the company to create a more personal, one-to-one rapport with its more than 30,000 users.
- *Focus groups.* When Tyler Phillips founded Partnership Groups, a child care and elder care referral service in Lansing, Pennsylvania, he created an information kit to explain the range of his company's services. Phillips sold these kits to corporations and counted on his corporate clients to in turn, promote these kits to their employees. But when clients' employees were interviewed in focus groups, they said they wanted their questions answered by a person, not just a kit. That was all Phillips needed to hear to

shift his company away from the kits and into more of a consulting service. Customers were given unlimited access to Partnership staff in getting their child care and elder care referral questions answered. Thanks to this increased interaction with employees, new options such as "FirstNest" for infant care were soon created. Ten years after focus groups helped redirect the company's service offerings, Partnership Group reports that the majority of its 109 corporate contracts are for three years and that the company is profitable, with sales of $9 million.

- *User groups/advisory boards.* SunWave Manufacturing of Leander, Texas, a maker of portable spas, uses a customer advisory board to stay in touch with customer needs. The advisory council is composed of SunWave spa dealers, who serve as a voice for other dealers in their regions. SunWave coordinates these meetings to coincide with industry events and trade shows, thereby reducing cost.

- *Voice mail.* The Beef Box is an electronic mailbox that Homes and Land Publishing Corp. of Tallahassee uses to get feedback from its franchisees, who publish magazines containing real estate listings for a specific region. "Anything they want senior management to hear" is the way Ron Sauls, executive vice-president, describes the comments or complaints franchisees call in with on the Beef Box. Saul's assistant transcribes the voice mail messages and then passes them along to company staffers for quick follow-up.

Collecting the information is only half the challenge. The information must be put in an accessible form by the company so that it can be acted upon. For example, Survivor Software Ltd., a developer of a personal finance program for the Macintosh, maintains a "suggestions" database. Reports Mike Farmer, president of the Englewood, California, company, "We have three categories: features that we'll implement immediately; features that are desirable, but we don't know how to do them; and features we intend to do on future revisions."

2. WHEN CUSTOMERS NEED HELP, PROVIDE IT QUICKLY

Once you get feedback from your customers, you must act quickly. If a customer calls with a complaint, you must respond immediately—preferably by fixing the problem, but at least by affirming your intention of fixing the problem as quickly as possible. If customers have to call more than once with a problem, they are much more likely to be dissatisfied, even if the second call results in a fix. A recent TARP (Technical Assistance Research Programs) study conducted among the 800-number customers of 460 companies found that the number of customers reporting complete satisfaction after one call was dramatically higher than when two or more phone calls were made.[11] (see Figure 9–1). The TARP study reinforces another study, which revealed that customer dissatisfaction does not increase in a linear way. After the first period of delay, a customer's dissatisfaction appears to increases sharply.

FIGURE 9–1

Customer Satisfaction Comparison One vs. Two Calls

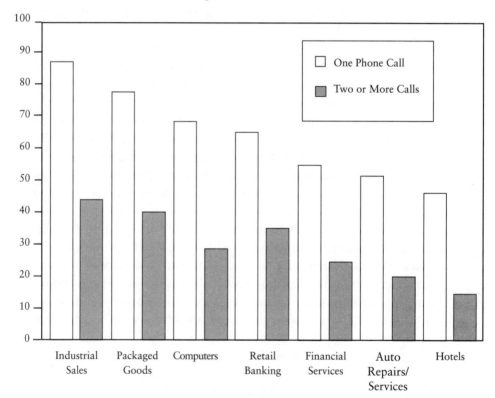

Source: "SOCAP 800 Number Study: A 1992 Profile of 800 Numbers for Customer Service," a survey of 460 companies, about 25 percent of them small- to midsize businesses, by Technical Assistance Research Programs, based in Washington D.C., for the Society of Consumer Affairs Professionals in Business, in Alexandria, Va.

3. REDUCE THE HASSLE OF REPAIRS AND REFUNDS AND WARRANTIES

Repairs, refunds, and warranties are often a source of frustration for customers. Consider how one business works to prevent dissatisfaction from brewing during these encounters:

Barry Fribush learned firsthand how frustrating repairs could be when he became a spa owner in the late 1970s. Still running a printing business and advertising agency in Washington, D.C., Fribush bought a spa when the product was still a West Coast phenomenon. Says Fribush, "When I finally found one, it was terrible. It kept breaking down and there was no easy way to get it repaired. I figured I could do a better job selling and servicing them."[12]

Soon after, Fribush founded The Bubbling Bath Spa & Tub Works, Inc., in Rockville, Maryland, and his early success stemmed from his ability to systematically provide good customer service. Well aware, because of his work in the ad industry, of the high price of advertising, Fribush realized he could not afford costly ads as a start-up. The easiest and least expensive way to get customers was through word of mouth from satisfied customers. So he set about creating a service system that would spawn satisfaction and evoke enthusiastic word-of-mouth advertising. A few of Frisbush's principles designed to make sure that problems get corrected early on include the following:

- *Stock only quality products.* You cannot have a satisfied customer if the product you sell keeps breaking down. As a result, Fribush carries only those spas with proven track records for reliability.
- *Trust repairs to the person who owns one.* All of Bubbling Bath's repairpeople are required to own a spa. Fribush makes them available at cost. It's the only way, says Fribush, that his repairpeople will truly understand the product they work on. By experiencing the problems they are asked to fix, his repair people are better service providers. Their technical skills go up and so does their sympathy for the customer.
- *Set the service hours according to customer calls.* Analyze when people call in for help and then staff as needed. For Bubbling Bath, a 9:00 to 5:00 service staff made no sense. Most of Fribush's service calls come in between 4:00 and 7:00 P.M., when people, home from work, turn on the spa and experience a problem. He runs a skeleton crew during the day and a larger staff during the evening rush.

- *Do it right or you won't get paid.* Every customer wants the repair job done right the first time, and when it's not, satisfaction takes a nosedive. In the beginning, callbacks were averaging 30 percent, or three out of every ten repair jobs. Fribush instigated a new policy: If Bubbling Bath has to fix the same job twice within a four-week period, the person who did the initial repair work does not get paid for that repair. The policy has made a marked improvement on the company's service record. Callbacks now average six a year.

4. LEARN HOW TO COMFORT AN ANGRY CUSTOMER

With enhanced customer feedback and complaint systems comes more customer interaction. The principles outlined to this point in the chapter are designed to help nip dissatisfaction at an early stage and prevent an escalation of customer anger. But even in the best of companies, an angry customer will occasionally surface. Even angry customers can be saved, however. Here's how:

When you come in contact with a customer who is angry, handle the person with care. It may help to visualize the irate customer as having a "psychological sunburn." If you touch the person when the sunburn is at its worst, you may get a violent reaction. Help the customer recover from the sunburn by reducing the "heat." Give him or her relief by following these six steps:

- *Let the customer blow off steam.* Encourage the customer to share by saying something like "I'm sorry you've had trouble. Please tell me the circumstances so that I can help you." Remain quiet and listen attentively to all the person has to say, and acknowledge his or her frustration. Do not act defensively. Do not interrupt. You're already on the road to resolving the complaint by first letting the person unload the discontent. When you do speak, ask open-ended questions, using words like *why, when, where, which,* and *what*. By keeping the irate customer talking, you will get more facts.
- *Let the customer know you understand his or her problem.* Paraphrase back to the customer his or her description of the problem. Your perception of the problem must match the customer's if the customer is ultimately to be satisfied. In addition, if possible, let the customer know you are recording the information in

writing. Such feedback as "Let me confirm this. We repaired your printer on Tuesday and by Thursday the problem had returned. Is that what happened? I want to write this down" helps the customer know you have heard him or her.

- *Find out what the customer wants.* Complaining customers do not want the problem handled; they want the problem resolved. Does your customer want a replacement, a refund, a store credit? Always ask the customer how he or she would like the situation to be resolved, by using such questions as "What would you like us to do?" This question is also important because often the customer will be satisfied with far less than the company is willing to offer.

- *Suggest a solution based on the customer's wishes.* If the customer's request is acceptable, then agree to the action and do it cheerfully and swiftly. In his book *Minding the Store*, Stanley Marcus says that giving customers what they ask for is better than bargaining. If you bargain, you are more than likely to lose their goodwill. Marcus tells of an experience early in his career when a woman bought a gown of handmade lace from his store. After wearing it once and clearly abusing it, she returned it and asked for her money back. Marcus gave it to her cheerfully, reasoning that it would cost more to replace her as a customer than the $175 cost of the dress. His instincts were right. "Over the years," writes Marcus, "this woman spent $500,000 with us."

- *If the customer is not happy with your solution, ask what he or she would consider fair.* Most customers will be fair. They are probably not asking for a refund or replacement simply to get your merchandise for free. If you have the authority, handle the request quickly. If you do not, find someone who can. If the customer leaves you unhappy with the outcome, the chances of winning future sales from the person are slim.

Several years ago, I treated myself to a series of facials and new skin care products. I purchased these products and services (which totaled almost $200) from the hair salon where I am a regular customer. Soon afterward, I had a reaction to one of the facial products. I had used about half of the cream before recognizing that the rash on my face was a result of one of the creams and not simply a result of changing my skin care routine. I asked for my money back. The facialist refused, saying she could not return the product given that so much had been used. She said she could do nothing about the problem. I took the problem to the salon owner, who refunded my money. But I never used the facialist's services or products again. Soon afterward, the facialist left the salon. She had not developed a large enough clientele to support her services. The point is this: Most people will be fair. Don't sacrifice a customer over the one-time cost of a product or service.

- *Make a follow-up satisfaction call.* This is your opportunity to firmly anchor the resolution and leave the customer more loyal to you than ever before. A follow-up call reinforces your commitment to service. A well-resolved complaint is a rarity in today's world. When you go the extra step to call back and confirm, you really stand out!

How to Win Back an Inactive Customer

Marketing expert Murray Raphel tells about a famous lion tamer named Frank Buck who, in the 1940s, put on his circus act throughout the United States using the theme "Bring 'em back alive." In other words, Buck would journey into the distant homes of the animals he wanted and would bring them back alive for people to see. How do you reconnect with those customers who have left your business and "bring them back alive?"

Answer: You ask them. You use such questions as "What steps can we take to win back your business?" Then you listen carefully and let your inactive client tell you what you must do to reearn his or her business.

AmeriSuites Hotel in Irving, Texas, lost and won back an important account. The American Honda account represented roughly $40,000 in annual sales for AmeriSuites. American Honda needed lodging for employees attending a three-week training program. New trainees rotated through the program throughout the year. The hotel's all-suite concept was ideal for extended-stay accommodations due to its refrigerator, microwave, sitting area, and ample space.

The hotel was located close to the Honda offices as well as to the Dallas/Ft. Worth airport. Despite these advantages, after approximately a year, AmeriSuites lost the account. The director of sales, Rich Gevertz, recontacted the decision maker at American Honda and asked, "What can we do to regain your confidence and win back your business?" The American Honda representative outlined the problems that made the company leave AmeriSuites and told Rich not to call back until each and every one of the problems was corrected.

AmeriSuites went to work. The staff focused on the key improvements that American Honda requested. It took two months to get the problems resolved. When the staff was sure its "house was in order," Rich called the company back and arranged a meeting at the hotel for purposes of demonstrating and discussing these changes and improvements. From changing transportation procedures and upgrading amenities offered to Honda guests to streamlining the billing procedures and creating customized hotel check-in information for Honda trainees, AmeriSuites met Honda's requirements. As a result of these actions, AmeriSuites won back the $40,000 American Honda account.

Consider these seven points to win back a lost customer:

1. Ask the question "What can we do to win back your business?"
2. Listen closely to what the customer tells you.
3. Meet the customer's requirements; communicate the changes you have made. Ask again for the customer's business.
4. Be patient with the customer. Be open. Remember, some wounds heal slowly.
5. Stay in touch with the lost customer.
6. Make it easy for customers to come back to you. Avoid the "I told you so" stance.
7. When the customer does return, earn his or her business every day.

Lost Customer Studies

AmeriSuites was fortunate with the Honda account. The hotel corrected its problems and persuaded the client to return before the car maker had formed a strong alliance with another hotel. Many "Bring 'em back alive" stories do not end quite so happily.

In the worse of cases, even when the account is irrevocably lost, there is a prize to be won: the knowledge of why the customer stopped doing business with you. Customers who leave you can provide you with a perspective about your business that is not available elsewhere. While often unpleasant to hear, this information can save you from losing customers under similar circumstances in the future.

Feedback from lost customers can be concrete and specific. Customers can respond to a direct question such as "What made you leave?" with information that will pay big dividends. For example, Staples, the discount office supply giant, carefully tracks customer purchases, and when it sees a lull or when a customer stops buying certain items, the company calls and gets feedback. The company may discover that the competition has a lower price, information that in turn enables Staples management to explore the issue further. This information is extremely valuable, because it allows Staples to continually pinpoint noncompetitive products and fine-tune pricing rather than making costly pricing adjustments across all products.

Lost customer studies can also help you decide which value-added services most help retention. One bank spent a considerable amount of money to improve the accuracy of its customers' monthly statements. Yet when it began to study customer losses, it discovered that less than 1 percent of customers left because of statement inaccuracy.

Finally, lost customer studies help you determine the kinds of customers you do not want. For example, when a health insurance company determined that certain companies bought only on the basis of price and switched insurers every year or so, it decided to eliminate such companies as future prospects. It instructed its brokers not to write policies for companies that had changed carriers two or more times over the past five years.

Summary

- People who have had their problems and complaints handled effectively will become your most loyal customers. They will trust and depend on you. You have proven yourself under fire.
- Lost customers represent more than one lost sale. They represent the loss of hundreds of sales in the future.
- Providing an immediate response to complaints goes a long way toward retaining a customer.

- Listening to and analyzing complaints can help your company have more satisfied customers, and keep customers loyal.
- It is always better to hear complaints than silence. You can fix a complaint, but it is nearly impossible to solve a problem you do not know exists.
- Listen, then act—these are the keys to satisfying dissatisfied customers and keeping customers loyal.
- Front line employees are the cornerstone to loyalty building. Their performance determines and shapes customers' opinions about your business.
- Responding quickly to customers' needs requires empowered employees.

10

How to Develop a Loyalty-Driven Culture in Your Company

When Doug Burgum bought Great Plains Software in Fargo, North Dakota, at the age of twenty-seven, he brought with him a unique perspective that originated from his summers as a kid working for his relatives' grain elevator business. Explained Burgum, "When you've got a grain elevator, the people you serve are landowners and they move the ownership of that land from father to son. My cousins are serving the grandsons of the people my grandfather served. That was the only business example I grew up with. You served customers for a lifetime. There was no such thing as a quick buck. When we bought Great Plains, [I] figured we had a great opportunity to build something where we'd instill in people that long-term mentality."[1]

Great Plains offers PC-based accounting systems that compete with those produced by the larger companies in Silicon Valley and other high-tech centers. With its North Dakota location, the company is a long way from those cities we associate with computer technology, but its success is generally attributed to Burgum's determination to build a loyal, long-term customer base. Said Burgum, "Accounting is not a fad. Nobody says, 'Gee, business is off, I think I'll stop keeping my books.' It's a fundamental thing you do in good times and bad. Our customers use this stuff for years and years. If you treat them right, you have them as long as they are doing accounting, so long as you listen to their needs and meet them."[2]

In order to listen to and meet those needs, Burgum began early on to compile a state-of-the-art customer list and turn it into the company's number one marketing weapon. Beginning in the early 1980s, the company designed into each user package a code that, after fifty transactions, blocked work. To unlock the software, customers were required to call Great Plains and get their individual ten-digit number that would serve as a key. When customers called in, the company registered them as users and asked about twenty research questions, including name, location, type of business, and company size. The company explained to the new users that by registering their names, Great Plains could contact them regarding any program changes, problems, or upgrades. The system continues today, and it is credited with enabling the company to have a database of every end user—now numbering in the tens of thousands—of its software.

Timely callbacks were key to offering quality technical support. "We had this policy of returning all calls the same day," said Burgum. "We'd fight to get them all done by 7:00 P.M. central time, but you'd end up leaving a lot of messages for people. That wasn't good enough. Given the pressures of accounting, the right answer a day or two late is the wrong answer."[3]

Beginning in 1987, Great Plains took a bold step and began guaranteeing response times to customer calls. The client was guaranteed a return call within one to three hours, depending on the terms of the service contract. A missed deadline meant the customer was given a $25 coupon, good for Great Plains products and services.

Soon after, Great Plains invested in a costly call distribution system that was bridged with the customer database. When users call, they are asked to punch in their ten-digit account numbers, enabling the system to determine who is calling, which software programs that user owns, and which technical support plan he or she has. The call is then routed to a Great Plains technical specialist trained in those programs. Moreover, the specialist can identify how frequently the user has called, who handled past calls, and what advice was given over the last six months.

The new phone system and computer support program cost the company in excess of $1 million, but the results from the investment have been exemplary. The number of calls on a typical day average 1,100, with more than half handled by a support specialist immediately. Since the creation of the guaranteed response, 99.13 percent have been returned on time; the record for the highest number of successive calls within the guarantee is a whopping 126,400.

And do customers appreciate the service? You bet. Thank-you letters, gifts, and flowers are routine occurrences. "More than 30% of the referrals I get are from existing customers," says Bill Sorensen, a Great Plains dealer in Dallas. "So you know there are lots of satisfied users out there, and support has a lot to do with it."[4]

Great Plains is a company that understood from its inception that it had to find a way to establish effective relationships with each of its customers. As its customer list grew from hundreds to thousands, the company was increasingly challenged with developing a system that would evoke loyalty. Sure, Great Plains was ahead of the game by marketing an accounting product that has natural, long-term loyalty-building properties, but Great Plains took these opportunities and leveraged them to the fullest. It began early on to pioneer a system that has evolved into what today is a state-of-the-art loyalty machine.

When you look at companies who have consistently built a loyal customer base, one common denominator surfaces time and time again: *Each company consciously created a system for getting and keeping a customer.*

In this chapter, we will examine the steps to building a loyalty system and examine how various businesses have initiated such steps to build a loyalty system in their company. In doing so, we will pull together many of the concepts about individual customer stages that we have discussed in prior chapters to illustrate how such a system can work.

Preparing to Build Your Loyalty System

Loyalty Measurement Factors

The first step in building a client loyalty system is to get familiar with the terminology and variables that define and drive loyalty:

- *Client base*. This is the total number of active customers and clients. You can calculate this number by adding together your total number of first-time customers, repeat customers, and clients. It is crucial that you count only customers and clients who are active and have made purchases or contacts with you recently enough to be considered current. Resist the temptation to include inactive customers and clients on this list. Be hard-nosed and brutally honest and include only current names.
- *New customer retention rate*. This represents the percentage of first-time customers that return for a second purchase within a specified period of time. This time period is governed by your typical customer's repeat purchase cycle. For example, in the hair salon industry there is typically no more than ninety days between salon visits; hence, to be classified as retained, a first-time salon customer would have to return for a second visit within a three-month time period.
- *Client retention rate*. This is the percentage of customers who have met a specified number of repurchases over a finite period of time. Continuing with the hair salon example, a person can be considered a client after having made five consecutive visits to the salon, with each visit falling within the average repeat purchase time frame of ninety days or less.
- *Share of customer*. This is the percentage of a customer's total purchases in a particular category of products and services spent with your company. A vendor has captured 100 percent share of a customer when the customer spends his or her entire budget for the vendor's products or services on that vendor. A salon whose customer buys all hair care services from the salon but purchases shampoo and styling products (also available at the salon) elsewhere has captured a 70 percent share of customer when 30 percent of that customer's total hair care budget is spent outside the salon. At the highest level of loyalty, a company consistently wins 100 percent share of a customer.
- *Average number of new customers per month*. This is the average of number of first-time customers who buy from your company each month. Use a six-month span of time to calculate this figure.
- *Purchase frequency*. This is the average number of times a customer or client buys from you per year.

- *Average purchase amount.* This is the average amount paid for products and services at each purchase.
- *Attrition rate.* This is the average annual percentage of customers that are lost or go inactive for any reason, including dissatisfaction and relocation.

As a first step to building your loyalty system, calculate these variables and use them to establish goals and to monitor the progress of your loyalty program.

Loyalty Program Basics

Your loyalty program should follow these eight steps:

1. Measure and track loyalty using the variables outlined above. Depending on your particular situation, it may be helpful to calculate a variety of retention rates, for example, including a total company retention rate, retention rates for each individual sales professional, and retention rates by account team or other group. Using these current rates as a base, set your customer retention objectives for the next five years. The same analysis could be done with share of customer, new customer retention rate, and so forth.

2. Introduce all company employees to the meaning and importance of client loyalty. If you have a small staff, you might choose to introduce this information in a meeting attended by all personnel. If you are a larger company, you will want to consider other communication tools, such as division meetings, corporate newsletters, and training videos, for getting and keeping the word out. A discussion of both current and projected loyalty rates should be an important part of this communication. Begin monthly performance evaluations with employees who have direct customer contact. Use the loyalty measurement factors as a basis for the review.

3. Build customer and client loyalty goals into employee performance and compensation plans. Reward excellent and improving loyalty rates with employee bonuses and raises. Address substandard and declining rates promptly. Set time lines for improvement and then train and coach employees accordingly. Release employees unable to meet loyalty goals.

4. Evaluate and review loyalty rates monthly. Consider posting rates in employee break rooms and/or other places highly visible to employees. This can help reinforce the company's commitment to loyalty and help motivate employees to strive for superior retention levels.

5. Get employees involved in the development and maintenance of the loyalty program. Staff members' input, recommendations, and ideas can play an important role in the program's success. It is no secret that employees are more likely to support a program they helped put together. One way to accomplish this involvement is to set up employee teams to perform specific loyalty "duties," such as retention evaluation and first-time customer program review.

6. Assemble an assortment of marketing, selling, and customer care tools aimed at cultivating loyalty at each customer stage. Develop at least of one key loyalty program for each customer stage. A new customer welcome promotion that motivates the first-time customer to buy again and a promotion for repeat customers that cross-sells other products and services are examples.

7. Identify the five biggest customer loyalty breakers in your company (the busy signal that callers often get when they call your business, an overly complicated return policy for items purchased, etc.) and develop plans for eliminating them. Begin implementation immediately.

8. Continue to modify, fine-tune, and course-correct your loyalty system as you go. Time and hands-on experience are great teachers.

Assembling Your Marketing, Selling, and Customer Care Tools

Learning from Your Customers, Your Counterparts, and Your Competitors

Harry Truman once said, "The things you don't know are the history you haven't read." While the former president probably had domestic and foreign policies in mind when he made that comment, he could just as easily have been talking about a company looking for ways to increase sales and loyalty in the 1990s. Answers to questions like "What has worked for you in the past?" "What has brought in new business?" and "What have you found to be the best routes to the market?" are often found in your sales records.

Remember Joan Silver of Reeves Audio Visual Systems, discussed in Chapter 7? By analyzing invoices and purchase orders, Silver was able to better understand the motivations behind her customers' purchases. Armed with these insights, Silver created effective new strategies for selling to both large and smaller accounts.

Understanding your own sales history is just part of the system planning process. Looking outward to your counterparts and competitors can also be a great source of information. Seek new ideas by asking, "What has been working lately?" and "How are they dealing with the marketing challenges I'm facing?" These are just two of the questions that can help you garner new ways to meet your challenges for developing a loyal customer.

Several years ago, the livelihoods of New England car dealers were jeopardized when their markets changed. Gone was the marketplace where car buyers traded cars every eighteen to twenty-four months. With sharply increased car prices, the trade-in cycle increased to fifty months. Suddenly, the service department was no longer simply a necessary evil. Instead, it became a key profit component for the dealers' long-term survival.

What did these dealers do next? They looked around the country and discovered that other dealers were successfully offering "planned maintenance" programs that were created by John Fisher, a former Chrysler dealer. At the center of the program was a computer-generated coupon booklet for preventive maintenance. Each coupon was redeemable for a prearranged appointment with the dealer's service department.

The coupon booklet was designed around a loyalty-building strategy: Encourage new car buyers to bring their cars in for regular check-ups. These regular visits helped a dealer build long-term customer relationships while also establishing the service department as a important profit center. No significant upfront investment was required by participating dealers—only a monthly service fee to Fisher, who in turn would process the coupons used and send owners reminders of upcoming appointments. By finding out what their competitors and peers were doing to increase business and cope with the changing habits of the market, these New England dealers were able to adjust their longtime practices to the new situation and continue to build a loyal customer base.

Evaluating Your Customer Chain

When assembling your marketing, selling, and customer care tools for your loyalty system, you must be sensitive to all aspects of your distribution chain. For example, Du Pont turned StainMaster stain-resistant carpeting into the most successful new product introduction in its history by listening to everyone who helps get its carpet to the market. Early in the product's development process, the director of Du Pont's flooring system division, Tom McAndrews, appointed a six-member committee made of representatives of the marketing, R&D, and financial departments. Tom's mandate to the committee was that they constantly ask themselves the question "How does what we're doing affect the customer?" Before the product was introduced, the committee spent three years in close coordination with retailers and mill operators, soliciting suggestions about how to price StainMaster and publicize its benefits to consumers.

The result? Du Pont launched StainMaster with the company's largest advertising budget for a new product. In return, the product produced more than $2 billion in revenues and single-handedly revived industrywide carpet sales. Reports McAndrews, "The key is, we looked at our customer as the entire distribution chain. You can't simply meet the needs of the end user."[5]

As you plan your loyalty system, start by outlining the distribution path by which your product or service gets to market and consider each member of that distribution path your "customer." For example, beauty product's distribution channel consists of distributors, retailers, and, ultimately, end users. Hair care and cosmetic manufacturers need to develop sell-through plans to influence each of these components of their distribution channel.

Why, as a manufacturer, for example, should you consider the distributor's customer stages? Or the retailer's customer stages? All the manufacturer really needs to do, you may argue, is to sell the product to the distributor. After that, it's the distributor's responsibility. The reason you want to consider the loyalty development stages of others in your distribution cycle is this: It is your opportunity to add value and nurture your customer's loyalty.

For example, Holly Farms, the poultry company, found that its fully cooked chicken was a big hit with busy consumers. Not so with grocers who stocked it. Their complaint? The sale expiration date was too short, so they refused to stock it. In response, Holly Farms improved its packaging, thereby extending the expiration date. Sales doubled. With a new sensitivity to its distribution channel, the company now makes a point of visiting store meat managers more often and sends them a quarterly newsletter, *Fresh News from Holly Farms*. All along the distribution chain, you have customers. At any point along the chain, a customer may decide to take his or her business elsewhere. It is wise, therefore, to try to keep all your customers happy and loyal—whether they are the ultimate users of your product or service or those who get the product or service to the final customer.

Developing a Loyalty Plan

After identifying all the groups in your distribution path, start to outline a plan for developing their loyalty by using the seven customer stages. It may be helpful to do this in the form of a chart, with your channels of distribution down the left-hand side and your customer stages across the top. Assuming the Holly Farms distribution channel comprises food broker, food store, and end user, then its loyalty planning chart could be organized as shown in Figure 10–1:

Next, examine your current marketing, selling, and customer care tools and chart beneath the stage or stages they address. This process will help you quickly identify stages you are currently addressing and those you are not. Do not assume that just because you have an existing program addressing a key customer stage, the program is sufficient in its present form. This is your opportunity to question every program that you do or do not have.

As a rule of thumb, a company needs at least one strong program for each distribution component and its corresponding customer stage. Remember that the average U.S. business spends six times more resources on capturing customers than on keeping them, yet customer loyalty is worth, on average, ten times the price of a one-time purchase. Look closely at your distribution of resources and consider whether you are allocating enough resources to the repeat customer, client, and advocate stages.

FIGURE 10–1
Hypothetical Loyalty-Planning Chart For Holly Farms Company

	Suspect/Prospect	First-Time Customer	Repeat Customer	Client	Advocate	Inactive
Food Broker						
Food Store						
End User						

When SuiteMark Hotels created a customer loyalty system for its five Westar hotel properties, the objective was to take various hotel influencers and convert them into loyal business providers. SuiteMark identified five key groups in the distribution channel: corporate travel arrangers, corporate trainers, travel agents, business and government travelers, and personal travelers. As with Du Pont's McAndrews, experience had taught SuiteMark to find ways to influence business at each of these levels.

In creating the system, SuiteMark charted a miniature Profit Generator system for each of the identified markets. For example, for the corporate travel arranger, the challenge was "What actions can we initiate to identify suspects, qualify prospects, turn prospects into first-time bookers, and turn first-time bookers into repeat bookers and then client bookers?"

In the case of SuiteMark, it was a matter of taking parts of a company's marketing, selling, and customer care programs that were already working and combining them with new programs. SuiteMark had already established an extensive frequent booker program called Westar Select. This program was designed to provide assistance and incentives to travel planners making reservations for a Westar property. The Select program included special promotions and incentives, Select reservation hotlines, Select member luncheons, a Select newsletter, and a special Select voucher system that regularly informed members of the number of Select Club points they had earned. These points were redeemable for special

Westar hospitality and travel privileges. This program was already working well for the company and earned a position in the travel arranger conversion system.

Using the Profit Generator customer stages as a guide, SuiteMark evaluated which of the company's existing arsenal of tools could be used within the Profit Generator system and what was missing. From that point, a detailed action plan was developed. Prewritten letters, questionnaires, telemarketing scripts, greeting cards, and other communications tools were created so the system user would simply have to insert the booker's name to customize the message.

A sample of the marketing and selling portions of SuiteMark's loyalty-building plan for the corporate travel arranger market segment is outlined in Table 10–1. Notice how the steps for the repeat customer and client stages are designed so that the communication is frequent, regular, and ongoing.

This system was designed to be supported by a personal computer or, if computers were not available, to be tracked manually. The system user had a master schedule template for each account and would use this template to track where the customer was in its customer stage development. Since this target group was travel arrangers, reservations determined the movement of the account through the system. Letters, questionnaires, and forms were composed and formatted for easy retrieval and use.

SuiteMark's system is built upon one overriding reality. These marketing and selling action steps are meaningful and loyalty inducing only to the extent that they are coupled with excellent, consistent delivery of the customer's basic hotel needs (easy reservation making, prompt front desk check-in of guest, clean rooms, accurate billing, etc.). Without this operational excellence, these loyalty-building actions cannot be effective. With them, loyalty can flourish.

The Strategy Behind the Loyalty System

Benjamin Franklin once said, "Human felicity is produced not so much by great pieces of good fortune that seldom happen as by little advantages that occur every day." The philosophy behind the loyalty system is similar. Rather than depending on miraculous happenings or extraordinary "once in a blue moon" feats, earn the

TABLE 10–1

Westar Hotels Loyalty Plan For Corporate Travel Arranger Market

---

I. Turning suspects into prospects

1. Identify suspects

   Corporatewide sources
   - National reservations system
   - Corporate telemarketing
   - Corporate sales program to key national accounts

   Property-specific sources
   - Site analysis
   - Visual survey of nearby business centers
   - Visits with property managers of nearby large commercial buildings
   - Chamber of commerce
   - Dunn's direct access "feeder city" list generation

2. Qualify suspects as prospects, using qualification criteria
   - Average hotel volume/month
   - Who is travelling? Purpose?
   - Decision maker names/titles
   - Lodging facility/facilities currently used and rate
   - Under current contract? expiration?
   - Criteria used to select hotel
   - Who makes lodging decision
   - Criteria used to select hotel
   - Who makes lodging decision?

II. Turning prospects into first-time customers

1. Send introductory direct mail package
2. Make telephone follow-up
3. Make initial sales call (introduce Select program to corporate accounts)
4. Schedule property tour
5. Conduct property tour
6. Send follow-up thank-you letter for taking tour
7. Establish ongoing sales call frequency based on account volume classification
8. Send Select Club fulfillment package upon request of prospect (including newsletter distribution)
9. Send goodwill:
   Birthday card
   Thanksgiving card
   Westar Annual Birthday Promotion
10. Repeat steps 7–9 until prospect turns into first-time customer

---

customer's loyalty and goodwill by using a well-conceived, companywide system that has effective front line implementation.

In a speech about customer service, Stanley Marcus, retired president of Neiman Marcus, described a recent shopping experience to the management group of a major jewelry retailer.[6] Marcus had accompanied a couple in search of jewelry on Fifth Avenue in New York. He recounted, "We passed a window, and my friend's wife said, 'Gee, that's just what I want! It could have been made to order

TABLE 10–1 (*cont.*)

III. Turning first-time customers into repeat customers, clients, and advocates

1. Send new booker welcome letter	Thanksgiving card
2. Conduct telephone questionnaire ("How'd we do?") after first visit	Westar Annual Birthday Promotion
3. Make regular sales calls/telephone calls	"You're Our Favorite Client" card
4. Send monthly *Select Newsletter*	7. Send mail-back questionnaire every six months
5. Send weekly Select points update	8. Repeat steps 3–7
6. Send goodwill: Birthday card	

IV. Making inactive customers active again

1. Send "We Miss You" card
2. Make follow-up telephone and/or sales call
3. Reevaluate the account based on information received in Step 2
4. Keep account in or remove it from "active" customer list
5. If "active," proceed with Steps 3–7 outlined in Part III

---

for me.' It was a pair of earrings. We went in for her to try them on. We found the first salesman and said, 'We want to see a pair of diamond earrings.' And he said—here Marcus points for emphasis—Well, I only sell gold earrings. If you want diamond earrings, go back there.' He pointed. We went back and there were diamonds in the case, and my friend said to another salesman, 'I want to see a pair of diamond earrings that are in the window.' And he said, 'Well, I don't sell earrings. I only sell bracelets. Over there.'"

Marcus continued:

Finally, after being told that the guard was away at lunch and that the show window could not be unlocked for an hour, the customer left, wandered across the street to Arpel and Van Cleef and purchased a $92,000 pair of earrings and, still later, a $675,000 necklace.

So I told this story to the group and said, 'Are there any questions?' Somebody asked, 'Would you mind telling us what store that happened in?' And I said, 'Well, hold on to your seats! That happened at your store.' Well, of course, you could feel the meeting suddenly disintegrate.[7]

An executive then rose and began providing reasons why the

jeweler does not allow salespeople to move from department to department, to which Marcus responded, "You're thinking like a merchant, not a customer. A customer doesn't give a damn about your security. A customer wants to be satisfied. Because you have an antiquated system of locking cases and entrusting a key to one man, you lost maybe six hundred thousand dollars worth of business."[8]

Thinking like a customer and not a merchant is the underlying premise of the customer development system. Outlined in Table 10–2 is a summary of the focus and key action steps for developing loyalty at each customer stage that were explored in previous chapters. The parameters are further summarized in Figure 10–2.

With these foci and action steps as a guide, your challenge is to create an arsenal of marketing, selling, and customer care tools for your business that address each of these stages. Regardless of the product or service you are offering, these customer stages and strategies, modified to meet your particular situation, can help you build a loyalty system.

Additional Applications for the Profit Generator System

Creating a customer conversion system for your business requires the melding of operations of every department in your company. Accounting, manufacturing, delivery, data processing, sales, marketing—all these functions must be united by one common denominator: to provide actions that directly or indirectly contribute to the company's ability to get and keep customers. The importance of getting and keeping a customer can sometimes be very remote to say, an accounts payable clerk buried in administrative rubble and with no direct customer contact.

The Profit Generator system and its concept of customer stages can provide an opportunity for demonstrating to all employees where and how their contributions fit in the company's big picture of building customer loyalty. For example, the Profit Generator customer stages could be used

- in an employee handbook, to provide all company employee with a common language about the cultivation and care of customers;
- to illustrate the role(s) each employee and his or her department plays in the company's system for "growing" a loyal customer;

TABLE 10–2
Loyalty Building Strategies by Customer Stage

SUSPECTS/PROSPECTS

Primary focus: Overcome suspect/prospect apprehension.

Action Steps

1. Project a leadership image.
2. Listen/look for buyer apprehension.
3. Address new buyer apprehension with
   - empathy/encouragement;
   - client "success stories";
   - free consultation offer; and
   - product/service guarantees.

FIRST-TIME CUSTOMER

Primary focus: Meet/exceed new customer expectations.

Action Steps

1. Exceed new customer expectations.
2. Build a vision for return visits.
3. Say thank you for business.
4. Invite customer to return.

REPEAT CUSTOMER

Primary focus: Provide value-added benefits with each repurchase.

Action Steps

1. Uncover/satisfy customer needs, using
   - value-added visits; and
   - cross-selling hooks.
2. Sell your loyalty-building products and services.
3. Analyze any competitive purchases for permanent shifts or temporary lapses.
4. Seek regular customer feedback.

CLIENT

Primary focus: Tailor service to the needs of the particular client.

Action Steps

1. Practice customized care. Look for ways to help customers "reinvent" themselves.
2. Don't take the customer's continued business for granted.
3. Let the client know it's smart to do business with you.
4. Continually seek input and feedback.

TABLE 10–2 (*cont.*)

ADVOCATE
Primary focus: Get clients to sell for you.
Action Steps
1. Encourage advocacy through letters of endorsement from clients, referral acknowledgments, and recommend-a-friend rewards.
2. Develop and regularly communicate with your network of clients and other business influencers.

INACTIVE CUSTOMER OR CLIENT
Primary focus: Develop "win back" plan based on inactivity diagnosis.
Action Steps
1. Detect inactivity as early as possible. Let the customer know that he or she is missed.
2. Activate special communication/purchase offers to woo customer back.
3. If defection is certain, ask "What can we do to win back your business?" and listen closely. Meet the customer's requirements, communicate changes, and ask for the business.
4. Be patient with the inactive customer. Stay in touch.

- in staff brainstorming sessions—how to get more prospects, how to turn repeat customers into clients, and so on; and
- as problem diagnostic tool—when sales are down, diagnose the problem by determining which customer stages are underperforming and how to improve them.

People Power: The Loyalty System Necessity
Attitude Is Everything

Having a "system to run on" is important for building loyalty; procedures, guidelines, tracking systems, and communication materials are important tools that help employees perform. But that's just part of the equation. The real success of your loyalty system is not just in having the right tools but in having those tools used by employees with loyalty-driven attitudes. Says Tommaso Zanzotto, American Express travel president, "When you want to increase

FIGURE 10–2

The Evolution of Customer Loyalty

Customer Stage	Suspect/ Prospect	First-Time Buyer	Repeat Customer	Client	Advocate
Customer/ Account Profitability	Little to None		More		Greatest
Marketing/ Selling Objective	Attraction	Transaction	Develop Relationship	Broaden Relationship	Leverage Relationship
Marketing/ Selling Strategy	Sell Benefits	Deliver on Benefits Promised	Provide Increasing Value Through Service and Support	Provide Value Beyond Product or Service	Provide Value and Get Clients to Sell for You
Cost of Marketing/ Selling		More		$ Less	
Knowledge of Customer Buying Preference	Little		More		Greatest

customer satisfaction, technical training—how to write a letter to a card member, for example—is easy. The quantum leap comes from improving employees' attitudes."

When this attitude is not present, even the best-conceived systems can break down. Consider Ruth Scherer's experience, as reported in the *New York Times*:

> I go into a branch of one of America's leading banks to make a deposit. Hallelujah! No one is there but me and one teller. So I skip the roped aisle and go directly to her window. She lifts her eyes to mine. "Please get in line," she says. I'm bewildered. "Please get in line," she repeats. I look around. "What line? I'm the only one here." "You have to get in line before I can help you." She sighs with impatience.
>
> Do I get nasty or shout? Do I explain that a line has two points or two people, and that I'm the only one there? No. I'm a mature woman.

I look at her. She looks at me. With check and deposit slip in hand, I go to the entrance of the roped aisle, walk between the ropes and turn to the right, then to the left, until I arrive at the front of "the line." I wait a few seconds. I almost don't hear her call, "Next."

The wrong attitude was also the culprit in the experience related by author and business consultant Murray Raphel about a super-market near his home. The store's management, seeking to pro-mote its friendly cashiers, ran a series of ads saying "If one of our cashiers ever forgets to say 'Thank you, have a nice day,' we will give you one dollar."

A few weeks went by. Murray and his wife, Ruth, stopped at the store. They shopped for a few items and arrived at the checkout counter. After taking their money, the cashier handed over the change—minus the friendly greeting.

"Aha!" Murray said. "You owe us a dollar."

"Why?" asked the bewildered cashier.

Murray, smiling, patiently explained the terms of the ad. The cashier smiled back. "I don't have to give you a dollar," she said. "That was last month's campaign."

Harvard Business Review editor Rosabeth Moss Kantor observes, "People at lower rather than higher organizational ranks make or break service strategies. No matter what strategy leaders inside the organization devise, what customers see is at the front line."[9] Effec-tively implementing strategy at the front lines is the true test of how a system is working.

It is estimated that 90 percent of all customer contact is through an organization's front line employees. The front line employees must understand the company's goals and the role they play in meeting them. Nowhere is that understanding more critical than in the implementation of loyalty-building programs like frequent buyer programs, cross selling, and life cycle promotions. The suc-cess of each of these programs is tied directly to the skill with which front line employees implement them.

Early in my career, I was the marketing director for a small hotel chain. My staff and I had spent substantial resources to identify well-qualified frequent travelers and to mail them free-night coupons to turn them into first-time customers. We had one hotel in the chain that was a particular challenge to market. It was hard to see from the interstate, and, to add to the problem, access to the hotel off the interstate was difficult. For this hotel, we needed every new guest we could get!

I got a call from the sales director at this location. He reported that a prospective guest had presented the coupon at the front desk but was turned away. It seemed that the coupon had expired the day before and, despite the fact that there were plenty of rooms available, the front desk would not honor it. The customer left angry and disappointed.

The incident taught me a valuable lesson: While I had communicated the mechanics of the promotion to the front line, I had failed to successfully build a larger vision to the staff about why the program was in place and why customer loyalty was the result we were after. Had I built the bigger vision, the coupon would have been honored and, by acknowledging the expired date to the new customer, the hotel could even have earned additional "points" in winning repeat business.

Creating a Vision

No one understands the importance of communicating a vision throughout a company better than Southwest Airlines Chairman Herb Kelleher. Kelleher oversees the "bargain fare" airline that is the seventh largest U.S. carrier and has just 2.6 percent of the nation's air travel market. The airline, based in Dallas, does not operate in thirty-five states. It flies only as far east as Cleveland, and its route map is a constellation of short hops. The airline keeps costs down in a number of ways. For example, no Southwest flights can be booked through the industry's big reservation computers (travel agents must call the airline directly), and there is no first-class or preassigned seating. Meal service is not offered, since most flights are fifty-five minutes or less. Instead, passengers are served peanuts and drinks.

Says regular Southwest passenger Richard Spears, vice-president of a Tulsa, Oklahoma, oil research company, "Sure you get herded on the plane and sure you only get peanuts and a drink, but Southwest does everything they can to get you to the right place on time and that's most important."[10] Lots of folks feel that way, and the airline has posted healthy profits while other airlines post losses.

Southwest employees understand Kelleher's philosophy that "those planes aren't making any money while there sitting on the ground," and they perform accordingly.

Consider crew leader Wally Mills. Southwest Airlines Flight 944 from San Diego lands on time in Phoenix. It's 3:15 P.M. Mills and six crew members must have the plane turned around and on its way to El Paso by 3:30. "I think of this as a game," says Mills. "I like to play against the [gate agents] up there working with the people to see if we can beat them."[11]

In order to win that game, the crew leader needs the cooperation, enthusiasm, and energy of every member of his crew. Workers must unload the bags for Phoenix and reload bags going to El Paso. The drinks and peanuts consumed on the flight have to be replaced and the plane tidied up. Thousands of pounds of fuel have to be pumped into the huge gas tanks. Passengers are boarded and the plane is ready to take off.

Mills and his team have accomplished their task in less than fifteen minutes. Most other airlines take almost three times as long to do the same tasks. Southwest flies approximately 1,300 flights every day, and 80 percent of them have speedy turnarounds like this one.

Major airlines have suffered dramatic losses in the past few years. Several have gone out of business or declared bankruptcy, but Southwest has continued to be profitable throughout the downturn. Significantly, Southwest has also won the industry's most coveted prizes: In a given month, it ranked highest in on-time performance, fewest customer complaints, and fewest lost bags. It is not surprising that customers are pleased with Southwest's performance, and one of the major reasons the company performs so well is that it has enthusiastic employees.

Southwest employees realize that their compensation and job security depend on productivity. Unlike employees at other large airlines, Southwest's people are paid only for the time they fly. As 12 percent owners, all Southwest employees share in company profits. This compensation system creates a considerable advantage for the airline. For example, pilots for American earn an average of $104,600 a year for flying midsize aircraft and actually fly about forty-eight hours a month. While earning about the same wages, Southwest pilots fly about eighty hours a month. Driven by higher productivity, Southwest's operating costs are 20 percent below American's and 37 percent below USAir's.[12]

Employees regularly praise the company and say it is a fun place to work as well as a good place to work. Kelleher has always included an element of goofiness in his strategy—whether it be marketing or employee relations. An orientation video for new employees is set to rap music. Flight attendants have costumes for holidays, including turkey suits for Thanksgiving and reindeer antlers for Christmas. Kelleher himself is known for wearing outlandish outfits to put a laugh in a generally hectic business.

Employees are willing to work hard when they know they are important and appreciated. Legend has it that Kelleher knows every Southwest employee by name. He's not afraid to pitch in and help out either. Flight attendant Raelene Chilcoat reported that on one flight, Kelleher filled the glasses with ice while she took drink orders. The mechanics and cleaners' union head, Tom Burnett, reports that Kelleher has been known to come to the cleaners' break room at 3:00 A.M. to pass out doughnuts and put on overalls to help clean a plane.

The attitude of top management obviously effects everyone in a company. If that management has a superior, hands-off attitude, it will extend to employees on down the line. If the head of the company is enthusiastic, appreciative, and upbeat, the employees are also likely to share that attitude. As mentioned in an earlier chapter, happy, positive employees are invaluable in growing happy, loyal clients. There is a direct connection between employees' attitudes and the way they deal with customers. As probably all of us know, a grouchy clerk can turn someone against an entire company.

Putting Employees First

When Marcus Rosenbluth founded Rosenbluth Travel in 1892, his main service was helping Europeans immigrate to America. Once they were settled and got jobs, many of those same immigrants gave Rosenbluth 5¢ and 10¢ at a time until they had saved the $50 required to bring over another family member. From these early beginnings, the company has flourished. Today the Philadelphia-based company generates revenues of $1.3 billion and is one of the largest travel companies in the world.

Marcus Rosenbluth's great-grandson, Hal Rosenbluth, is now at the helm of the business, and he and his staff are busy reinventing the company to meet the customer-driven demands of today. After graduating from the University of Miami in 1974, Hal joined his dad at Rosenbluth, but Hal didn't start at the top or even in the middle—he started as a gofer, running errands and stamping brochures. A year or so later, he moved to the meetings department, and then gradually, by 1978, worked his way to head of the department.

Rosenbluth describes his observations from his first few years with the company: "What I saw was a tremendous focus on the customer, and it began to bother me that the focus so often created problems for our people. Everyone felt pushed to do heroic deeds for the client, which was fine in its way, except that the competition for hero status sometimes got a little out of hand. Booking agents competed. Vacation consultants fought over who got to sit at the desk nearest the entrance. People played up to the receptionist who directed calls. There was a lot of politics, a lot of scorekeeping, and a lot of stress."[13]

It was when Hal became involved in the business travel market that he truly learned what teamwork was all about. In contrast to the petty backbiting he had seen in other departments, the corporate travel agents worked with one another.

Airline deregulation brought opportunity to the travel market, and Rosenbluth Travel found ways to capitalize on it. Business travel expanded rapidly, and everyone at the company was working long hours—many spending ten to twelve hours a day at work.

"I understood—for the first time during that period of rapid expansion—that the people in a company have to come first, even ahead of the customers. . . . [I]f your people aren't happy with their jobs, the customer will never be uppermost in their minds. When they ought to be focusing on the customer, they'll be thinking about their own frustrations."[14]

The true front liners in any travel agency are its agents. Commenting on the enormous day-to-day demands on these staff members, Rosenbluth explained, "They needed the nerves of an air traffic controller and the brains of a magna cum laude, but we'd been paying them as if they planted flowers." As a way to compensate agents more fairly, the company instituted a "Pay for Quality" program. The program is based 60 percent on accuracy, 20 percent on professionalism (going the extra mile for colleagues), and 20 percent on productivity (but only if the other two criteria are satisfied).

The Pay for Quality program increased individual agent take-home pay by 32 percent and reduced the total payroll by 4 percent. Since people began doing things right the first time, the position to rework mistakes was eliminated. Internal competition between coworkers was reduced. Moreover, the company experienced a decrease in turnover, training costs, and human resource expenses, while seeing an increase in productivity.

Concludes Rosenbluth, "What we have is a hierarchy of concerns: people, service, profits. We focus on our people, our people focus on service and profits result—a by-product, you might say, of putting our associates ahead of our customers. I know it sounds simplistic, but I know it works."[15]

Keeping Customers Loyal: The Only Constant Is Change

Just like the world we live in, your loyalty system must be ever changing. The particular methods you employ to earn loyalty today may need a major overhaul twelve months from now. You must keep modifying, upgrading, and changing your system to meet the changing demands of your marketplace and your customer. As we have seen, there are no loyalty guarantees. Unless you continue to provide value, as your customers define it, even your most seemingly loyal customers and clients will eventually go elsewhere. In the 1980s, Stouffer and its Lean Cuisine line took bold steps to change the frozen food market as it was known at the time. Stouffer offered products available from no other source: low-calorie, ready-to-cook dinners that actually tasted good. The success of the line was immediate and dramatic. Stouffer grabbed a 18.6 percent market share in a $3 million market, and the company expanded to twice its original size. Pleased and proud, Stouffer rested on its laurels.

But as we pointed out, everything changes. Profits and revenues began to drop, and before Stouffer realized what was happening, sales had fallen 27 percent. Executive vice-president Edward Marra attributes the loss to complacency. The company assumed that its loyal customers would stay loyal, but they did not. As Lean Cuisine succeeded, other companies came along to compete. Competitors offered equally delicious low-calorie meals, at better prices.

Marra understood the message that consumers were sending: "We were no longer a good value, and value had become increasingly important to consumers."[16] The company took steps to respond to that message. Prices came down, the product line was updated and reformulated, and profits began to rise again. Since 1990, Stouffer has again claimed the number one market share with its Lean Cuisine line and profits have increased fivefold.

Chairman Stanley Gault provides the best prescription for maintaining a loyalty clientele: "There's no magic formula for staying close to your customer. It's basic consideration, time, effort, commitment, and follow-up."

Others have learned the same lesson: Doug Burgum of Great Plains Software, Joan Silver of Reeves Audio Visual Systems, Du Pont's McAndrews, and Hal Rosenbluth of Rosenbluth Travel have all discovered that the real solution to loyalty lies in creating an ever-changing system that develops and nurtures the loyal customer.

Start right now to devise new ways to get and keep your customers. You can always find new solutions in the concept of customer stages and in the fact that loyalty is developed and earned one step at a time.

Summary

- Measurement and tracking are key to every successful loyalty program.
- Incorporating customer and client retention goals into employee compensation is an important component of loyalty systems.
- Businesses can learn how to keep customers loyal from their own past experience, from the customers themselves, and from their competition.
- Implementing a companywide loyalty system in phases is important to establishing a workable program.
- Before a company can engender loyal customers, it must have loyal employees who understand their role in the company's success.
- A successful strategy for building loyalty is not static. It must constantly be updated, improved, and adjusted as conditions and people change.

References

Chapter 1. Customer Loyalty: The Way to Many Happy Returns

1. David Stum and Alan Thiry, "Building Customer Loyalty," *Training and Development Journal*, April 1991, 34.
2. Frederick F. Reichheld, "Loyalty-Based Management," *Harvard Business Review*, March–April 1993, 71.
3. Christopher Fay, "Can't Get No Satisfaction? Perhaps You Should Stop Trying," white paper, Juran Institute, (Wilton, Conn.: n.d.), 1.
4. Fay, 4.
5. Robert A. Peterson and William R. Wilson, "Measuring Customer Satisfaction: Fact and Artifact," *Journal of the Academy of Marketing Sciences*, Winter 1992, 6.
6. Peterson and Wilson, 65–67.
7. Fay, 5
8. Fay, 5
9. Paul B. Brown, "Return Engagements," *Inc. Magazine*, July 1990, 99–100.
10. Brown, 99
11. Frederick F. Reichheld and W. Earl Sasser, Jr., "Zero Defections: Quality Comes to Services, *Harvard Business Review*, September–October 1990, 110.
12. Clases Fornell, "A National Customer Satisfaction Barometer: The Swedish Experience," *Journal of Marketing*, January 1992, 12.
13. Brown, 99–100.
14. Reichheld, 65.
15. Reichheld and Sasser, 106.

Chapter 2. A Closer Look at Loyalty

1. Christopher Power, Walecia Konrad, Alice Cuneo, and James Treece, "Value Marketing," *Business Week*, November 11, 1991, 132.
2. Ibid.
3. Paul B. Brown, "Return Engagements," Inc. Magazine, July 1990, 99–100.
4. Alan S. Dick and Kunal Basen, "Customer Loyalty: Toward an Integrated

Conceptual Framework," white paper. Journal of the Academy of Marketing Science, Spring 1994, Vol. 22, Number 2, 99.

5. John Case, "A Business Transformed," *Inc. Magazine*, June 1993, 84–91.
6. Ibid.

Chapter 3. *Growing a Loyal Customer: The Seven Key Stages*

1. Eric Larson, "Strange Fruits," *Inc. Magazine*, November 1989, 80–88.
2. David Stum and Alan Thiry, "Building Customer Loyalty" Training and Development Journal, April 1991, 34–35.
3. "The Ride's the Thing," *Newsday* newspaper, Nassau and Suffolk edition, December 7, 1992.
4. Frederick Reichhold and Earl Sasser, Jr., "Zero Defections: Quality Comes to Services," *Harvard Business Review*, September-October, 1990, 105.
5. Tom Richman, "Come Again," *Inc. Magazine*, April 1989, 177–78.
6. Ibid.
7. Paul Brown, "A Bird in the Hand," *Inc. Magazine*, August 1989, 114–15.
8. Stan Rapp and Thomas Collins, *MaxiMarketing* (New York: McGraw-Hill), 213.
9. Kevin J. Clancy and Robert S. Shulman, *The Marketing Revolution* (New York: HarperBusiness), 136.

Chapter 4. *Turning Suspects into Qualified Prospects*

1. McGraw-Hill magazine advertisement, in Jerome McCarthy, *Basic Marketing* (Homewood, Ill.: Richard D. Irwin, 1975), 396.
2. Tom Heyman, *On an Average Day* (New York: Fawcett Columbine, 1989), 154.
3. William O'Connell and William Keenan, Jr., "The Shape of Things to Come," *Sales and Marketing Management*, January 1990, 37.
4. Udayan Gupta, "Costly Marketing Research Pays off for Biotech Start-Up," *Wall Street Journal*, August, 2, 1993, B2.
5. Interview with Steve Tran, sales representative for MacHaik Chevrolet, Houston, Tex., June 27, 1990.
6. Ibid.
7. Michael Schrage, "Fire Your Customers," *Wall Street Journal*, March 16, 1992. B2.
8. Frederick Reichheld, "Loyalty Based Management", *Harvard Business Review*, March-April, 1993.
9. Paul B. Brown, *Marketing Masters* (New York: Harper & Row, 1988), 152.
10. Ibid.
11. Ibid.
12. Peter Pae, "Advanta Finds Edge with Careful Customer Screening," *Wall Street Journal*, April 8, 1993, B4.
13. Kevin Hilliker, "Hair Is Big in Dallas and That Troubles Roger Thompson," *Wall Street Journal*, December 29, 1991, A8.

14. Ibid.
15. Peter Laundy, "Image Trouble," *Inc. Magazine*, September 1993, 81.
16. Laundy, 80.
17. Laundy, 82.
18. Divinia Infusino, "Brash and Bold," *Profiles Magazine*, May 1993, 36.
19. Laundy, 84.
20. Allen R. Myerson, "This Man Wants to Bury You," *New York Times*, August 1, 1993, sec. 1, 1.
21. *Auto Week*, August 19, 1991, 10.
22. Jerry Fried, "Prospects Are Expensive, So Give a Damn," *Furniture Advantage*, November 1988, 1.
23. Drawn from Wayne Morgan's Selling Seminar for Real Estate Agents, Austin School of Real Estate, Austin, Tex., September, 1990.

Chapter 5. Turning Qualified Prospects into First-Time Buyers

1. John Graham, *Competitive Advantage*, August 1991, 5.
2. William O'Connell and William Keenan, Jr., "The Shape of Things To Come," *Sales and Marketing Management Magazine*, January 1990, 37.
3. Jeffrey Lant, *Money Making Marketing* (Cambridge, Mass.: JLA Publications, 1987), 172.
4. "Painting a Sales Portrait," *Success Magazine*, May 1990, 35.
5. Tom Peters, "60 Minutes" (Chicago: Nightingale-Conant Corporation, 1987), side 1.
6. Pam Caroll, "Sales Detectives: How to Exploit the Information Edge," *Success Magazine*, May 1990, 43.
7. Rick Barrera, "A Direct Approach to Sales Prospecting," *Small Business Reports*, October 1990, 34.
8. "Go out of Your Way," *Creative Selling Newsletter*, 3.
9. Verne Newton, "We Still Haven't Learned Our Lessons," *Boardroom Reports*, May 1, 1992, 5.
10. Ibid.
11. Paula C. Kringle, "Training Salespeople to Sell Services," *Sales Training Magazine*, May 1989, 14.
12. Ralph G. Nichols and Leonard Stevens, *Listening to People* McGraw (New York: McGraw-Hill, 1957).
13. "Through the Customer's Eyes," *ANA/The Advertiser Magazine*, Fall 1991, 59.
14. Jan Ozer, "Roadmap to the Sale," *Competitive Advantage*, March 1992, 4.
15. Brian Azar, "Be a Sales Doctor," *Success Magazine*, December 1989, 24.
16. Ibid.
17. "Learn to Think like a Sales Doctor," *Competitive Advantage*, August 1992, 8.
18. Charles Burck, "Launching in a Storm," *Fortune Magazine*, August 9, 1993, 93.
19. Guy Anderson, "Tale of the Sale," *Selling Advantage Newsletter*, 1993, 3.

20. "What Are the Shared Qualities of Top Sellers?" *Selling Advantage Newsletter*, 1993, 2.
21. Teri Lamers, "Lost Job Survey," *Inc. Magazine*, April 1992, 78.
22. Ibid.

Chapter 6. Turning First-Time Buyers into Repeat Customers

1. Richard Shapiro, "One Step Ahead," *Boardroom Reports*, September 15, 1992, 5.
2. Mark Shapiro, "Business Joke of the Week," *Austin American Statesman*, Business sec., B1.
3. Michael Miller, "Ordering IBM Ambra PC Can Be a Hassle," *Wall Street Journal*, August 27, 1993, B1.
4. Benson P. Shapiro, V. Kasturi Rangan, and John J. Sviokla, "Staple Yourself to an Order," *Competitive Advantage*, 3.
5. Ibid.
6. Thomas Teal, "Service Comes First: An Interview with USAA's Robert F. McDermott," *Harvard Business Review*, September–October 1991, 119.
7. Teal, 126.
8. Teal, 120.
9. James A. Perkins, "How Does Service Drive the Service Company?" *Harvard Business Review*, November–December 1991, 156.
10. Russell Belk, "Situational Variables and Consumer Behavior," *Journal of Consumer Research*, December 1975, 157.
11. George Walther, "Reach out to Accounts," May 1990, 24.
12. John Goodman, "Customer Education," *Boardroom Reports*, April 15, 1992, 9.
13. "Doctor's Letters Are Linked to Patient's Satisfaction," *Wall Street Journal*, October 11, 1991, B2.
14. Jennifer Potter-Brotsman, "The New Role of Service in Customer Retention," *Forum*, no. 14, Summer 1993, 10.
15. Ibid.
16. Ibid.
17. Murray Raphel, *Mind Your Own Business* (Atlantic City, N.J.: Raphel Marketing, 1989), 91.
18. Drawn from letter to Beth Anderson from All county Plumbing and Heating Corporation, Brooklyn, New York.
19. "A Mail Campaign Helps Saab Find and Keep Its Customers," *Wall Street Journal*, June 21, 1993, B1.
20. Howard Upton, "Do They Understand What You Do?" *Spirit Magazine*, January 1992, 38.
21. Ibid.
22. Ibid.
23. Ibid.
24. Mort Mandel, "Shrewd Thinking," *Boardroom Reports*, May 1, 1993, 16.
25. Richard Shapiro, "Retaining Profitable Customers: A Targeted Approach,"

paper presented at the QUIS 3 conference, University of Karlstad, Karlstad, Sweden, June 16, 1992, 12.

26. R. Shapiro, 12.
27. Jay Finegan, "Survival of the Smartest," *Inc. Magazine*, December 1993, 88.
28. Ron Smothermon, *Winning through Enlightenment* (San Francisco: Context Publications, 1980), 137.

Chapter 7. Turning Repeat Customers into Loyal Clients

1. Michael Treacy and Fred Wiersema, "Customer Intimacy and Other Value Disciplines," *Harvard Business Review*, January–February, 1993, 85.
2. Paul B. Brown, "Paper Trail," *Inc. Magazine*, August 1990, 113.
3. "Targeting Your Best Customers," *Inc. Magazine*, December 1992, 25.
4. Josh Hyatt, "Ask and You Shall Receive," *Inc. Magazine*, September 1989, 93.
5. Ibid.
6. Susan Gibson Breda, "Empowerment," *Travel Counselor*, March 16, 1992, 44.
7. Ibid.
8. Ibid.
9. Larry Armstrong, "The Customer as Honored Guest," *Business Week*, Annual Quality Issue, 1991, 104.
10. Claudia H. Deutsch, "Stronger Ties with Customers Makes Sense," *Competitive Advantage*, April 1991, 7.
11. Ibid.
12. Ibid.

Chapter 8. Turning Loyal Clients into Advocates

1. Michael Phillips and Salli Rasberry, *Marketing without Advertising* (Berkeley, Calif.: Nolo Press, 1986), 1:8.
2. Bob Fenster, "The New Auteurs," *Harper's Magazine*, June 1991, 34.
3. Ibid.
4. Ibid.
5. Phillips and Rasberry, 1:6–7.
6. Paul Y. Brown, "The Real Cost of Customer Service," *Inc. Magazine*, September 1990, 50.
7. "Making Money out of Mellow," *New York Times*, May 4, 1986, B1.
8. Ibid.
9. "The Sound of Success," *Washington Post*, April 24, 1983, H1.
10. "Making Money," B1.
11. "Sound of Success," H1.
12. Paul Y. Brown, "The Real Cost of Customer Service", Inc. Magazine, September 1990, p. 50
13. Brown, 90.
14. John Case, "Customer Service: The Last Word," *Inc. Magazine*, April 1991, 90.

15. Ibid.
16. Case, 92.
17. Teri Agins, "Clerking at SteinMart Is a Society Lady's Dream Come True," *Wall Street Journal*, December 2, 1992, A1.
18. Ibid.
19. Ray Considine and Murray Raphel, *The Great Brain Robbery* (Altadena: GBR), 131–135.
20. Bradford Wernle, "Food for Thought: Restaurants Keep in Touch with Diners via Newsletter," *Data Courier*, December 17, 1990, sec. 1, 3.
21. Ibid.
22. George Griffin, "Dissecting a Successful Newsletter," *Graphics Art Monthly*, October 1992, 102.
23. Ibid.
24. Ibid.

Chapter 9. Customer Inactivity: How to Prevent It And What to Do When It Strikes

1. Tom Peters, "Creating Total Customer Responsiveness," in *Thriving on Chaos* (New York: Harper & Row, 1987), 120.
2. Jeff Bailey, "Why Customers Trash the Garbage Man," *Wall Street Journal*, March 17, 1993, B1.
3. Susan Greco, "Winning back a Lost Customer," *Inc. Magazine*, September 1993, 25.
4. Ibid.
5. Linda Goldzimer, "Business through Customer Feedback," *America West Magazine*, September 1989, 87.
6. Edward O. Welles, "How're We Doing?" *Inc. Magazine*, May 1991, 80.
7. Mack Hanan and Peter Karp, *Customer Satisfaction* (New York: Amacon, 1989), 157.
8. Jacqueline S. Gold, "Customer Service," *Financial World*, September 28, 1993, 56.
9. Ibid.
10. Susan Greco, "Every Employee a Service Rep," *Inc. Magazine*, November 1993, 123.
11. TARP, "SOCAP 800 Number Study: A 1992 Profile of 800 Numbers for Customer Service," reprinted in *Inc. Magazine*, June 1993, 30.
12. Paul Brown, "For You, Our Valued Customer," *Inc. Magazine*, January 1990, 109.

Chapter 10. How to Develop a Loyalty-Driven Culture in Your Company

1. Jay Finegan, "Taking Names," *Inc. Magazine*, September 1992, 122.
2. Ibid.
3. Finegan, 125.
4. Finegan, 126.

5. "Getting Customers to Love You," *Fortune Magazine*, March 13, 1989, 48.
6. Mark Seal, "Life of a Salesman," *Inc. Magazine*, December 1992, 175.
7. Ibid.
8. Ibid.
9. Rosabeth Moss Kanter, "Service Quality: You Get What You Pay For," *Harvard Business Review*, September–October 1991, 8.
10. Bridget O'Brian, "Southwest Airlines Is a Rare Air Carrier: It Still Makes Money," *Wall Street Journal*, October 26, 1992, 1A.
11. O'Brian, 11.
12. Hal Rosenbluth, "Tales from a Non-Conformist Company," *Harvard Business Review*, July–August 1991, 27.
13. Rosenbluth, 28.
14. Rosenbluth, 33.
15. Rosenbluth, 34.
16. Howard Schlossberg, "Markets Changing as Never Before," *Marketing News*, April 12, 1993, 7.

Company Index

Subject Index